LEARNING TO COMPETE IN AFRICAN INDUSTRY

T0384400

Learning to Compete in African Industry
Institutions and Technology in Development

BANJI OYELARAN-OYEYINKA
United Nations University-Institute for New Technologies,
The Netherlands

Routledge
Taylor & Francis Group

LONDON AND NEW YORK

First published 2006 by Ashgate Publishing

Reissued 2018 by Routledge
2 Park Square, Milton Park, Abingdon, Oxon OX14 4RN
605 Third Avenue, New York, NY 10017

First issued in paperback 2021

Routledge is an imprint of the Taylor & Francis Group, an informa business

© Banji Oyelaran-Oyeyinka 2006

Banji Oyelaran-Oyeyinka has asserted his right under the Copyright, Designs and Patents Act, 1988, to be identified as the author of this work.

All rights reserved. No part of this book may be reprinted or reproduced or utilised in any form or by any electronic, mechanical, or other means, now known or hereafter invented, including photocopying and recording, or in any information storage or retrieval system, without permission in writing from the publishers.

A Library of Congress record exists under LC control number: 2005030375

Notice:
Product or corporate names may be trademarks or registered trademarks, and are used only for identification and explanation without intent to infringe.

Publisher's Note
The publisher has gone to great lengths to ensure the quality of this reprint but points out that some imperfections in the original copies may be apparent.

Disclaimer
The publisher has made every effort to trace copyright holders and welcomes correspondence from those they have been unable to contact.

ISBN-13: 978-0-815-39019-0 (hbk)
ISBN-13: 978-1-351-15408-6 (ebk)
ISBN 13: 978-1-138-35636-8 (pbk)

DOI: 10.4324/9781351154086

Contents

List of Tables

Tables

List of Figures and Boxes

Figures

Boxes

Acknowledgements

This book is one outcome of research in four African countries carried out in my first three years at the United Nations University-Institute for New Technologies (UNU-INTECH). An important motivation was the desire to bridge the information and knowledge gap on the structure and nature of learning in African industry. While the literature on the political and social-economic conditions in African has grown, the same cannot be said about the role of institutions supporting technical change in the continent.

My focus however has been on Sub-Saharan Africa. The aim is to contribute in a small way to the understanding of the ways in which technology is utilized at the enterprise level and what institutions support the process of learning and knowledge accumulation. In preparing this book, I have received the assistance of colleagues particularly the country coordinators of the studies that form the basis of the book and I thank them immensely.

The following are the country project leaders: Uganda, Dr Z. Nyiira and his team; Zimbabwe, Kenneth Kodero; and Nigeria, Prof. Olufemi Bamiro and Dr. Boladale Abiola both of the University of Ibadan, while the Kenya study was coordinated by Geoffrey Gachino, UNU-INTECH. I received tremendous support and cooperation from the field coordinators, enterprise owners, and government officials that were interviewed.

I also express my appreciation to colleagues and friends who took the time to read parts or all of the manuscript and gave me useful comments without which this book will have been far less comprehensible and readable. These individuals include: Richard Nelson, Rajneesh Narula, Rajah Rasiah and Calestous Juma. My gratitude to Lynn Mytelka, the director of UNU-INTECH when the research was carried out. Lynn was very supportive of the African projects and gave useful advice on different aspects of the work. Kaushalesh Lal gave useful insights on statistical techniques. Sophie Gross did a wonderful editorial job while Mr. T.O. Ogunmola of NISER, Ibadan provided valuable support in analysing the data.

I thank anonymous reviewers of a Journal version of Chapter 3 which was published in the International Journal of Technology and Sustainable Development (IJTSD).[1] In the course of writing this book, I had wide ranging discussions at a meeting in Jamaica with Alice Amsden, a good friend and human being on the book and related academic concerns. She inspired me more than she probably realized and I am grateful to her.

---

1   Oyelaran-Oyeyinka (2004).

My able secretary, Eveline in de Braek did a marvellous job all through the time of preparing the manuscript and my employer the UNU-INTECH provided both the funding and the intellectual environment for the projects that led to this book.

Finally, I thank my wife and family for their support and indulgence, through the time of research and preparation of the book manuscript.

List of Abbreviations

CI	Competitiveness Indicator
LDCs	Least Developed Countries
NSI	National System of Innovation
RDIs	Research and Development Institutions
R&D	Research and Development
SAPs	Structural Adjustments Programmes
SI	System of Innovation
SIs	Systems of Innovation
SMEs	Small and Medium Enterprises
SOEs	State-Owned Enterprises
SSA	Sub-Saharan Africa
S&T	Science and Technology

Foreword

Africa's economic woes hit the news headlines almost every day. The mainstream view today is that the problem is structural. Numerous natural and historical factors from tropical climate, landlockedness, ethno-linguistic fragmentation, to abundant natural resources (in the so-called 'resource curse' thesis) have been mobilized to 'explain' why Africa is destined for under-development and poverty. The only solution, according to this view, is to make up for the continent's structural handicaps by providing them foreign aid and making sure that the aid money is not stolen or wasted.

Oyelaran-Oyeyinka's book goes against such 'fatalistic' view and tries to find solutions to Africa's economic problem by investigating what is actually happening on the ground. To do this, the book analyses in depth what is going on in the industrial firms of Africa, looking at their technological capabilities, management strategies, training programmes, inter-firm cooperation, and many other things that those who are into 'grand' theories may regard as trivial but are in fact what determine the industrial success or otherwise of enterprises and ultimately the economies. The book also looks very closely at the relationship between enterprise performance and government policies regarding R&D, industrial clustering, and infrastructure provision – once again, things that may look mundane but are at the centre of industrial development.

The book's findings are sometimes 'obvious', as in the case of the impact of inadequate electricity supply on industrial performance. However, the issue has been rather neglected in the recent period, possibly because of our excessive fascination with the internet, against which electrification looks rather dull. However, the book reminds us that the failure to solve this 'obvious' problem is proving to be a major obstacle to the continent's development.

Other findings in the book are less obvious and give us a lot of food for thoughts. For example, the finding that the small size of the firm reduces its 'institutional memory', thus hampering knowledge accumulation, is an extremely important point that has numerous policy implications: should the African countries therefore try to promote larger firms?; should that prove impossible for whatever reason, is it possible for the government or the industry associations to create certain institutional mechanisms beyond the firm level that will be long-term repositories of technical knowledge?; if so, what are the exact institutions that need to be constructed? These are some of the fascinating questions that this apparently 'little' finding throws at us.

What makes the book really valuable is that it is able to situate all these findings in a robust theoretical framework that draws diversely and deftly from the recent developments in the theory of knowledge, the economics of technical change, the theory of the firm, the literature on industrial cluster, the literature on the national systems of innovation, and last but not least institutional economics. It is because of such theoretical foundation that the book allows us to understand the realities of Africa and come up with some sensible solutions to its problems with the depth that is missing in the 'fatalistic' mainstream literature. The book is a truly valuable addition to the study of the continent that has been subject so much to prejudices and sweeping generalizations.

Ha-Joon Chang
Faculty of Economics
University of Cambridge

Chapter 1

Introduction

Introduction

This book examines the institutional roots of the persistent differences in the economic performance of firms, industries and countries in Africa. While there is slow overall progress towards sustainable industrialization and economic progress in African countries, there is evidence of some firm-level success in the region. Firms require a combination of competitive capabilities, working within the right sets of institutions in order to gain and sustain domestic and global competitiveness. While individual enterprises are learning how to compete in a changed and hostile economic environment, we posit that one of the greatest problems constraining the learning and competitive effort of enterprises is the absence of the right kinds of institutions. We follow the definition of institution provided by North (1996): 'Institutions are the rules of the game of a society or more formally the humanly-devised constraints that structure human interaction. They are composed of formal rules (statute law, common law, and regulations), informal constraints… and the enforcement characteristics of both'. However as Nelson and Nelson, (2002) correctly observe, to see physical and social technology as 'constraints' is problematic. He illustrates: 'A productive social technology is like a paved road across a swamp. To say that the location of the prevailing road is a constraint on getting across is basically to miss the point. Without a road, getting across would be impossible, or at least much harder'.

We take the view that institutions and continued technological innovations both broadly defined, are central to the process of economic development. Large numbers of countries in Africa have neither succeeded in acquiring technology effectively, nor built effective institutions to support technical change. Subsequently, the region has suffered the loss of competitiveness not only in manufactures but also in traditional commodity exports. Loss of opportunities in global trade and technology exchange has meant that African countries have so far benefited only marginally from globalization. For most Sub-Saharan Africa (SSA) countries, manufactured exports which remains a small proportion of global exports, declined over the years (Table 1.1). While SSA has realized some increase in manufactured exports, this has been due to in part to the effects of reduction in the prices of commodities relative to manufactures in the last twenty years (UNCTAD, 2001). Oil and non-oil commodities constitute more than 80 per cent of Africa's exports. More disturbing is the decline of traditional exports. According to a recent study by Ng and Yeats (2002) for the World Bank in 1962, Africa's exports of palm nuts and kernels accounted for 91 per cent of world total amounting to $75 million. Exports fell to $3 million by 1999 while global market share was less than 10 per cent of 1960s. Also, global market shares for groundnuts, palm kernel oil, and palm oil was between 51 to 83 per cent, but have now fallen to only between 2 to 3 per cent, with the combined exports of these products now much lower than it was four decades ago. If Africa had maintained its 1960 global share of markets, current exports would be about $7.7 billion higher than current export value. According to the World Bank, 'competitive share losses for palm oil are of major importance ($1.8 billion) and are about $1.1 billion for both alumina and unmilled maize' (Table 1.2).

Structural Adjustment Programmes (SAPs) embarked upon by almost all the countries in the region imposed severe conditionalities, but the gains in competitive share of manufactures, for which much pain was endured, met with limited success or none at all. The transition to processed exports of so-called traditional exports did not materialize. In the years after independence more than forty years ago, Africa seemed destined to become a major exporter of various types of vegetable oils, tin, iron, bauxite and copper ore products. It was also not difficult to conjecture the export of sizeable global shares of meat products, fish oils, maize, and rice products, fruit jams, and animal feeds. This promise has not only failed to materialize, the region has also lost price competitiveness of traditional products. According to Mg and Yeats (2002), only tropical beverage groups recorded an overall positive change over the last decade due largely to more than 20 per cent increase in coffee prices.

Diversification into manufactured exports was an important objective of economic reforms with the aim of reducing dependence on commodity exports; however the effort has not been successful. For instance, the composition of manufactures in merchandise exports in 1983 was below 10 per cent of total exports and remained so in the year 2000 at 8.8 per cent in contrast with South East Asia where exports of manufactures rose from 52 per cent to 78 per cent in the same period. As Stein (1994) remarked, this is as much an indictment of the orthodox policies of the World Bank/IMF in Africa as it is of the contrasting emphasis on developmental approaches in the two regions. While the role of long lasting institutions was clearly recognized in East Asia, much of the efforts in constructing structural adjustments in Africa was focused on short-term balance of payment issues, and much less on building institutions.

In an analysis of the international competitiveness of nine African countries over the 1980 and 1990 period, UNCTAD (2001) found that positive competitiveness indicator (CI) largely explained successful export performance. CI is explained in terms of the evolution of unit labour costs in dollars, which is positively correlated with labour productivity and real exchange rate but inversely related to real wages. Labour productivity is the most permanent and significant predictor of manufactured exports. Mauritius and Egypt, both of which displayed dynamic

Table 1.1 Exports, Manufactured Exports, Current Account Balance and Net Barter Terms of Trade for SSA, 1980-2000*

Year	1980	1990	1992	1993	1994	1995	1996	1997	1998	1999	2000
Merch. Exports	53 049	45 738	42 033	38 178	39 558	48 476	56 563	56 025	46 590	50 875	64 308
Manuf. Exports		3899	3808	3867	4196	5027	5248	4131	5687	5884	5715
Percent		8.5	9.1	10.1	10.6	10.4	9.2	9.1	12.2	11.6	8.8
Bal. On Cur.Act	-4226	-9550	-15084	-15030	-10911	-11527	-5745	-9022	-17022	-17878	-7181
Bal/GDP	-2.3	-5.2								-9.3	-3.6
Terms of Trd.	177.1	113.9	102.4	97.6	96.2	100.0	110.3	101.6	90.1	96.8	119.7

* All figures are in millions of current dollars except for percentages; balance of payments exclude net capital grants; figures exclude South Africa.

Source: World Bank (2001a and 2002).

Learning to Compete in African Industry

Table 1.2 Implications of the Demise of Some African 'Historical' Exports

	African Exports ($000)		Africa's World Trade Share (%)	
Commodity (SITC)*	1962	1999	1962	1999
Palm Nuts & Kernels (2213)	75 061	2 861	91.1	9.9
Groundnuts Green (2211)	184 279	24 542	83.4	3.2
Palm Kernel Oil (4224)	8941	15 816	53.4153.1	2.2
Palm Oil (4222)	36	11 634	50.9	1.0
Natural Abrasives (2752)	13 247	2059	27.6	0.2
Fixed Vegetable Oils, nes (4229)	8555	10 131	16.0	1.3
Alumina (5136)	25 608	60 330	13.8	0.7
Unmilled Maize (0440)	18 762	20 725	13.2	0.2
Fur Skins (2120)	37 855	757	12.3	0.1
Vegetable Oil Cake (0813)	47 401	49 264	10.9	0.8
Copper Ore & Concentrates (2831)	11 492	44 633	8.7	0.9
Oil of fish (4111)	7825	1453	7.6	0.4
Bovine & Equine Hides (2111)	18 155	24 627	8.0	0.9
Unwrought Tin (6871)	21 761	267	7.8	0.0
Meat Extracts (0133)	2120	759	7.6	0.6
Tine Ores and Concentrates (2835)	5851	9139	6.0	0.5
Plywood (6312)	12 149	48 659	5.2	0.6
Glazed or Polished Rice (0422)	6346	601	3.5	0.0
TOTAL OF ABOVE	505 444	328 257	13.9	1.0

* Since Revision 2 data were not available until mid-1970s, these statistics are based on the earlier Revision 1 classification which first became available in 1962.
Source: African Region Working Paper Series No. 26, www.worldbank.org.

and stable export profiles for the last two decades, exhibited the most sustained productivity growths.[1]

---

1   Mauritius sustained an average manufacturing productivity growth of 4.5 per cent for 18 years, and Egypt an average of 3.5 per cent productivity for 16 years in spite of real appreciation in real exchange rates, and without lowering wages. Most countries attempt to

Table 1.3 Composition of Exports from Sub-Saharan Africa

	1980	1990	1997
Crude Petroleum	75.6	61.3	54.7
Non-oil primary commodities	19.7	22.8	26.6
Manufactures	4.0	15.5	18.4
Unclassified	0.7	0.4	0.3

Source: UNCTAD (2001).

Explaining Africa's development dilemma

Several explanations have been advanced to explain Africa's dismal economic performance. They range from policy-related issues (World Bank, 1982); structural and institutional factors (for example, Easterly, 1997; Sachs and Warner, 1997); the paucity of technological and managerial capabilities which result in the failure to effectively transfer technology and the under utilization of human and physical resources (Enos, 1992; Lall, 1992a; Lall, 1993; Lall and Pietrobello, 2003; Wangwe, 1995) and the long-term effects of historical factors (Engerman and Sokoloff, 1997). While these factors explain parts of Africa's growth problems, a systemic explanation of the nature of institutions in long-run development is still lacking. Africa is far from having uniform initial conditions and varies widely in economic and political governance systems. Thus, cross-country analysis tends to hide the considerable intra-regional variations, particularly, the significant influences of specific national systems. This book therefore calls attention to the role of institutions supporting technical change in long-term industrialization and how technological capability is central to competitiveness in the new global context. The role of initial conditions such as levels of literacy and natural endowment, the structure of industry, as well as resource endowment have been emphasized (Sandberg, 1982; Abramovitz and David, 1994). The unique contribution of this book is its emphasis on institutions shaping the evolution of the systems of innovation in Africa. This first tentative attempt to explore long-run development in Africa within the systems of innovation framework therefore follows the line of inquiry suggested by Lundvall et al. (2002). According to the authors, 'a principal task for future research based on the concept of national systems of innovation is to adapt it in such a way that its application in less developed countries…helps to stimulate policy learning. We will argue that a major step in this direction is to broaden and deepen the concept and make it more dynamic' (ibid: 225). This challenge is taken up in Muche et al. (2003), where for

---

achieve competitiveness through wage suppression and sharp currency depreciation. However wage suppression often leads to social problems as well as impacting negatively on long-term productivity growth.

the first time a group of scholars took up the idea of a system of innovation in Africa.[2] The concept, they argue, is highly relevant also for the South. To this end, a broad approach where innovations are conceived as activities rooted in the daily routines of firms as well as in the capabilities of managers and engineers would be the preferred research programme.

Human capital and organizational roots of industrial stagnation

The observed shortcomings in the technology development efforts could be located within a much broader social and economic policies failure. We argue that the combined impact of low institutional capacity and the low levels of human capital, both with roots in low educational and skills attainment, have had major negative consequences on the observed pattern of development and the national systems of innovation in Africa.

The present-day African state, while vested with considerable economic and political power concentrated in the executive president, has relatively weak control over the rural peripheral areas (Callaghy, 1987; Aron, 1996). The centralized-bureaucratic state, with the fusion of politics and bureaucracy, is a direct legacy of its colonial past (Burke, 1969; Van Arkadie, 1995; Allen, 1995).[3] Such an administrative structure, weakened by its poor initial human capital base, possesses very little capability to manage industrialization. Indeed, despite strong executive control, the state's administrative and institutional capacities are weak. It appears that the limited administrative and institutional capabilities of the African State are mainly a result of its colonial legacy and the 'transplanted' nature of its institutions.

These transplanted institutions were superimposed on indigenous, informal institutions that characterized civil society, and cultural norms and tradition. These institutions are inefficient since they fail to generate loyalty and ownership (Dia, 1996). Indeed, Van Arkadie attributes the inefficiency of the African bureaucracy to the absence of a 'deep-rooted tradition' of bureaucracy in Africa. He notes that Africa's postcolonial bureaucracy did not possess the 'deep historical roots' of the Mandarin tradition that influenced many East Asian countries. Hence, he argues that the new bureaucracy to which science and technology institutions belong, which emerged in the post independence era, did not possess the requisite self-confidence and coherence to hold the state together (Van Arkadie, 1995: 197).

Africa's institutional infrastructure is largely structurally weak. Technology infrastructure (for example, research and development (R&D) institutions, design,

---

2   See Muche et al. (2003).

3   Burke (1969), for example, cautions that it is important to examine the administrative system of the colonial era when analysing the present system of governance in Africa. He posits that the colonial bureaucracy generally monopolized power in its African territories. Directives were issued from the colonial office in Europe, but it was the administrative hierarchy of governor at the top, together with the lower-level functionaries including African chiefs and headmen, who actually formulated and executed administrative policy.

metrology, testing, quality assurance, technology information) is largely ineffective (for example, Lall, 1995a; 1992a). While some technology institutions certainly exist in Africa, there appears to be limited interaction between them and the industrial sector. They thus operate in isolation from the productive sectors. In addition, many are not only poorly funded and given conflicting objectives, but also have inadequate equipment and unmotivated staff. Further, poor coordination among agencies competing for relevance, the limited skills of policy makers, together with the paucity of scientific and technical personnel with the requisite understanding of the science and technology system, jeopardized development objectives. Moreover, there seems to be a paucity of institutions that are critical to the development initiative. For example, Nissanke (2001) notes the dearth of institutions providing industrial finance to the micro, and small and medium-sized enterprises in Africa.

The limited administrative and institutional capabilities of Africa's 'lame leviathans' (Callaghy, 1987) have been further diminished by the structural adjustment programmes implemented since the early 1980s. Technology institutions were equally severely undermined by the reforms with key emphasis on budgetary cuts and the hollowing out of the state. According to Aron,

> The state in Africa has come full circle to the small government of pre-colonial days; but with the additional hysteresis effect from past shocks of a seriously depleted current institutional capability, deterioration in the current quality and scope of fiscal services and infrastructure provision, coupled with a fiscal position highly vulnerable to changes in foreign aid (Aron, 1996: 117).

Despite the diminished administrative and institutional capacities of the African State in the post structural adjustment era, it is now left with tasks that are not only critical but also more complex. They include the manipulation of market-related policy instruments; the implementation of technological investment programs; the management of physical and engineering infrastructure; and the delivery of social services. Van Arkadie (1995) suggests that if the private sector is to further develop in Africa, the state will need to be endowed with the requisite capabilities to meet the needs of this development. It will need *inter alia* to develop a well functioning legal system, sponsor the growth of new markets such as finance, and foster the emergence of coordinating organizations such as business associations and chambers of commerce.

The economic performance of successful latecomers such as the South East Asian economies in part rests on their efficient, high-quality technology institutions, highly skilled engineers, and professionally managed enterprises, (Amsden, 1989). The major weakness of the innovation policies of African states was the neglect of the evolutionary character of technological advance in long-run economic development. Policies also overlooked the highly systemic nature of innovation. While states established ministries of science and technology (S&T) that had little interaction with other economic policy ministries and R&D agencies that were isolated from the private sector, these efforts inadvertently alienated the policy-making machinery from mainstream policy making. They are also insulated from politically driven economic parastatals that ordinarily should be natural customers of the S&T agencies. The formulation and implementing of industrial policy was also quite separate from the S&T policy-making process. In effect, national technological infrastructure gave little support to domestic firms that would benefit from the evolutionary process of technological deepening through learning that is the hallmark of dynamic latecomers. In sum, the legacy of colonialism, the weak bureaucratic capacity to manage a modern system of innovation, together with the adverse effects of the structural adjustments programmes (SAPs) have combined to severely limit the administrative and institutional capabilities of the African State.

Understanding the persistence of low growth in industry

African industry is presently made up largely of micro-enterprises and small and medium enterprises (SMEs), and clusters, a sector that conventional analysis does not credit with significant technical change and inventive activities. While the economic contribution of micro-enterprises differs across countries in Africa, their significance in the provision of goods and services cannot be underestimated. In some African countries without a well-developed factory system, the micro and small enterprises contribute as much as 90 per cent of goods and services produced in the economy. This group of enterprises produces largely for the low-income group and employs low-level techniques. The medium and large enterprises on the other hand, depend largely on imported technologies, particularly the enterprises in the engineering and related sectors. Their presence and distribution in countries vary considerably and depend on a number of factors such as resource endowment and availability of human capital. Relatively resource-rich countries like Nigeria, using its oil wealth, invested relatively heavily in chemicals, extractive and metallic core sectors in the 1970s and 1980s. From these core sectors were expected spin-off firms emerging from the development of Hirschman-type backward and forward linkages. A generation of enterprises, in response to the import substitution industrialization (ISI) strategy, including small firms was established. However, the shallow nature of endogenous technological capacity led to the failure to move beyond the elementary phase of industrialization. The causes of industrial stagnation in Africa have their roots in several factors (for example, Ogbu et al, 1996). Among these factors are unfriendly macroeconomic policy environment, low worker productivity and low skill levels, and high transaction costs. We suggest that these are consequences rather than the causes of the present state of African industry. Pre-existing conditions are just as important as the immediate reasons.

For instance, in colonial Africa, European multinational enterprises operated in enclaves in the mineral or agriculture sector, juxtaposed with expatriates and immigrants dominating the retail and distribution sector, while the indigenous population, especially those in East and Southern Africa, operated in the informal sector (Blakemore and Cooksey, 1982; McCarthy, 1982; Cantwell, 1997). Thus, in the pre-independence era, the African presence in the private sector was considerably overshadowed by expatriate and immigrant groups such as the Asian in East Africa, the Lebanese in parts of West Africa, and the European settlers in Zimbabwe and Kenya. Colonial policies, such as graduated licencing systems, credit restrictions and controls on itinerant trading, stifled the growth of African entrepreneurship (McCarthy, 1982). In the post independence era, however, attempts were made to rectify this situation by creating a class of national entrepreneurs. To this end, strategies of increasing public ownership (as in Ghana, Nigeria and Tanzania) or supporting the transfer of wealth to a nascent African property-owning class (as in Kenya) were implemented (Van Arkadie, 1995).

However, public ownership of industry achieved minimal success. Parastatal industries, which were largely import substituting, tended to be among the most inefficient. They were generally plagued by excess capacity because of the inability to maintain plants locally, to substitute local for foreign materials, and to provide basic technical management skills (Lall, 1992a). Plants also faced perennial shortages of basic components and parts, which are commonplace items within the system of innovation in advanced economies. It would seem that misplaced assumptions by African planners concerning the nature of industrial systems underpinned the establishment of these industries. Public servants, with the advice of young engineers relying on no more than theoretical knowledge of how industry works, assumed the enormous responsibilities of planning and managing large-scale process plants, roles for which they were ill-prepared.[4] The conditions for a successful operation of plants, that is, a vibrant system of innovation (SI), which guarantees a minimum interdependent relation among economic agents, were completely absent. Not surprisingly, the financial performance of state owned companies was dismal with the attendant drain on the treasury.[5]

---

4 The Nigerian steel project provides a ready example. The government of Nigeria invested proportionally heavily on this project in terms of physical capital as well as in the training of engineers and technicians in foreign countries all through the 1970s to the late 1980s. However, much of the assumptions on the availability of the requisite raw material, particularly coking coal were spurious. While planning and investment was based on the availability of local coal, subsequent tests showed that local coal could not support the plant's nominal capacity even in the first stage. According to the conclusion in a report by the *British Mining Consultants* which carried out the pre-feasibility report: 'It is evident that proved commercial reserves of the Obi deposit (the coal mines) cannot guarantee either the qualitative or quantitative long term needs of the proposed metallurgical industry'. The French mineral consultants, *Sofremines*, came to much the same conclusion: 'Not a single test has good correlation with coking properties. In these conditions, we consider that as well as 20% as 40% of Enugu coal in the blend as assumptions without serious basis', see Oyelaran-Oyeyinka, 1994. The *Sofremines* report was submitted in 1975, however investment went on unabated without a serious re-examination of the original planning basis. The industry continues to have serious problems and to date has been unable to operate.

5 Ariyo, A. and Jerome, A. (1999) *World Development*, **27**, 201–213, citing cases from Ghana and Nigeria, notes that one-third of the state-owned enterprises in Ghana incurred operating deficits ranging from 0.2 to 3.4 per cent of GDP during the years, 1980 to 1982. The outstanding public debt of these state owned enterprises was an astounding 37 per cent of total domestic debt. The situation was no better in Nigeria. The government's investment

However, we do know that countries with highly effective SIs have successfully operated equally successful state-owned enterprises (SOEs) (Chang and Cheema, 2001). Chang and Cheema cite the examples of Austria (with a SOE sector contributing 14.5 per cent of GDP in the 1970s), France (11.9 per cent of GDP) and Norway, as well as East Asian countries such as Taiwan, with the largest SOEs in non oil-producing countries. In other words, direct control of production may well not be the issue, rather it is the effectiveness of the systems of innovation and the robustness of institutions. Apart from SOEs, the private sector landscape of Africa is dominated by a 'mass' of private business activity, the majority of which is occupied by micro and small enterprises (Schulpen and Gibbon, 2002). The larger private enterprises, which are capital-intensive and import dependent, are concentrated in traditional sectors such as apparel and furniture manufacturing. The SAPs implemented in Africa adversely affected these enterprises. Indeed, Lall, examining the Ghanaian situation notes, 'large swathes of the manufacturing sector were devastated by import competition' (Lall, 1995b, 2025). The industrial survivors and the new entrants are again mainly small-scale enterprises making low-income or localized products. The progressive graduation of these firms into a dynamic cluster of internationally competitive, small-scale manufacturing firms is highly doubtful without strong state support. In most cases, the firms lack the entrepreneurial ability to organize, establish and run modern industry, which require longer scales, longer time horizons, and more advanced technologies and organizational skills than informal activities (Lall, 1992b).

The emergent enterprises in Africa tended to have concentrated more on trading and other non-productive sectors, a carry-over perhaps of the past. The absence of a nexus between private enterprise and large-scale state enterprises is a result of this parallel strategy pursued by these two economic agents in the national system.

There also appears to be poor coordination between the private sector and government in Africa. Several reasons have been advanced to explain this. The absence of a business class with substantial finance, together with organizational resources and entrepreneurial skills prevented the newly independent African states from cooperating with it in its development process. Moreover, the state was largely financially independent of the private sector since it was rarely a source of public revenue: in the mineral-rich economies, the state had access to alternative sources of public finance; whereas in other economies it resorted to peasant revenues (for example, Allen, 1995; Mkandawire, 2001). It also seems that African governments tended to perceive the business class with suspicion, especially minority ethnic groups or former colonial powers. Indeed, there were initiatives to restrain or displace them (for example, Van Arkadie, 1995; Akyüz and Gore, 2001).

---

in state-owned enterprises was estimated at N23 billion and the average return from this investment was a mere N500 million. Moreover, 40 per cent of the federal government's non-salary recurrent expenditure and 30 per cent of its capital investment was spent on these enterprises.

This lack of interaction between the private manufacturing sector and the government had meant that industrial policy making (when it was done) was left in the hands of bureaucrats and politicians.[6] In many cases, their judgement had been flawed or undermined by a mixture of non-economic considerations, inexperience, poor understanding of business dynamics, and the politicians' private agenda (Hawkins, 1991). The end result had been the persistence of the weak systems of innovation due in part to a limited contribution of its private economic agents.

In summary, the pattern of institutions mediating the process of development varies widely. Indeed, economic historians have seriously questioned the traditional perception that the industrialization undertaken in the earlier industrialized countries was an essentially market-driven process (for example, Vartainen, 1995). It seems that the role of the state was not limited solely to the provision of a basic legal framework, public order and external security. Institutions, which were favourable to industrialization, were actively encouraged, several public services were organized and the state, itself, undertook direct organizational activities in production.

Vartainen (1995) cites the example of the Nordic countries where the state had undertaken the establishment of institutional research structures to support the development of natural resources. He noted that that it is difficult to envisage how progress could have taken place if it were solely entrusted to private entrepreneurs. Nations necessarily build on pre-existing national capacity constrained by historically framed contexts. Further, Zysman (1994) states that institutions were built by the politics of nation-building in response to economic crises which threaten social positions. They were not created by the problem of organizing innovation and production.

What this means is that innovation systems are shaped by fundamental social processes outside the domain of the firm at the material time.[7] Observed patterns of production and innovation cannot be explained in purely social, economic or technological terms. Innovation systems are rooted within localized learning organizations even in the context of a globalizing learning context. The idiosyncratic character of firms and organizations is developed by the efforts of individual engineers and managers through an evolutionary process, in which the state remains an important coordinator. Since tacit knowledge constitutes an important asset of organizations, firms remain rooted in local socio-economic milieu. Unfortunately, in Africa, attempts to substitute for past imbalances using the state have been singularly unsuccessful due in part to the poor capacity of the state as an actor in the national system but also due in large parts to inherited

---

6   Hawkins (1991) asserts that the role of policy making in Africa's industrialization initiative is controversial. He observed that few countries formulated industrial policies per se. Instead, manufacturing was perceived as an integral part of the national development plans, which set targets for industrial growth and outlined the policy framework for achieving these targets in very general terms.

7   The French centralized systems of innovation has its roots in the historical decision by kings seeking means of control and taxation, and the subsequent nation building through a revolution.

characteristics of the industrial system. Initial conditions as we see persist and continue to be important, but there has also been successes and this is what this book examines and attempts to understand, with a view to finding patterns for generalizable principles.

Institutional and evolutionary basis of innovation systems

The systems of innovation thinking which guides our discussion in the book has its roots in evolutionary economics[8] and the Neo-Schumpetarian theories.[9] They provide the theoretical underpinning for the key concepts that explain the dynamic and transformational processes of evolution which are: diversity (variety and variation), selection, replication (innovation), inheritance, path-dependence and bounded rationality.

An understanding of the processes of diversity, selection and replication is important in explaining systemic dynamics and change. Evolutionary theory provides an explanation for the persistent change in economic systems that is in constant flux. Structures and complexity arise in evolutionary systems that may have had quite simple origins to which they may not return. Understanding the current state of a system may therefore necessitate a return to a previous historical state. In other words, path dependence is an important concept in evolutionary phenomena. Again actors do not always have complete information for 'rational' decision making. Organizations and individuals therefore behave in accordance with adapted habits and practices.[10]

Variety generation in evolutionary technical change relates to the existence of a population of agents (firms, organizations and individuals), products, processes and technologies. For instance, organizational variety creation is observed in the emergence of new biotechnology research units within universities and public research institutes in response to the biotechnology revolution (Henderson et al., 1999). New types of firms have been created in telecommunication as the competitive environment change and as old economic regimes of state monopoly give way to liberal market regimes. The new actors rely on new sets of knowledge bases, competencies and specialization. Technological innovation can therefore not be divorced from institutional and organizational innovation and the centrality of innovation to the persistent changes in the economy equally stems largely from the persistent national, sectoral and firm-level differences in capabilities. For its part, selection reduces variety in organization, firms, products, processes and technologies. There are market and non-market selection mechanisms that vary in intensity depending on the environment in which they are embedded (Metcalfe, 1998).

---

8   See in particular Nelson and Winter (1982), Witt (1993).

9   Dosi et al., 1988.

10   As Malerba (2002: 140) observed "Boundedly rational" agents act, learn and search in uncertain and changing environments.

Evolutionary thinking has quite a long antecedent[11] but the work of Nelson and Winter (1982) represents an important point of departure in understanding firm and industry level behaviour of agents and how the processes of technical change stimulate economic growth. Their model focuses on micro-level 'behaviour' represented by organizational routines and search behaviour within a selection environment. The organizational routine of a firm is likened to the gene in biological evolution (although they are not similar). Routines are equated to habits that involve individuals in the firm with their skills and experiences.[12] In short while routines apply to an organization, skill is an attribute of the individual.

Search behaviour arises because firm and organizational routines tend to lock actors in a certain direction that might be difficult to change. Alteration to existing routines would take firms on a search process that is highly uncertain and dependent on its extant knowledge base. A technological learning process has a great deal of in-built technological variety. The complex character of knowledge (particularly the idiosyncratic tacit and localized nature of firm-level knowledge) that may be completely outside the current domain of the firm makes the search behaviour of firms a relevant concept in evolutionary thought.

However, there are limits to a firm's search process in Nelson and Winter's evolutionary model, which incorporates Herbert Simon's bounded rationality in that there is a limit to the knowledge available to a firm due to accessibility conditions. In other words, a firm has access to only a small part of all possible knowledge and such knowledge may not necessarily translate to innovation as a result of limited technical and managerial capability of a firm. For this reason, firms develop routines because they are boundedly rational in their learning, production and innovative activities where they face transaction costs. In effect, firms would not necessarily process knowledge of all available technical, production and marketing possibilities.

The learning process and performance of a firm is conditioned by the selection environment which could be market or non-market selection resulting from the demand and supply conditions in markets, as well as from the institutional and policy context. Selection exerts powerful influence at another level, which is as a determinant of the sources of learning. A learning trajectory as Malerba argues, is a result of the structures of learning which in turn generates the pattern of observed innovation (Malerba, 1982; Metcalfe, 1997). There are diverse sources of learning apart from doing R&D which include learning-by-doing, learning-by-using and learning-by-interacting. Other forms of building up what Edquist (2001) called structural capital (knowledge capital controlled at the organization level by individuals) include training and hiring skilled individuals.

---

11   We will not go into the debate but see Dosi et al. (1988) for different perspectives and theoretical reviews.

12   Nelson and Winter (1982: 72) define a skill as: "Capability for a smooth sequence of coordinated behaviour that is ordinarily effective relative to its objectives". Skills contain elements of tacitness that is neither easy to communicate nor written down.

Thus organizational routines, search behaviour and selection environment are the main pillars of the theory of micro-evolution.

Institutions and systems of learning and innovation

The observed differences in national economic performance is traced in large parts to the differences in their institutions (North, 1996). The comparative empirical work of Nelson (1993) on national systems of innovation showed that countries have developed different knowledge bases in research and development (R&D), and the capacity for innovation. Various authors have emphasized directly and indirectly, the centrality of institutions to systems of innovation in the way the concept is defined. The broad definition provided by Edquist (1997: 14) underlines the point. He defines an innovation system as: 'all important economic, social, political, organizational, and other factors that influence the development, diffusion, and use of innovations'.[13]

In sum, we infer from the above that the systems of innovation framework has roots in evolutionary economics as well as its Neo-Schumpetarian variant (Dosi et al, 1988). Having outlined the evolutionary technical change dimension, we turn to the links with institutional foundation and we summarize them in five broad theoretical connections, which we state without elaboration.[14] First, institution is a strong selection mechanism for innovation. This has market and non-market origins and the latter provides the leverage for policy intervention at several levels of the economy (Metcalfe, 1997). Second, learning processes are key determinants of innovative activities and relatedly, institutions are the carrier of knowledge. This is particularly so for tacit, non-codified knowledge at the firm-level.

> The speed of economic change is a function of the rate of learning, but the direction of that change is a function of the expected payoffs to acquiring different kinds of knowledge (North, 1996: 346) (emphasis mine).

Third, path-dependence is a central concept of institutional change and it equally underpins learning and innovating activities that are essentially heuristic with feedback loops (Edquist, 1997). Fourth, as Sampat and Nelson (2002) rightly observe technical innovation relies strongly on institutional innovation, the absence of which has been responsible for much of the policy failures in developing countries technology acquisition efforts. Fifth, considerable diversity is generated through learning in much the same way as the economic change is brought about by market and non-market selection mechanisms that create diversity (Edquist, 1997: 7).

In the next section we outline the broad methodological and conceptual direction of the book.

---

13 Beije (1998: 256) defines it as 'a group of private firms, public research institutes, and several of the facilitators of innovation, who in interaction promote the creation of one of a number of technological innovations (within a framework) of institutions which promote or facilitate (or hamper) the diffusion or application of these technological innovations'.
14 Chapter 2 of this book is devoted to a theoretical review of institutions.

Concepts and methodological issues

The unit of analysis in the two different studies reported in this book is the SME and the countries covered are Nigeria, Uganda, Kenya and Zimbabwe. Details of the sample and methods are provided within the individual chapters. The underlying principles are the forms of industrial organizations and varieties of institutions that have emerged to explain the sources of firm, industrial and national level competitiveness, which we discuss in the subsequent chapters in this book. The chapters are complimentary and focus on the central issues in the innovation systems framework such as learning processes in firms and organizations, the types of institutions promoting technological and production networks, the role of infrastructure in the growth of SMEs and institutions promoting SMEs and SMEs' clusters growth. In what follows, the key concepts are briefly discussed.

Why focus on small and medium enterprises?

While the development of small and medium firms remains central to the economic development of African countries, they have not fulfilled their expected mandate due to a number of well known structural constraints (Pyke and Sengenberger, 1992). Small firms lack the managerial and technological capabilities that are routinely internalized by large firms. In recent times, the exposure of African industry to international competition from the eighties further laid bare the structural fragility of the region's industrial system.

The traditional technology policy framework advances two broad reasons for supporting small firm activities. The first is the perceived market failure in the labour and technology markets and the second is the incidence of weak or absence of markets and institutions in developing countries (Metcalfe, 1994; Lall, 2001). As most analysts agree, there is pervasive market failure in developing countries, while widespread institutional dis-articulation exerts far greater impact on small rather than large producers. Institutional weaknesses raise transaction costs thereby constraining firms from taking advantage of market opportunities while market failures[15] limit access to markets and innovation possibilities. From a policy perspective, small and medium enterprises (SMEs) expansion generates employment and does it in ways that create positive externalities due to their wider geographic spread and quantitatively larger numbers. Support to SMEs is therefore seen as a way of attenuating the negative effects of unemployment and to generate economic growth.

---

15 Markets fail due to the problems of 'asymmetric information' and the so-called 'appropriability' factor. On the former, the difficulties in obtaining information on borrowers lead to the rationing out of such agents, notably small producers, by lenders in the financial markets. Concerning the latter, the inability of firms to capture the full benefits for instance, of R&D investment and workers' training, often lead to under-investment in these activities relative to what is socially optimal, see Biggs (2001) for empirical evidence from developing countries.

The policy response to the internal resource scarcity of SMEs and recent competitive pressures had been for state and private agencies to attempt to develop institutions and services to promote competitiveness within small firms. Central to this approach is the effort to upgrade product quality, improve design and packaging, and to raise the overall human skills of firms through *real service* provision (Pyke, 1994; Schmitz, 1992). Services are supposed to be delivered by an array of agencies that are themselves technically weak, poorly funded and largely ineffectual. The shortcomings in the types of public intervention point analysts to private options to eliminate policy biases (Hallberg, 2000). However, much of the alternative prescriptions would still require considerable state action. They include: (a) eliminating market failures that led to cost disadvantages, restrict access to markets, (b) facilitating access to information; (c) removing discriminatory practices against small producers; and (d) improving public goods.

In the recent past, there has also been a move towards greater systemic support in contrast to the previous orientation of traditional technology policy that deals largely with the conception of firms operating in isolation. This view suggests that small and medium enterprises and clusters in developing areas will need sustained systemic support to cope with the new competitive domestic and global market (Pyke and Sengenberger, 1992; Levy et al., 1999; King and McGrath, 1999; Pietrobello and Rabelotti, 2004). Greater systemic coordination in the provision of infrastructure and information for instance would lead to gains in *collective efficiency*. The aim of the SMEs' studies reported in the different chapters is to examine the role of institutional support and the ways SMEs and clusters in African countries learn through the provision of individual and collective support. In doing this we attempt to answer the question whether for instance clustering as an industrial organization strategy does foster collective learning and promote enterprise performance.

Types and sources of learning

Technological learning is the way organizations and firms accumulate technological capability (Malerba, 1992). Technological capability is the knowledge, skills and experience necessary in firms to produce, innovate, and organize marketing functions (Lall and Wignaraja, 1998; Ernst et al., 1998). Much of the technological knowledge required by small and medium firms in developing Africa is incremental and could often be acquired through what (Lall, 1992b) described as 'elementary learning' although there are exceptions within firms that have moved up in the supply chain. As a firm climbs the ladder of manufacturing complexity, the types of knowledge it requires, the nature of its organization and the forms of institution to support it become increasingly complex. In the last decade we have come to know much more about the nature of learning and capability acquisition in firms and, in what follows, I provide a brief overview.

First, learning in firms is a major source of incremental technical change and as such a firm is a learning organization, and through the knowledge it accumulates, it continually transform its knowledge assets to operate at higher orders of

Box 1.1   Ten Features of Technological Learning in Developing Countries

1. Technological learning is a real and significant process. It is conscious and purposive rather than automatic or passive. Firms using a given technology for similar periods need not be equally proficient: each would travel on a different learning curve according to the intensity and efficacy of its capability-building efforts.

2. Firms do not have full information on technical alternatives. They function with imperfect, variable and rather hazy knowledge of technologies they are using.

3. Firms may not know how to build up the necessary capabilities – learning itself often has to be learned. The learning process faces risk, uncertainty and cost. For a technological latecomer, the fact that others have already undergone the learning process is both a benefit and a cost. It is a benefit in that they can borrow from the others' experience (to the extent this is accessible). It is a cost in that they are relatively inefficient during the process (and so have to bear a loss if they compete on open markets).

4. Firms cope with uncertainty not by maximizing a well-defined function but by developing organizational and managerial 'satisfying' routines (Nelson and Winter, 1982). These are adapted as firms collect new information, learn from experience and imitate other firms. Learning is path-dependent and cumulative.

5. The learning process is highly technology-specific, since technologies differ in their learning requirements. Some technologies are more embodied in equipment while others have greater tacit elements. Process technologies (like chemicals) are more embodied than engineering technologies (machinery or automobiles), and demand different (often less) effort. Capabilities built up in one activity are not easily transferable to another.

6. Different technologies have different spillover effects and potential for further technological advance. Specialization in technologies with more technological potential and spillovers has greater dynamic benefits than specialization in technologies with limited potential.

7. Capability building occurs at all levels – shop-floor, process or product engineering, quality management, maintenance, procurement, inventory control, outbound logistics and relations with other firms and institutions. Innovation in the sense of formal R&D is at one end of the spectrum of technological activity; it does not exhaust it. However, R&D becomes important as more complex technologies are used; some R&D is needed just for efficient absorption.

8. Technological development can take place to different depths. The attainment of a minimum level of operational capability (know-how) is essential to all activity. This may not lead to deeper capabilities, an understanding of the principles of the technology (know-why): this requires a discrete strategy to invest in deepening. The deeper the levels of technological capabilities aimed at, the higher the cost, risk and duration involved. The development of know-why allows firms to select better the technologies they need, lower the costs of buying those technologies, realize more value by adding their own knowledge, and develop autonomous innovative capabilities.

9. Technological learning is rife with externalities and interlinkages. It is driven by links with suppliers of inputs or capital goods, competitors, customers, consultants and technology suppliers. There are also important interactions with firms in unrelated industries, technology institutes, extension services, universities, associations and training institutions. Where information flows are particularly dense, clusters emerge with collective learning for the group as a whole.

10. Technological interactions occur within a country and with other countries. Imported technology is generally the most important initial input into learning in developing countries. Since technologies change constantly, moreover, access to foreign sources of innovation is vital to continued technological progress. Technology import is not, however, a substitute for indigenous capability development – the efficacy with which imported technologies are used depends on local efforts to deepen the absorptive base. Similarly, not all modes of technology import are equally conducive to indigenous learning. Some come highly packaged with complementary factors, and so stimulate less learning.

Source: Lall (2000).

operations (Lundvall et al., Malerba, 1992). Secondly, following from above, a firm is characterized by a certain level of technical and organizational knowledge base.[16] Third, a firm draws upon a wide variety of knowledge sources (suppliers, subcontractors, machinery suppliers) that may be within its locale, but often outside the national boundary (Lundvall, 1988; Von Hippel, 1988). Fourth, there are different modes of learning and the widely known learning-by-doing, and learning through R&D are only some of these sources. Fifth, learning processes are linked to specific sources of technological and productive knowledge such as apprenticeship, equipment manufacturers and others. Six, learning does not take place in a vacuum and firms do not innovate in isolation. External actors with whom firms interact are crucial to learning in firms. Learning processes are linked to the trajectories of incremental technical change through the accumulated stocks of knowledge in firms (Malerba, 1992). Box 1.1 provides a summary.

Networking dynamics among SMEs

Systemic interaction among firms and other agents are important for the exchange of knowledge, skills and experience to engage other firms and institutions in the process of production and innovation (Ernst et al, 1998). What these authors describe as linkage capability is a most important firm asset that has not been fully explored in the literature of underdeveloped economies. In addition to internal firm capabilities, a firm succeeds on the strength of its ability to gain access to, and process a whole range of, knowledge outside of itself. It does this by internalizing such knowledge, and by continually engaging in networking with sources of knowledge within the national system and outside of it. In doing this, it contends with various actors, diverse knowledge channels and in the process develops process paths to transform knowledge into firm capabilities for production and innovation. Knowledge flows into firms arise from both within and outside the national system but in this book we are concerned with all possible interactions between internal and external sources of knowledge.

Networking could also be conceptualized as information flows and knowledge interactions, which may take several forms. The first are inter-firm flows of knowledge and skills in a user-producer type relationship, through the movement of skilled staff from one firm to another, sub-contracting (manufacturing and trade types), joint ventures, franchise, and supplier-customer relations. These diverse forms of interaction constitute important channels of flows in advanced and developing economies (Pavitt, 1984; Von Hippel, 1988; OECD, 1999). Second, there is firm-institution interaction in which public agencies such as technology development centres (of different varieties across countries), and public R&D laboratories are among the most prominent in Africa. Their mandate, in broad terms, is in assisting firms in process and product adaptations, and in gaining comparative advantage

---

16   Several but similar taxonomies have been advanced on the types of capabilities at the firm level (Ernst et al., 1998).

through utilizing natural resources. Ideally, through this mode of interaction, support institutions will assist firms in gaining access to what otherwise will be expensive information (about processes, products and competitors), and testing and quality control costs, which firms are unable to undertake, will be provided or subsidized. These are services which firms traditionally regard as 'public goods' in much the same way as power supply, water and telecommunication, but which are often completely absent, or poorly provided (Biggs et al., 1995; Oyelaran-Oyeyinka, 1997c; Romijn, 2001).

Clustering and industrialization

An industrial cluster is a dense sectoral and geographical concentration of enterprises comprising manufacturers, suppliers, users and traders. However, an innovative cluster is more than a geographic phenomenon, rather strong inter-firm interaction and sectoral specialization are the defining features of a sustainable cluster (Nadvi, 1994). In this respect, three factors distinguish an innovative cluster. First, high rates of learning and knowledge accumulation lead to continual changes to the knowledge base of the cluster. Second, high levels of networking between key agents and institutions (suppliers, producers, and so on). Third, the existence of a dense network of formal and informal institutions (Becattini, 1990; Schmitz, 1995; Saxenian, 1991). The clusters in the highly industrialized countries are characterized by high economic performance while clusters in developing areas exhibit lesser degrees of inter-firm collaboration, lower intensity of learning and have weaker institutions.

SMEs in early industrialization are largely imitative innovators drawing on a variety of market mechanisms or formal sources such as joint ventures, licencing and informal sources such as reverse engineering, learning-by-doing (Kim, 1997). As widely reported in the literature, while this category of firm may not engage in frontier technologies, the technical change processes in which they are engaged constitute important sources of learning and do lead to substantial productivity growth (Bell and Pavitt, 1993; Mytelka, 2000; Ernst et al., 1998).

Innovation, innovation systems and development

As Abramovitz (1986) observed, capital accumulation and increase in the labour force are not enough to explain variation in economic growth. 'Social capability', that is, the capacity to create and manage institutional changes specifically, the variants that support innovation, is important in fostering effective systems of innovation.

Latecomers[17] in particular need a supportive system of innovation as examples from the acquisition of semiconductor, steel and chemical industry in Korea show (Freeman, 2002). The plant scale advantage, which latecomers could exploit, impose exacting requirements in the form of high-level skills as well as a network

17 A 'latecomer' is a country that industrialized initially by borrowing foreign technology (Amsden, 1989).

of engineering, R&D and testing facilities, among others. All of these take time and efforts to build, as List (1885) aptly summed up more than two centuries ago:

> The present state of the nations is the result of the accumulation of all discoveries, inventions, improvements, perfection and exertion of all generations which have lived before us: they form the intellectual capital of the present human race, and every separate nation is productive only in the proportion in which it has known how to appropriate those attainments of former generations and to increase them by its own acquirements (quoted in Freeman, 2002: 193).

List therefore anticipated the way in which an innovation system[18] would build on past innovations and the learning efforts that need to accompany imitation by later comers' technological efforts.

While some developing countries, described by Amsden (2001) as 'the rest', have succeeded well in building up technological capabilities, African countries have been generally unsuccessful. We propose the notion of dynamic and non-dynamic latecomer systems of innovation (SIs) to describe the successful and the not so successful countries learning to imitate and industrialize. Early industrializers developed dynamic SIs and have a long history of technical (not necessarily formal scientific) culture as well as institutions supportive of entrepreneurship and a mix of skill, experience and knowledge, codified in human capital. As Lall (1992b) and Lall (2001) points out, successful SIs are characterized by a certain optimal skills structure in engineering, mathematics and sciences that support industrial development. It is not enough for a country to produce manpower per se, but also the right kinds for its level of development. While general knowledge acquired from formal educational institution forms an important component of a nation's human capital, firm-level training, R&D and production are necessary for the idiosyncratic knowledge bases of firms. Freeman, (2002) cites the human capital base of dynamic SIs, which contrasts sharply with non-dynamic SIs in SSA. Lately, attempts have been made to apply the SI concept to the situations of developing countries (Arocena and Sutz, 1999; Gu, 1999; Cimoli, 2000); following the earlier path breaking work of Freeman (1987); Lundvall (1992); Nelson (1987); Edquist (1997). Lundvall et al. (2002); Muche et al. (2003) applied the concept in a variety of situations, which has hitherto concentrated on the most advanced industrial nations to the study of the less developed economies.

---

18   Viotti (2001) suggests that developing countries should rather adopt the notion of national learning systems since they do not undertake innovation and because current application of the concept excessively dwell on R&D as a measure of innovation capability. We see no reason for a change in nomenclature inasmuch as innovation is broadly defined to include routine incremental activities on the shop floor. Secondly, our operative concept is the phrase system of innovation, rather than take the two words apart, which causes confusion, we suggest they be so understood. Systems are sets of elements standing in interaction (Von Bertalanffy, 1968). Nations, technical systems and sectors consist of elements and interact in certain complex fashions, which we need to explain. Whether advanced as in human systems or simple as in amoeba, systems are a different matter.

Box 1.2   Ten Characteristics of Innovation

- Firms do not innovate in isolation but do so within a network of other economic agents, making interaction an important element. More importantly, innovation takes place in all sectors (not only in high-tech such as biotechnology and information technology but equally in traditional sectors such as foods and beverages); and across all firm sizes (small and medium).
- All agents are involved in a continuous process of learning and as such the notion of knowledge 'producer' and 'user' has limited conceptual and policy relevance. Learning in turn is heuristic taking place over a long period of time and possessing systemic and incremental character.
- The role of knowledge has become increasingly central to an analysis of economic progress and *institutions*, carriers of knowledge. In the 21st century, innovation will be the main driver of competitive industries and enterprises.
- Innovation is intertwined with economic and technological considerations.
- The processes and systems of innovation are complex and variable.
- For these reasons there are no easy ways to measure innovation.
- The nature of market problems and constraints, and as a result, the manner of innovation generation differs from industry to industry.
- The nature of knowledge differs from industry to industry and from firm to firm.
- The nature and profitability of innovation outputs, significantly among industries at any point in time, require different efforts and expectedly yield different rates of return on investment.
- Innovations often generate benefits far from their industrial source of origin.

However, the SI in underdeveloped and industrialized countries differ in many several respects and distinctly so in three attributes. First, a large part of advanced economies are highly technology and R&D intensive. Second, industry is becoming progressively knowledge-based and innovation driven in these countries. Third, and complementary to the two, the economies have high levels of skilled manpower, its importance accentuated by the intensified global competition, driven in large parts by the twin forces of technological change and elements of globalization. Again, systems of innovation are conceptualized narrowly or broadly,[19] but in both contexts they take on the functions of the management of uncertainty, the provision of information, the management of conflicts and the promotion of trust among groups (Edquist, 1997; North, 1989). The work of Nelson (1993) was carried out within the narrow conception of SI. Other sets of studies referred to earlier, as well the series of studies undertaken at the United Nations (UNCTAD, 1999 and 2000), have widened the locus of actors considered in the national system of innovation (NSI).[20] The characteristics of innovation employed in this book are summarized in Box 1.2.

---

19   In a narrow sense, institutions correspond to organizations such as universities, technological service organizations; while in broad terms, it includes political context governed by constitutions and the rules regulating innovation activities.

20   The UNCTAD studies include the Science, Technology and Innovation Policy Reviews (STIPS) carried out for Colombia, Jamaica and Ethiopia.

Box 1.3   Characterization of Innovation

- Innovation is a product;
- innovation is a new process of production;
- the substitution of a cheaper material, newly developed for a given task, in an essentially unaltered product;
- the reorganization of production, internal functions, or distribution arrangements leading to increased efficiency, better support for a given product, or lower costs; or
- an improvement in instruments or methods of doing innovation.

The role and importance of human capital

The notion of human capital regards education as directly contributing to the formation of knowledge and skills in productive work. Human capital is the sum total of the skills level of a country's entire workforce which includes managers and administrators. We make a distinction here between formal education, which is clearly very important, and non-formal education, which has been built upon pertinent knowledge, skills and experience. The potential real income per capita of a country is a function of the productivity of its labour (Sandberg, 1982; Tortella, 1994).[21] More importantly, this experience and skills is located within an organized system, which in this case, we take to be the modern industrial enterprise.

> The firm is thus the strategic locus within which organized human capital produces new products and processes and thereby advances the productivity of nations (Amsden, 1989).

The firm itself is located within a network of other economic agents, however, systems effectiveness is a result of the competencies of actors and their interaction within the particular system.

Outline of the book

The chapters address various aspects of the theme of this book and are organized as follows. Chapter 2 places the book in the overall context of the theme of the book by discussing the theoretical aspects of institutions, technology and the path dependent character of institutional change. It advances three propositions on the nexus of institutions and technology in Africa. First, it argues that traditional technology policies in Africa failed to stimulate the desired endogenous technological dynamism because the policy process assumed away the role of institutions. Second, the capability building efforts through international technology transfer processes

---

21   See Tortella (1990) for various country studies that examine this issue.

has equally been flawed because it focuses largely on machinery purchase and the imitation of organizational forms for R&D with little consideration for the underlying institutional forms and practices in which they were embedded. Third, because the path of development is highly dependent on past decisions and actions, S&T institutions in Africa are entrapped in sub-optimal systems configurations. To the extent that institutions determine the efficiency of the knowledge creation and exchange among critical actors, the artificial separation of technology from the institutional structures in which it is created was a major conceptual and policy mistake. Moreover, organizations created for advancing technology development had little connection with the enterprise, the locus of industrial production and innovation. The influence of institutions in long-run economic development is discussed with illustrations from the technological and institutional lock-ins in the extractive industries and the evolution of formal educational institutions in Africa.

Chapter 3 examines the links between different forms of technological knowledge and the learning processes by which they are created in African industry. The growth of knowledge has much to do with the effectiveness of past as well as current institutions and the depth of available stock of local knowledge. Local stocks of knowledge develop through local efforts as well as from imported technical skills from outside the national system. We make a distinction between formal and 'non-formal' local learning institutions. It is upon the latter that small firms rely for growth, but this category of enterprise is either overlooked in conventional analysis, or in the extreme, regarded as inferior to formal learning. In this regard, a substantial part of knowledge in modern economies is attributed to measurable codified knowledge while non-formal learning, which is largely tacit in nature and far more difficult to measure, is unaccounted for. For instance, Africa's small firms, rooted in crafts apprenticeship, are likely to learn through this kind of knowledge system, and enterprise performance may therefore signal how well such institutions of knowledge are serving the firm. Learning, based predominantly on information and knowledge, is regarded as the defining concept in a world that is increasingly characterized by rapid changes in the modern sectors. In addition the chapter provides a theoretical discussion of the role of small and medium enterprises (SMEs) in African industrialization and the support institutions that undergird their growth and innovation activities. We examine the effects of clustering and the typology and nature of clusters in the region.

Chaper 4 examines the types and sources of skills and knowledge in African industry. The chapter as with the ones that follow, employ field data from the sample African countries.

Chapter 5 employs new firm-level data to analyse the nature of networks and collaboration within Africa's emergent systems of innovation. Efforts to promote systemic interactions among economic agents through political and policy coordination have not been very successful. Market coordination is weak, and private user-producer interaction among firms and other organizations have been the dominant mode of collaboration. This chapter reports statistical significance between firm performance and a number of networking variables supporting the hypothesis that inter-firm collaboration yields efficiency benefits.

Networks are increasingly important organizational forms and we need to understand their nature in order to determine their influence in systems. By networks we mean the structuring of linkages among economic agents, such as firms, in a way that results in permanency to create patterns of persistent interaction. This makes networks more than mere channels of information exchange because persistence of relations suggests structure and relative stability. The chapter compares network structures across countries in Africa. Much of the research carried out in Africa in the past focused largely on organizations making policy for S&T (agencies and ministries), and public institutions responsible for R&D. They focus much less on the systemic links between knowledge generating institutions and the agents of production, the kernel of this chapter.

Chapter 6 examines the ways in which physical infrastructure such as roads and energy constrain the productive activity of firms. Indivisibility confers a system's character on infrastructure and, in so doing, constrains or fosters production and innovation.

Chapter 7 discusses the broad rationale for small firm support and the limited success of the traditional technology policy methods. The underlying theoretical argument is the perceived market failure in the labour and technology markets and, secondly, the incidence of weak or absence of markets and institutions in developing countries. There exists pervasive market failure in developing countries, as well as widespread institutional disarticulation, which exert considerable impact on small rather than large producers. Institutional weaknesses raise transaction costs, thereby constraining firms from taking advantage of market opportunities, while market failures limit access to markets and innovation possibilities. Policy makers view support for SMEs from the perspective of employment generation and the creation of positive externalities due to their wider geographic spread and quantitatively larger numbers. Support to SMEs is therefore seen as a way of attenuating the negative effects of unemployment and to generate economic growth.

Consistent with the central theme of the book, Chapter 8 analyses the informal and formal institutions that promote the processes and the dynamics of cluster growth and clustering in Africa. The importance of clustering has been widely discussed in the context of dynamic European conditions and the importance of support mechanisms recognized. In this chapter, our interest is to raise the issues of localization of clusters within the communities and locale in which they are embedded. Tacit knowledge, which underpins much of the dynamism of small producers (see Chapter 3), constitutes an enduring strength of clusters, which need to be developed. Porter (1998) suggests the strength of clusters can be found 'increasingly in local things – knowledge, relationships, motivation – that distant rivals cannot match'. Institutions, both informal and formal, provide the framework for cluster embeddedness, and act as the 'social glue' (Porter, 1998: 12) for cluster cohesiveness. 'The mere co-location of companies, suppliers, and institutions creates the potential for economic value; it does not necessarily ensure its realization' (ibid:12). Institutionalization is more than the mere presence of organizations, it connotes repeated patterns of behaviour on the part of the actors over a long period of time. I therefore proceed with the 'obvious' proposition that clustering may have been slow in developing for the precise reason that institutions that promote specialized services and firms are absent to take on manufacturing linkage roles. Manufacturing subcontracting in different clusters with contrasting history, habits, and practices are examined to provide some evidence for the proposition. We analyse the nature, content and factors that determine the pattern of collaboration among SMEs in one rural-based and one metropolitan cluster, viz., Nnewi and Lagos in Nigeria respectively, as well as small enterprise clusters in Ghana, Uganda and Kenya. The influence of social networks on manufacturing that have persisted and deepened because of weak institutions of contract enforcement is also examined. However for clusters to move to innovation systems, formal institutions support would be required to strengthen embedded nord practices.

Chapter 2

Institutions and Technology in African Development

This chapter advances three propositions on the relationship of institutions and technology. First, it argues that traditional technology policies in Africa have failed to stimulate the desired endogenous technological dynamism because the policy process assumed away the role of institutions. Secondly, the capability building efforts through international technology transfer processes have equally been flawed because they focus largely on machinery purchase and the imitation of organizational forms for R&D, with little consideration for the underlying institutional forms and practices in which they were embedded. Third, because the path of development is highly dependent on past decisions and actions, institutions of S&T in Africa are entrapped in sub-optimal systems configurations that took root over the last four decades. To the extent that institutions determine the efficiency of the knowledge creation and exchange among critical actors, the artificial separation of technology from the institutional structures in which it is created was a major conceptual and policy mistake. The influence of institutions in long-run economic development is widely recognized (Nelson and Nelson, 2002; Mokyr, 2002; Rosenberg, 1976; Edquist, 1997).

Technology has long been recognized as a social process shaped by institutional structures in which they are embedded. While the cumulative increases in workers' productivity in industrial countries has been driven largely by technological advance, investment in physical capital and the growth of human capital, these factors are shaped in very profound ways by institutions. Institutions supporting technical advance are to that extent extremely important to long term economic growth precisely because technology underpins the introduction of new products and processes in the economy. In an industrially dynamic context, causing changes to the machinery and equipment, the introduction of new forms of industrial organization will be accompanied by 'new institutions, the institutionalization of... new social technologies may require new law, new organizational forms, new sets of expectations' (Sampat and Nelson, 2002: 49). The corollary is that, in a situation of economic backwardness, changes to institutions are rare just as technological innovation might be equally rare or non-existent.[1] Institutional changes become

---

1   Nelson and Sampat (2001) cite North (1990) re-articulation of the 'institutional obstructionist' notion of economic backwardness as being responsible for the failure of poorly performing economies to adopt productive technologies.

even more crucial at a time of human engineered structural change. Indeed structural adjustment must necessarily be attended by deep-going structural shifts.

While quantitative performance of institutional innovation may be difficult to measure, aggregate structural changes revealed by indicators such as the composition of GDP, trade and labour distribution, are undergirded by, and reflect the long-run outcome of institutional and technological changes. The difficulty in measurement may well explain the rather casual treatment of institutional innovations. According to Mensch (1978), institutional innovation co-evolves with technological innovation and introducing new technologies is always accompanied by organization change.

There are varying levels at which the impact of institutions could be analysed depending on whether one is interested in more micro or macro issues. Scott (2001) identifies six categories, namely, the levels of world systems, society, organizational field, organizational population, organization and organizational subsystem. Our focus is on the level of societies in Africa and the level of organizational field, a category similar to the vocabulary of innovation systems.[2]

Again, institutions are conceptualized narrowly or broadly,[3] but in both contexts they take on the functions of the management of uncertainty, the provision of information, the management of conflicts and the promotion of trust among groups (Edquist, 1997; North, 1989).[4] For these reasons, institutions are necessary for innovation for two reasons. First, the innovation process is characterized by considerable uncertainty. Institutions act to provide stability and to regulate the actions of agents, and to enforce contractual obligations. Second, learning and knowledge creation, validation, and distribution are prerequisites of modern economic change mediated by institutions such as R&D, finance and investment organizations and as rules, such as intellectual property rights, patent laws and so on. This chapter will examine institutions and their role in supporting technical advance in the process of development, the meaning of institutional path-dependence and lock-in, the configuration of institutional systems in Africa, and what prospects exist for deploying the productivity-enhancing properties of technology to build Africa's systems of innovation.

---

2   Quoting from Scott (2001), DiMaggio and Powel (1983) define an *organizational field* as 'those organizations that, in aggregate, constitute a recognized area of institutional life: key suppliers, resource and product consumers, regulatory agencies, and other organizations that produce similar services or products' (p. 143).

3   In a narrow sense, institutions correspond to organizations such as universities, technological service organizations, while, in broad terms, it includes political context governed by constitutions and the rules regulating innovation activities.

4   Coriat and Dosi (1998) refer to the broad meaning of institutions as having three components, which are: (a) formal organizations (ranging from firms to technical societies, trade unions, universities and state agencies); (b) patterns of behaviours that are collectively shared (from routines to social conventions to ethical codes); and (c) negative norms and constraints (from moral prescriptions to formal laws).

Path dependence in institutions and systems

This chapter employs the broader concept of institutions and locates it within a historical context that admits the evolution of institutions themselves (David, 1994; Zysman, 1994; Coriat and Dosi, 1998) and calls attention to a set of issues in understanding institutional evolution. First is the origin of the institutions, and the need to explain institutions that preceded them and the mechanisms that led to institutional transition. Secondly, they refer to the degrees of intentionality of institutional constructions. In other words, whether institution arose out of a *self-organizational* process or derived from a collective *constitutional* process. Third, there is the concern for institutional efficiency. The point is whether institutions are merely 'carriers of history' in the sense of David (1994) and simply 'path-dependently reproducing themselves well beyond the time of their usefulness (if they ever had one)' (Coriat and Dosi, 1998: 7).

Path dependence refers to a decision-making process in which the present and future depends on the history of past actions and in which self-reinforcing dynamics is present. In this way, the trajectory established by initial conditions persists and conditions the choices made afterwards. As North (1990: 98–99) puts it: 'Path dependence is a way to narrow conceptually the choice set and link decision-making through time. It is not a story of inevitability in which the past predicts the future'. Making choices on new directions is constrained by the increasingly high cost of reversing previous ones, and the narrowing[5] of the scope of new ones. In the vocabulary of Nelson and Winter (1982), path dependence is the persistence of routines and the institutionalization of habits and practices. There are numerous examples of technological lock-ins in the literature, but as North (1990) tells us the same characteristics that lead to technological lock-in such as sunk costs and network externalities apply to institutional lock-in. For instance, industrial societies are described to be in a state of carbon lock-in, where increasing returns to fossil technologies makes the adoption of more sustainable technological and institutional alternatives difficult. Institutional path dependence could be conceptualized as the pre-eminence of sub-optimal norms, regulations and rules in the face of better alternatives (Pierson, 2000; Mahoney, 2000; Woerdman, 2003). An institution could therefore approach a situation of temporary or permanent stasis: a state of lock-in. Five broad causes are identified as being responsible for institutional lock-in namely: the emergence of a superior alternative, the perceived or real increasing problem-solving capacity of an existing stable policy, incomplete information, external shocks, and lastly high set-up costs.

---

5   Woerdman (2003) resolves administrative costs into set-up costs of establishing an institution structure and the running costs of day to day operation. Set-up costs are resolved sunk costs (of existing structure) and the switching costs to a new establishment. Examples of organizational set-up costs include information collection and processing costs, establishing legal frameworks, of (re)allocating property rights, and the costs of making contracts.

Institutions and development

As Mokyr (2002) correctly noted, institutional structures produce different outcomes and certain distinct factors define the trajectories of national and local institutions. The role of institutions in African societies from the perspective of path-dependent development is widespread.

At the macro level, three types of institutional structures have been identified as accounting for the observed development of the SI in Africa. First is the pre-existing level and pattern of postcolonial education enrolment as a proxy of human capital, a strong determinant of national technological capacity. Second, factor endowment, which had been the starting point for wealth creation in other regions, may well be an obstacle to development.[6] Factor endowments have strongly determined the course of investments and subsequently, the path of endogenous technical change. Conceived as rules and norms of behaviour that structure repeated human interaction, institutions strongly influence the pattern of endogenous technical development. In an increasingly interdependent global context, institutions may not necessarily be endogenous to regions and societies; they may be, and are often, imported.[7] In any event, much of the economic prosperity of latecomer countries is ascribed to technologies and institutional forms borrowed from the west (Amsden, 1989). For this reason the institutional assignment of latecomers is different from that of the west: they are largely dedicated to the search for and the adoption of, technologies transferred from advanced industrial countries.

While analysts agree on the role of institutions, our knowledge of the origins of institutions in Africa is limited. The literature identifies three distinct institutional forms shaped largely by national resource endowments, which are said to have created three kinds of 'societies'. They have been classified as enclave societies, industrializing 'Western' societies (including Japan) and colonial societies (Engerman, 2000). In enclave societies, factor endowments pattern the evolution of institutions leading to high-income inequalities and skewed levels of human capital, which tend to favour certain groups. Enclave economies are created by a combination of local political interest and foreign investment in agriculture, and mineral resources with a strong export orientation. These sectors are characterized by 'extensive scale economies' requiring exacting technological capabilities in investment and production.[8]

Enclave driven institutional structures are found in mineral producing countries of Africa such as Zambia, Nigeria, South Africa and Ghana, and the Sugar Islands and Latin America. The resource profile of enclave economies exhibits broadly

---

6   The term 'resource curse' has been used to describe the lack of growth-generating effect of natural resources in developing countries, see Mikesell (1997) and Aunty (1993).

7   For instance, the system of organized R&D within laboratories is an invention of the West. See Rosenberg (1986).

8   This necessary conjunction of domestic and international partnerships is referred to as 'disproportionate political influence' and 'extensive scale economies' by Engermann and Skoloff (1997).

similar characteristics, consisting of plentiful land to support plantations (tea, coffee, banana and sugar), or minerals (copper, gold, diamond, iron ore, bauxite). Capital and technology intensiveness are normally higher than average in setting up mineral processing complexes, and so are skill requirements. While specialization grows, the imperative for manufacturing through alternative industrial organizations such as small and medium enterprise is reduced. Institutions supporting enclave production systems often get locked in, with a strong exclusionary effect. Alternative modes of industrial organization are foreclosed and the dominant institution exhibits persistence and self-reinforcing attributes.

The second type of society is well known. Rosenberg and Birdzell (1986) trace the evolution of western scientific and technology society that culminated in the pattern of the extant innovation system in much of the OECD countries today. The third type has three broad variants, which we may broadly classify as dynamic latecomers and non-dynamic latecomer systems of innovation.[9]

The weaknesses and the pattern of evolution of institutions in Africa have been identified as major causal factors in Africa's development (Aron 1996; Engelman and Sokoloff 1997; Clark 2000). There is a plethora of literature on the slow and episodic development of Africa's economy, but we know of no empirical studies that have attempted to identify the technological roots of Africa's so-called 'growth tragedy' (Easterly and Levine, 1995). Yet, African economies had initial technical conditions that might have provided the basis for building endogenous technological capabilities.[10] However, in the four decades since colonialism, they have failed to do so.

Again, while poor institutions have been identified as central to the growth crisis, few studies have identified the nature and type of such institutions.[11] Endogenous

---

9   The first variant is made up of the 'Asian Tigers': South Korea, Singapore and Taiwan, and following closely, India, Brazil and China. The second variant consists of the 'newly industrializing countries'– for example, Thailand and Malaysia, countries relying on foreign direct investment for the development of their systems of innovation. The third variant is largely found in Africa and South Asia. These societies have strong colonial legacies, low levels of technology, a rudimentary system of R&D and an industrial structure based on low value products requiring non-complex technologies.

10 For example, around 1500, major centres in Sub-Saharan Africa (SSA) had higher rates of urbanization than North America. According to Bairoch (1988: 58): 'Leading examples of urbanization around the time of 1500 are to be found in the Kingdoms of Ghana, Songhai, Benin, Congo, Zimbabwe and the Yoruba States. Around 1500, the city of Benin had a population in the range of 60-70,000 and was a well ordered urban centre with a system of water conducts and a sizable artisantory working at an advanced technical level.' Moreover, as Acemoglu et al. (2000: 9) noted: 'There were sizable cities in Black Africa by 1000 BC, if not earlier.' In the Middle Ages, Kano City (in modern Nigeria) had a population of 30,000 while Yorubaland (in Nigeria) had a dozen towns with population of over 20,000 and its capital, Ibadan possibly had 70,000 inhabitants (ibid: 9).

11   A recent exception is Kayizzi-Mugerwa (2003) Reforming Africa's Institutions Ownership, Incentives and Capabilities UNU-WIDER.

institutions have shaped the path of development and have in turn, been deeply moulded by development. For instance, Kenwood and Longhead (1992) noted that the immediate changes to aboriginal institutions included the reorganization of laws and institutions according to the interests of metropolitan entrepreneurs and states. British colonial policies systematically pursued policies that created 'extractive institutions', as did the Portuguese and the Dutch.[12] The political structure, which constitutes part of the broad system of innovation, as different from the narrow restriction to organizations (R&D, university, and so on), experienced considerable changes as a result of external influences.

As Acemoglu et al. (2000) observe, institution building was far removed from the strategy pursued under a colonial policy, whose primary objective was to exploit natural resources. The institutions of property rights, law and order that took root in the colonies of Australia, Canada, New Zealand and the US persist in African countries till today; so also the colonial institutional legacy and its variant, the extractive-induced institutions. The nature of these institutions essentially turned the colonies into sources of primary products, while discouraging the growth of potentially competitive manufacturing industries.[13]

Institutional discontinuity[14] in the colonies therefore patterned the trajectory of industrial evolution in non-trivial ways. Meanwhile institutional continuity, which is the hallmark of the long-term cumulative accumulation of industrial capacity in Britain resulted in sustained export advantage:

> During the nineteenth century the development and utilization of labour resources provided the British cotton industry with its unique sources of competitive advantage... No other cotton industry in the world could readily acquire Britain's highly productive labour force; no other industry in the world had gone through the century-long development process that had produced the experienced, specialized and cooperative labour force that Britain possessed (Mass and Lazonick, 1990), cited in (Freeman, 2002: 197).[15]

---

12   For example, the philosophy of King Leopold of Belgium was patterned after that of the Dutch in Indonesia, which was that 'the colonies should be exploited, not by the operation of a market economy, but by state intervention and compulsory cultivation of cash crops to be sold to and distributed by the state at controlled prices' (Acemoglu et al., 2000: 9). A classic illustration of the disruptive policy of colonialization is the following statement by a French official: 'The European commandant is not posted to observe nature ... he has a mission ... to impose regulations, to limit individual liberties ... to collect taxes' (Young, 1994: 101).

13   Pre-colonial India, for instance, had a thriving textile industry, which was practically destroyed in order for India to be a major source of cotton for British industry. This policy was uniformly applied in most of the colonized areas in Africa such as Kenya, Nigeria and Ghana.

14   We define institutional discontinuity, as North (1989) did, as a major change to the routines, rules and norms of behaviour that repeatedly structure human interaction in a society. Major reversals to institutions require equally massive organizational and technical investments to learn and sustain the new institutional routines.

15   In other words, while British colonial policy might have been responsible for industrial continuity in its conquered territories, there was more to its long-term success. The SI that

African states are not *new* states, but a continuation of old societies as well as 'successors to the colonial regime inheriting its structures, its quotidian routines and practices, and its more hidden normative theories of governance' (Young, 1994: 283). Institutions persist even as they evolve, but they take their cue from initial conditions.[16] In an account by Wittfogel (1957), control structures erected by large empires of China, Russia and the Ottoman Empire persisted for over 500 years into the twentieth century. Unlike in other African countries, French settlers in Mauritius supported the institutions of property rights and gave strong backing to business, and later expanded the country's export-processing zones. Mauritius' success is in large part traceable to these institutions.

The persistence of initial conditions

The notion of hysteresis has been applied to the persistence of initial conditions in Africa (for example, Aron, 1996). It is particularly relevant to the process of industrialization, which takes place over a long period of time. Insights into how unequal opportunities resulted from different institutional structures come from the divergent evolution of countries in the Americas in the last three centuries (for example, Engerman and Sokoloff, 1997). For example, Mexico, Barbados, Cuba and other colonies were either richer than, or had similar per capita incomes with, the United States in the sixteenth century. Today, in a process that started with the Industrial Revolution, the United States has become the richest country in the world, while these countries, formerly rich in natural resources, fall behind. Two sets of explanations are offered: the first is the role of technological innovations and the rapid productivity growth of industry in the United States and Canada. Secondly, institutions that promote technical innovations and wider participation through mass literacy and human capital flourished in the US and Canada, and much less so in the other countries. Limiting access to education effectively restricts the advance of entrepreneurship and subsequently, industrialization.[17]

Initial institutional conditions therefore seem to shape the pattern of institutional changes over time and thereafter dictate the outcome of the State and individual efforts.

Another important outcome of initial conditions is the creation of *discontinuity* in the nature of institutional power structures, the social processes of learning

---

evolved in Britain robustly supported production. It is for this very reason that institutional reversal in the colonies could be an explanatory variable since curtailment of export and the promotion of primary products specialization could be said to have effectively killed export capacity. See Acemoglu et al. (2000).

16 Persistence of institutional forms have been documented by Wittfogel (1957), Engermann and Sokoloff (1997), and North et al. (1998). Citing Acemoglu et al. (2000) provide strong evidence that colonial institutions persist.

17 By the mid-1800s, countries in Latin America had a fraction of the literacy rates of those in the United States and Canada, since Latin American countries did not provide universal primary education until the twentieth century.

and knowledge accumulation. Based on historical and econometric evidence, Acemoglu (2000) shows that European colonialism not only led to major change in the organization of these societies, but also an 'institutional reversal'. European colonialism led to the development of relatively better institutions in previously poor areas, while introducing *extractive institutions*[18] or maintaining existing bad institutions in previously prosperous places.

The kernel of their thesis is that interaction between institutions and the opportunity for wider participation in the industrialization process through human capital accumulation was important to the long-run development of former European colonies such as the United States and Canada. The initial conditions such as geography and natural resources were instrumented to the earlier higher rates of per capita income in many countries. However, the process of industrialization changed the path of development resulting in the central role of institutions in development.

To place the foregoing historical and resource-based factors shaping institutional systems in context, we draw specifically on a modified version of Carlsson (1997) treatment of technological systems defined as a network of agents interacting in a particular area of technology to generate, diffuse and utilize technology. He identified four important elements that are important to the functioning of systems. They are: the initial conditions and nature of technology spillovers, receiver competence or national absorptive capacity; linkage capacity of the system (connectivity); and, lastly, the variety creating mechanisms. The role of path-dependence on each of these elements in the evolution of innovation systems in two different environments is summarized in Table 2.1. In this approach, we take institutions as 'products of their environments', as well as the carriers of the history, which helped in forming them. Historical precedent thus assumes an important place in the analysis in addition to the basic assumption that industrialization is an evolutionary process. As David (1994: 215) observes: 'institutions typically evolve new functions and because these are added sequentially they are shaped by internal precedents'.

In the context of development, we define two types of systems for ease of analysis. The first is a dynamic and a rapid learner termed *First Tier System of Learning Innovation in Development (SLID1)* and the second is non-dynamic and slow learning termed *Second Tier System of Learning Innovation in Development (SLID2)*. For instance, East Asian countries that achieved rapid economic progress through learning industrialization represent the former, while many African countries fall in the latter category. There are several measures that differentiate developed from underdeveloped areas.[19] Complementary indicators of SLID1 and SLID2 will be

---

18 The term 'extractive institutions' means the rules and norms that support the concentration of political power in the hands of the small elite that appropriate wealth from natural resources. On the other hand, institutions of private property encourage wider spread of opportunities to all citizens to take advantage of industrialization opportunities.

19 Notably GDP per capita (high income countries have GDP/capita above US$ 9266 in 2000), high literacy levels, 100% adult literacy, low mortality rate typically less than 10 per 1000. See World Bank Annual reports and UNDP Human Development Reports.

Table 2.1 Institutional Characteristics of SLID1 and SLID2 Countries

Elements of Innovation Systems	Dynamic Systems of Innovation: SLID1	Non-Dynamic Systems of Innovation: SLID2
1. Initial conditions and nature of production system	Pre-existence and continued existence of large local entrepreneurship. Knowledge bases quickly developed through imitation of advanced industrial countries; beneficial interactions with foreign and domestic suppliers.	No pre-existing entrepreneurship; largely traditional craft-based or artisan industries. Systems of subsistence trade but no factory-type system at the onset of efforts to industrialize. Importation and import substitution characterize initial technology learning efforts, which were largely unsuccessful.
2. National technological capabilities	Built up strength in mechanical engineering, strong in electro-mechanical, rapidly acquired telecommunications, information and computers technology.	Weak capabilities in mechanical or engineering industries. Trade-based commodity economies. Largely users of new technologies
3. Linkages and networks capacities	High to average degree of: Buyer-supplier links (global and domestic) Technical community network. Building of institutions through policy and spontaneously. Buyer and supplier competence in public and private domains, resulting in institutional clusters. Integration of academic and industrial institutions and with international actors leading to 'excellent observation post'.	Very weak: Global buyer-supplier links, and domestic linkages. Technical problem solving network largely absent and almost complete reliance on foreign technical services. Informal networks at the level of informal enterprises. Institutions are weak or absent. Low buyer-supplier competencies. Hardly any institutional cluster; R&D and universities only marginally important to production.
4. Education and human capital	High levels of literacy and great emphasis on human capital even in the early periods. Formal education translated to high skills attainment in industry and R&D organizations.	Inherited enrolments in education that was highly skewed; education was selective and limited to a few; educational attainment low and persists in spite of 40 years of substantial investment in education.
5. Institutions	Institutional types could be: Pre-existing organizations for generating innovations. Co-evolution with technological system of formal and non-formal types of behaviour and rules of the game.	No pre-existing organizations to generate modern innovation. Policy derived institutions are de-linked from production, much of it destroyed by colonial policies encouraging 'extractive' production type institutions.

levels of investment in R&D, hi-tech and basic infrastructure conditions, proportion of technical and scientific manpower and cohesion in the SI based on interaction intensity and ease of information exchange and flows. The learning dimension accentuates the importance of competence building that stresses both the individual skills development and organizational learning, in long-run development.

It also calls attention to the weakness of the techniques, currently employed in measuring "institutions" that tend to be static (no sense of path dependency) and largely abstracting contents and outcomes from the form. For instance if a country in Africa replicated a R&D laboratory from the USA, then it is assumed to be developing and institutional for research capable of the same level of effectiveness.

Institutional systems features in developing countries

It is generally accepted that SIs in developing countries are poorly developed and known to be subject to widespread systemic disarticulation. The analysis of policy failure from a systems perspective has been described variously as systemic failure or systems failure (OECD, 1998: 102; Edquist, 2001, 235). A fundamental position of evolutionary theory[20] is that institutions are not neutral, but are subject to x-efficiencies much in the same way that firms do not always perform at optimal levels (Niosi, 2002a). The inefficiency of institutions stems from their history and their connectedness to previous environment. In other words, institutional evolution is path-dependent, and inefficiency could arise from any of several sources. In analysing institutional features, we identify three broad systemic categories in developing countries. They are a pointer to the strengths and weaknesses of national systems and at the same time provide a rationale for new sorts of interventions to build competencies and promote greater systemic cohesion where they are needed.

Rigidities in organizations and institutional intertia

While organizations may be subjected to strong inertia pressures, lack of perceptible change may not necessarily mean that an organization is not changing. There could be either of two possibilities. First, an organization may respond too slowly relative to the changes in the local, national or global contexts. This might well be the case with much of the perceived slow speed of adoption of quality standards imposed on firms in the least developed countries (LDCs) in the wake of liberalization of financial markets and production. Secondly, organizations may be subjected to much too strong structural inertia, relative to their internal capabilities, to make on-going changes inadequate. Dissipative forces, arising from rapid structural reforms for instance, re-focused the attention of organizations and firms to non-core activities that render real substantive changes difficult or impossible. For instance, reform 'conditionalities', such as forced budgetary cuts, led to widespread closures of universities through

---

20   In broad terms, and in whatever discipline, evolutionary theories have properties by which they explain the processes of self-transformation, an issue central to our thesis. According to Witt (2002), an evolutionary theory is: (i) dynamic – such that the dynamics of the processes, or some of their parts, can be represented; (ii) historical – in that it deals with historical processes which are irrevocable and path-dependent; (iii) self-transformation explaining – in that it includes hypotheses relating to the source and driving force of the self-transformation of the system.

strikes and created instability in other levels of the educational sector. Faced with this situation, universities were unable to pay the desired attention to developing necessary knowledge and physical infrastructure that over time suffered decay. Firms had to cut back on foreign imports and technical services all too suddenly due to massive devaluation of local currencies. Subsequent reduction in the number of production shifts and lay-off of staff resulted in industry-wide decline in capacity utilization. Under this condition, quality improvement and learning through staff development became a second-order priority. Staying in the market and not falling further behind becomes a major objective.

However, learning speed and the nature of structural inertia have to be viewed relative to what (Hannah and Freeman, 1984: 154) have described as, 'temporal pattern of changes in key environments'. Deeply entrenched organizations should have been more intensely institutionalized. However, the forces of inertia from the environment might also accompany higher levels of embeddedness. Through repeated learning, organizations develop and modify their routines by which their legitimacy is established and competencies recognized. These routines are institutional memory that are often difficult to change or change very slowly. As Nelson and Winter (1982: 96) observe, routines are 'the sources of continuity in the behavioral patterns of organizations'. This is evident in the evolution of the S&T systems in the western world and in the lessons they hold for evolving institutions in Africa.

The linkage of science to production had been preceded by a long history of technological advances. Indeed the systematic wedding of science into industry could not have been possible without certain basic prerequisites. First was the development of large-scale manufacturing, especially the machine tools industry. Secondly, scientific disciplines did not develop at the same rate. The lack of adequate understanding of certain natural phenomena constrained further advances in other fields. For example, the compound steam engine could not be commercialized until cheap, high-quality steel came into the market (Rosenberg, 1986).

Similarly, hard alloy steels found very limited utility until complementary machine tools were invented to work them. In his *Science in History* (1954), Bernal talks of a definite succession of the order in which areas of experience are brought within the ambit of science. Roughly it runs: Mathematics, Astronomy, Mechanics, Chemistry, Biology and Sociology. Marx had also observed that, of all the disciplines that found use before the industrial revolution, it was mechanics that attained a certain degree of perfection. Mechanics and the machine industry undergirded the industrial revolution.

By 1875, science had begun to develop explanations for some natural phenomena in a coherent and systematic manner. Bridging the gap between science and industry might have been aided by two related reasons – the potential practical applicability of the explanations offered by science and the translation of the potentials of science into unprecedented economic growth. According to Rosenberg (1986), the need for the coupling of science with the economic sphere resulted in what amounted to a system for innovation, first at the level of the firm and then at the level of the economy as a whole. What emerged in organizational terms was a novel combination of the manufacturing and marketing functions of the business enterprise with scientific organizations, under the same management, and pursuing common goals and incentives. This revolutionary scientific-technical regime was anchored at one end in industrial research laboratories invented to apply scientific methods and knowledge to commercial problems, and, at the other end, in consumer purchase and use of a product or service embodying that knowledge.

Basic science thus became an increasingly powerful force in the productive sector. Gradually the skill of the artisan and the genius of the lone inventor became increasingly subsumed in the Galbraithian technostructure. As Marx perceptively noted, 'Invention then becomes a business, and the application of science to direct production itself becomes a prospect, which determines and solicits it' (Marx, 1973: 704). This leads to our second observation. The technical foundation of industry having been laid, the post scientific era found a secure anchorage. Without the endogenous technical capability accumulated during the pre-scientific era, when metallurgy and machine tools industries developed, it would have been near impossible to erect the present complex industrial structures. This is a lesson easily missed by structural adjustment advocates and African policy makers themselves. Systems of innovation support production, while production systems take a long time to build. 'Getting the price right' cannot possibly be a panacea, neither could it be a substitute for the fundamental evolutionary assignment of *getting the institutions right.*

But these developments seem more like consequences than causes of the West's unique institutional invention: a large, highly organized body of scientists seeking explanation of all natural phenomena by a common method based on observation, experiment and reason. This achievement can be credited to a large extent to the successful invention of an institutional form that suits the context of that particular environment. This unique characteristic of modern industry distinguishes it from the nineteenth century industrial revolution. Indeed, it is doubtful if the scientific-technical revolution of the twentieth century could have been possible without it. Galbraith (1985) sums it up very succinctly:

> The real accomplishment of modern science and technology is in taking ordinary men, informing them narrowly and deeply and then, through appropriate organization, arranging to have their knowledge combined with that of other specialized but ordinary men. This dispenses with the need of genius (ibid: 64).

Most African countries, in an attempt to achieve scientific and technological progress, engaged in the wholesale imitation of industrialized country models such as the establishment of specialized R&D institutes, whose function was to generate scientific knowledge from which industry and agriculture would then draw, as and when needed.[21] We do not need to belabour the fact that this great experiment

---

21   The establishment of R&D organizations seemed to have been taken to represent a system of innovation. This idea unfortunately persists in conception and practice. The so-called 'linear model' of innovation has had a profound influence on the thinking of African policy makers for decades. See Vitta (1990).

achieved very limited success. We suggest that the two most important causes of this failure is the *lack of an institutional base* for innovation, and, secondly, the right kinds of human capital to build and sustain a technical foundation for industry. Rather than aim to draw more on the *underlying principles and processes* that had generated the diversity of past and present institutions, African countries tend to have focused on building organizations without paying much attention to institutions to sustain them. By this, we mean the evolutionary process of innovative design and development, which had fitted institutions to differing and changing contexts, while usually embedding individual components within functionally coherent structures. By simply imitating structures that work for the present context in the industrialized countries, African countries ignored the fact that these institutions were products of an *organic* process, rather than mechanically given forms. The institutional forms were created, refined and adapted to given contexts over a long historical period. As a result, problems of functional incoherence were designed into the structure from the beginning. The present institutional structures observed in the industrialized countries were radically different from what they were half a century ago.

The impact of initial conditions, the quality of pre-existent national human and industrial capabilities is well illustrated with the persistence of educational institutions established several decades earlier.[22] For instance, whereas African governments have recorded substantial progress in educational attainment, very few changes have been made to the structure of the education system that had existed during the colonial era. King (1991) suggests that African policy makers had very little influence over the development of their education systems. He argues that foreign donor agencies and other international institutions operating in the continent largely influenced the education system that evolved in post-colonial Africa. The donor/client dependency relationship that emerged hindered the capacity of Africans to develop educational policies that were socially relevant and financially feasible (King, 1991).[23] It seems that the combination of this legacy and the lack of significant African involvement in education policy formulation resulted in an education system, which still remains elitist in ethos and does not cater for the employment and skill needs of the continent.

---

22 Some of the materials used in this section provided the basis for our argument in a recent book chapter, 'Human capital and systems of Innovation in African Development', Oyelaran-Oyeyinka and Barclay (2003), pp. 93–108.

23 For example, at the Addis Ababa conference of 1961, which was one of the first conferences that sought to address the education system in Africa, King notes that the African voice appears to have been 'indistinct'. This also seems to have been the case for subsequent conferences, such as the UNESCO/ECLA of 1962, and research reports, such as the Faure Report of 1972, which were all influential in shaping educational policies in Africa. See King (1991: 73–90). In addition, it is interesting to note that it was only in the late 1980s that the World Bank began to make a conscious attempt to include African nationals in analytical work for their various education sector studies. Prior to this, the Bank used its own staff or those of UNESCO for such work. See World Bank (2001a; 64–65).

The education system, specifically at the tertiary level, produces an inappropriate mix of skills. African institutions of higher education presently enrol 60 per cent of students in the arts and humanities and 40 per cent in science and engineering. Enrolment in technical subjects presently lags behind that of other regions. While in 1995, only 0.04 per cent of persons as a percentage of the population were enrolled in technical subjects such as engineering and mathematics, the figure for the four Asian Tigers was 1.34 per cent (Lall, 2001). In a technical enrolment index constructed by Harbison-Myers,[24] Norway ranked first with 73.52, while South Africa, the most industrialized country in SSA, had a total of 23.61, Nigeria, 5.85 (less than 9 per cent of the Norwegian figure) and most of SSA ranged from 1 to 5. Policies of the past that limited emphasis on technical enrolment may have been appropriate in the early independence period when most African countries were faced with a paucity of administrative staff. However, this skill mix has remained unchanged for the past four decades despite the declining demand for arts and humanities graduates and the rising and unfulfilled demand for science and engineering graduates (World Bank, 1988; Fabayo, 1996).

Learning has proceeded very slowly, and institutional change has equally been slow. The quality of education offered in Africa, considered to be well below world standards, tends to be falling further. Education standards are increasingly declining with the gap in achievement between African students and those in industrialized countries 'widening to unbridgeable proportions' (Clark, 2000: 82). Notably, the student/teacher ratios at the primary and secondary schools have steadily increased in the post 1990 period especially in low-income, semi arid countries such as Gambia and Chad, as well as in middle-income, oil importers such as Botswana and Zimbabwe (see Figure 2.1). In addition, there has been a drastic decline in the quality of physical inputs (for example, African staff, especially at the senior levels, and learning resources and facilities) that are essential for the successful operations of knowledge institutes. The declining quality of education is largely a result of constant budget cuts (since 1980) together with rapid increases in enrolment rates. This has made the financing of education recurrent costs more difficult (World Bank, 1988). As Figure 2.2 shows, the expenditure per student at all levels has declined drastically since 1970. This decline is more severe for secondary and tertiary education, with most low-income countries experiencing the most severe declines. Indeed, in countries such as Chad, Gambia and Niger, government expenditure per secondary student fell from US$ 536 in 1970 to a mere US$ 90 in 1995. Expenditure on tertiary education fared no better: spending per student dropped from US$ 5,054 in 1980 to US$ 1,185 in 1990.

---

24 See Lall (2001). Technical enrolment index is tertiary enrolment (times 1000) plus tertiary enrolment in technical subjects (times 5000), both as percentage of population.

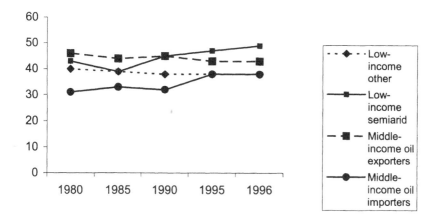

Figure 2.1   Student/Teacher Ratios in Primary Schools in Africa, 1980–1996
Source: ADEA, Statistical Profile of Education in Sub-Saharan Africa (1999).

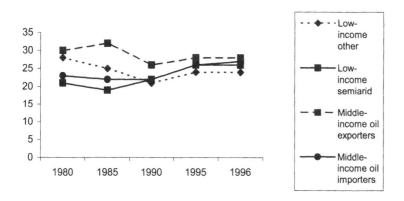

Figure 2.2   Student/Teacher Ratios in Secondary Education in Africa, 1980–1996
Source: ADEA, Statistical Profile of Education in Sub-Saharan Africa (1999).

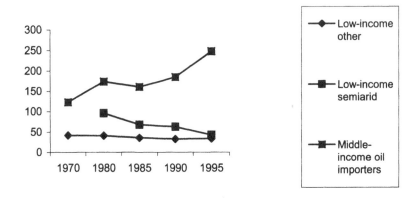

Figure 2.3   Government Expenditure on Primary Education per Student (Constant 1990 US$)

Source: ADEA, Statistical Profile of Education in Sub-Saharan Africa (1999).

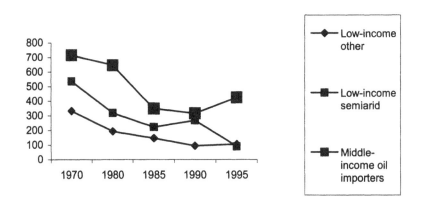

Figure 2.4   Government Expenditure on Secondary Education per Student (constant 1990 US$)

Source: ADEA, Statistical Profile of Education in Sub-Saharan Africa (1999).

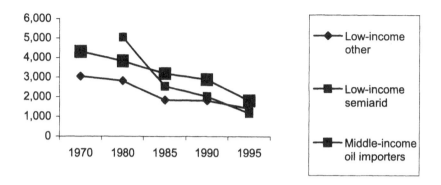

Figure 2.5 **Government Expenditure on Tertiary Education per Student (constant 1990 US$)**
Source: ADEA, Statistical Profile of Education in Sub-Saharan Africa (1999).

Moreover, firm-level training, which complements the education system, is weak in Africa (see Chapter 3 for details). Enterprises, with the exception of the major multinationals, invest very little in training. In addition, the apprenticeship system that exists in Africa is more geared to the development of traditional skills, which are of a very low level of technological sophistication (Lall, 1995).

Institutional systems lock-in is aptly demonstrated by the structure of Africa's extractive industry. For instance, while Ghana has a fairly long history of mining, it has not developed a viable local system of engineering supplies and services in the way we have seen in a country like Peru; which in any case is estimated to be some ten years behind the Chilean mining system, the regional leader. The relative contribution of mining to GDP for an industrialized country, for example, Canada, may not be too different from that of Ghana and South Africa, but mining contribution to export earnings is considerably higher for developing countries. With Canada's 14.9 per cent, the Guinea's (largely bauxite) 90 per cent and Botswana's (diamond) 80 per cent, these figures suggest two possible reasons: (a) significant dependence of resource-rich developing countries on export earnings from these commodities; and (b) limited diversification of the developing economies and, as a result, poor domestic linkages of mining with the national system.

Aryee (2001) computes a contribution to export earnings per unit to GDP index for three countries. The index shows the linkage intensity of the mining sector to the economy. The higher the value of the index, the more an enclave the mining sector tends to be. The index reflects the extent of Canada's mining sector integration with the local economy with the least index figure in contrast with which Ghana has the highest. Commenting on Ghana's mining, he concluded, 'Linkage with the rest of the economy is predominately fiscal' (ibid, 73). While the mining sector in Ghana employs some 13,000 persons, they are mostly with the mining companies and little or no capital goods and service companies. While mining contribution to national earnings continues to improve, '[o]verall multiplier tends to be low. Linkage with the production sector of the economy are weak; much of the technology and machinery continues to be imported with most sub-contracting work going to established overseas firms' (Aryee, 2001: 73). In Ghana 12 of the 16 currently operating mines are 90 per cent foreign-owned with practically all machinery and equipment imported and minerals exported with little linkage to the national economy. Consistent with the nature of large-scale mining established several decades earlier, machinery and equipment are imported due in part to the enclave institutional nature of the sector.

Transforming a traditional enclave sector into a dynamic system requires efforts on all fronts and by all agents in the national system. More importantly, it might take considerable effort to break from an essentially inferior practices and norms or what is referred to in the literature as 'unlocking lock-in or exit from lock-in'. In other words, building and maintaining organizations depend, to a considerable extent, on available public resources and the ability of actors to honour contractual and political commitments. Government involvement tends to create its own idiosyncratic lock-in conditions for two main reasons. First, governments have the authority to override market forces, thereby creating alternative institutions to which actors have to respond. Second, state institutions tend to persist for much longer periods due to in-built processes that make alterations to essentially constitutional rules slow and difficult (Walker, 2000; Unruh, 2000). Institutional gaps may in part be traced to the inability of African governments to establish necessary agencies due to financial constraints and poor or a lack of information on what institutions are required. Private involvement in institutional creation is very limited.

The lessons for African policy makers seem at once complex yet simple. The role of institutions is sharply illustrated by examples cited above, but the context is as different as the past century is from the present one. What worked in the last fifty years may not be applicable now, and what worked for Europe may not be entirely suitable for the present state in Africa. What seem important are the underlying principles: the role of institutions and their path-dependence, and the importance of investment in human capital at all levels from formal schooling to industry.

Organizational ineffectiveness

Different types of organizational ineffectiveness manifest as system inefficiency (Niosi, 2002a). The relevance of existing research and training institutes, for example, has been questioned; the former for their lack of linkages with the productive sectors and the later for their limited ties to dominant actors in the economy such as SMEs. This gives rise to the poor coordination of knowledge and economic production functions, leading to imbalances in the demand and supply for skills of the right kinds, quantity and quality mix at sectoral levels and over time. Poor resource commitment for meeting organizational commitments, including poor funding and inadequate staffing, are also common and may lead to x-ineffectiveness. While there is a general agreement that developing countries need to create organizations and institutions where they do not exist and reform those that are functioning poorly, institutions for policy making themselves lack both broad and specific competencies in their coordination functions. This is a serious drawback for developing countries and leads to a situation in which policy coordination is largely politically driven in the absence of strong market coordination.

Institutional gaps

In developing countries, the systemic weakness found in the innovation system is, in part, a result of the fundamental weakness of political-policy institutions and processes. There are institutional inadequacies that manifest themselves as lack of rules of the game, poor enforcement of contractual laws, and inadequate intellectual property laws, which may constitute disincentives to innovation and technological learning. These lead to inefficiencies in the functioning of innovation systems. Building S&T institutions in Africa is almost totally a public[25] sector endeavour.

Efforts to stimulate the evolution of a formal system of innovation could be said to have commenced in the 1950s and 1960s, when African countries embarked on the establishment of research and development institutions (RDIs) as a means of acquiring technology. This was done in tandem with the setting up of policy institutions such as 'national research councils' for S&T or ministries of S&T. In terms of numbers and range of RDIs, it would appear that considerable progress was made. National research councils were established in Ghana, Mali and Niger. Ministries of S&T were set up in Senegal, Burkina Faso and Nigeria; Ethiopia and Tanzania had commissions for S&T; an Academy of Scientific and Technological Research was established in Somalia, while Sudan had a national research council. Between 1974 and 1987, these bodies grew from four to 28, with a consequent increase in the number of research personnel. However, while there have been considerable increases in the number of institutions and agencies and some success in agriculture, the qualitative impact of the exercise remains, arguably, little, in the industrial sector (see Chapter 1). One important reason is that S&T policy institutions remain distant from top-level decision and planning machinery of governments because S&T policy was interpreted to mean R&D policy. What should have been a systems-wide cross-sectoral policy for industrialization was conceptually frozen into 'councils' and ministries of S&T. The policies, unknowingly, encouraged the isolation of RDIs from the mainstream productive sector, and it is on these agencies that much of the money budgeted for S&T in SSA is expended

Maintaining these organizations to achieve effective service delivery depends to a considerable extent on available public resources. However, government involvement tends to create its own idiosyncratic lock-in conditions for two main reasons. First,

---

25 Unruh (2000) cites Williamson (1997). Williamson's (1997) observation that formal governmental institutions change over timescales of decades, while informal institutions such as values and culture, change over centuries.

governments have the authority to override market forces, thereby creating alternative institutions to which actors have to respond. Second, state institutions tend to persist for much longer periods due to in-built processes that make alterations to essentially constitutional rules slow and difficult. However, institutional gaps may in part be traced to the inability of African governments to establish necessary agencies due to financial constraints and poor or a lack of information on what institutions are required. Private involvement in institutional creation is very limited.

Summary

In this chapter, we advanced three propositions on the relationship of institutions and technology. First, we argued that traditional technology policies in Africa have failed to stimulate the desired endogenous technological dynamism because the policy process assumed away the role of institutions. Secondly, the capability building efforts through international technology transfer processes have equally been flawed because they focused largely on machinery purchase and the imitation of organizational forms for R&D with little consideration for the underlying institutional forms and practices in which they were embedded. Third, because the path of development is highly dependent on past decisions and actions, institutions of S&T in Africa are entrapped in sub-optimal systems configurations. To the extent that institutions determine the efficiency of the knowledge creation and exchange among critical actors, the artificial separation of technology from the institutional structures in which it is created was a major conceptual and policy mistake.

Chapter 3

Learning Knowledge and Skills in Small and Medium Enterprises: A Theoretical Review

Introduction

This chapter takes off where chapter two ends by examining the links between different forms of technological knowledge and the learning processes by which they are created in African industry. It links knowledge generation with the behaviour and institutional support for small and medium enterprises (SMEs) and clusters. A particularly relevant concept to the system of innovation is the interaction of different actors through three broad learning channels namely, R&D, competition and networking. The chapter first discusses the relevance of institutions to knowledge and skill creation and in the sections that follow, elaborates on the notions of inter-organizational collaboration, and the nature of systemic support for SMEs and clusters. The chapter closes by discussing how learning is related to enterprise support systems.

Institutions and types of knowledge

The growth of knowledge is related both to historically generated learning institutions as well as the depth of available stock of local knowledge.[1] This stock of knowledge could come from outside the national system or developed through domestic efforts. There are also the so-called 'non-formal' local learning institutions, upon which the growth of small firms rely, but which are either overlooked in conventional analysis or, in the extreme, regarded as inferior to formal learning. In this regard, a substantial part of knowledge in modern economies is attributed to measurable codified knowledge, while non-formal learning, which is largely tacit in nature and far more difficult to measure, is unaccounted for. For instance, Africa's small firms, rooted

---

1 However as Johnson and Lundvall (2003) observe, what is important is the process of learning rather than the stock of knowledge. They offered the notion of the 'learning economy', 'as an economy where the ability to learn is crucial for the economic success of individuals, firms, regions and national economies...the learning economy is not necessarily a hi-tech economy. Learning is an activity which takes place in all parts of the economy, including so-called low-tech and traditional sectors' p. 143.

in crafts apprenticeship, are likely to learn through this kind of knowledge system; enterprise performance may therefore signal how well such institutions of knowledge are serving the firm. Learning based predominantly on information and knowledge is regarded as the defining concept in a world that is increasingly characterized by rapid changes in the modern sectors. Whatever the source of information and knowledge, 'low income countries and regions are as strongly affected by the learning economy and, in a sense, experience the need for competence building even more strongly than the metropolis'.

Forms of knowledge and the relevance of skills transfer processes have been altered significantly by advances in digital technologies as well as by the changes in the economic contexts particularly the liberal regimes of trade and production (Lundvall and Johnson, 1994; Johnson et al., 1994; Ducatel, 1998). However, debates about the most appropriate mix of skills and the most important sources of knowledge accumulation are likely to continue in the foreseeable future. For instance, the discussion on how to assign the relative weights of formal and experiential or non-formal knowledge in firms underlines the conceptual dichotomy of tacit and codified knowledge. Despite the increasing propensity to codify technical functions, tacit knowledge remains an important component not only in the context of traditional sectors and small firms, but also as a necessary cognitive basis for interpreting codified knowledge including digital and mathematical functions.

Institutions as carriers of knowledge

The concept of 'institution' is often used interchangeably with that of 'organization'. While the normative and cognitive aspects of institutions are stressed, greater emphasis is laid on the structural dimension of organization. 'Institutions are transferred by various carriers-cultures, structures and routines' (Scott, 1995: 75).[2] Institutions, being far more pervasive and often more influential in their impact than the economic system, tend to exert profound effects on the internal processes of producing entities. Herein lies the importance of institutions in determining the rate and direction of technical change.

Organizations may be set up to perform technical functions, but being embedded in a social context, they take on 'value-impregnated status' and, in the process of time, their goals or procedures become institutionalized (Selznick, 1949: 256–257, quoted in Scott (2001: 23). Several organizations for science and technology research and policy in the last four decades were established in Africa, but their objectives remain largely unfulfilled. One of the explanations for the poor performance of these organizations may well be the mechanistic conception that guided their establishment

---

2   Scott (1992) defines organizations as entities set up around definite processes that result in the attainment of particular goals. To this end the structure of an organization will be shaped by the different functions, roles, and rules that promote good performance.

with little consideration for path-dependent parameters defining their evolution.3 Organizations find their meaning and legitimacy through this process and ultimately, support and resources for their existence. As Selznick (1948: 16–17; emphasis in original) observed, organizations are the 'structured expressions of rational action', but they are also organic social systems and to that extent, they are transformed over time.

> Institutionalization is a process. It is something that happens to an organization over time, regarding the organization's own distinctive history, the people who have been in it, the groups it embodies and the vested interests they have created, and the way it has adapted to its environment...In what perhaps its most significant meaning, 'to institutionalize' is to infuse with value beyond the technical requirements of the task at hand (quoted in Scott, 2001: 24).

Types of knowledge

We follow the taxonomy proposed by Johnson et al. (2002) (hereafter JLL) that views knowledge in terms of what, who, why and how we know things. In this treatment we focus narrowly on what Kuznets (1965) termed 'useful knowledge', by which he meant technological knowledge as the source of modern economic growth.[4] JLL identified four forms of knowledge, namely, 'know-what', 'know-why', 'know-how', and 'know-who'. At the organizational level these categories of knowledge translate into 'shared information databases', 'shared models of interpretation', 'shared routines' and 'shared networks'. Know-what refers to knowledge about facts which is largely codified, while know-why is the knowledge of principles, rules and ideas of S&T. This form is primarily codified, but relies considerably on tacit knowledge for interpretation – particularly at the level of individual understanding. Know-how is the skill and knowledge of doing things reflected in such activities as industrial production and, due to the process of acquiring it, has a significant tacit component. Lastly, know-who is the knowledge of individuals gained through shared social interactions and networking. Mokyr (2002) confined his analysis to 'know-what', which he defined as propositional knowledge[5] and which can be used to create 'know-why' or instructional or prescriptive knowledge, otherwise called

---

3   According to Parson (1956: 16–58) organizations are differentiated vertically into three broad but distinct levels, namely, the technical that does production; the managerial, that is concerned with control, coordination and resources and product procurement; and, lastly, the institutional. The last function relates the activities of the organization to the norms and convention of the community and society in which it is located.

4   See Mokyr (2002), *The Gifts of Athena: Historical Origins of the Knowledge Economy* for a seminal treatment

5   Know-what, according to Mokyr (2000: 5), takes two forms: 'one is the observation, classification, measurement, and cataloguing of natural phenomena. The other is the establishment of regularities, principles, and "natural laws" that govern these phenomena and allows us to make sense of them. Such a definition includes mathematics insofar as mathematics is used to describe and analyse the regularities and orderliness of nature.'

Table 3.1 Learning Processes and Types of Knowledge

	Know-What	Know-Why	Know-How	Know-Who
Knowledge type	Codified	Codified	Tacit	Tacit
Sources	Facts and information	Scientific principles and laws	Skills acquired through experience	Developed and maintained through personal contacts in research groups and production networks
Transfer processes	Formal joint	Formal	Non-formal	Non-formal
Learning context	Digital libraries Formal institutions (Libraries)	Digital libraries Formal institutions	Workplace Research and Training centres	Workplace Research and Training centres

techniques. What this means is that know-what (episteme) provides the basis for know-how (technique);[6] for instance, to translate a model or an invention into practical instructional manual. One knowledge form would feed on the other. Table 3.1 presents the taxonomy.

This way of looking at knowledge has several implications for transfer mechanisms, and for the development of institutional forms (formal education, the role of firms, and training). Ducatel (1998) talks of the learning triangle consisting of theoretical, vocational and experimental forms, which, translated to institutional terms, suggests a closer interaction between formal schooling and workplace training. For African countries there are four broad implications. First, a large part of knowledge in these societies is tacit in nature; African societies thrived on oral history and much of techniques are passed on from master craftsman to the apprentice. Even if this is hardly acknowledged in official documentations, much of learning takes place through this institution of apprenticeship and, for much of

---

6   Techniques are the fundamental unit of the technological knowledge set. They are essentially sets of executable instructions or recipes on how to manipulate nature, much like Nelson and Winter's 'routines'. When these instructions are carried out in practice, we speak of production and they are no longer knowledge but action. It is comparable to DNA instructions 'being Mokyr' (2002).

history, knowledge of nature was regarded as secrets to be passed on to the chosen, this most often being the offspring.

Secondly, institutions for codification of knowledge were hardly developed and 'modern' organizations for doing this are embedded in many widely accepted social systems and practices. Thirdly, orthodox measurements of knowledge generation and flows concentrate largely on measurable data such as patents, scientific publications and R&D statistics. These practices, having been adopted by developing countries' policy makers and scholars, tend to underrate institutions of apprenticeship with a vast knowledge base that is largely tacit. Attention is focused on formal schooling, such as universities, to the exclusion of enterprise level skills and traditional crafts. Fourthly, while scholars and multilateral organizations call for increased investment in knowledge of the type that is rewarded with certificates, the precise mix of such skills, which we acknowledge is very important, is not specified and the tendency is to assume that formal training is all that developing countries require. On the contrary, skills required for building modern economies are far more complex and cannot all be acquired in formal schooling, important as they are. Ducatel (1998) identified seven sets of skills, namely: (1) the capacity to manage models mentally; 2) the workings and interactions of machines; (3) the capacity to make inferences from statistics; (4) willingness to take responsibility for work process and products; (5) oral and visual communication capacity; (6) combining technical and business skills; (7) ability to make good judgement. These skills are not acquired through formal schooling but are extremely important for industry.

Varieties of learning and types of knowledge

Non-formal learning, which often takes the form of learning-by-doing, is an important component of human capital, but this is particularly so in economic contexts where traditional craftsmanship, often acquired through apprenticeship, predominates. Knowledge of production, which is largely tacit, relies largely on the skills (know-how) of workers although skill itself draws on know-why to find reasons for particular procedures or routines.[7] In this chapter we will examine, in some depth, the nature, prevalence and role of apprenticeship, and the links with tacit knowledge in promoting learning in firms.

Tacit knowledge is a bundle of information that is more easily expressed than spoken. It is built from considerable practice and accumulated experience in some narrow tasks, for instance by an apprentice learning from the master. For this reason it is idiosyncratic, but not necessarily inapplicable to other situations. For instance,

---

7   A metallurgical technician could mix iron ore, coal and other materials under the right kind of temperature and obtain molten iron without any knowledge of why this reaction had taken place. Yet skill is not the domain only of technicians; an accomplished mathematician requires elements of both know-why and know-how to be effective in solving complex problems. To master calculus, one requires consistent practice, the domain of skills and tacit knowledge.

a great many people use the computer to perform quite complex operations, yet cannot define what an operating system means; neither is it necessary for individuals to be able do so. There are many dimensions to tacit knowledge,[8] but much of the tacit knowledge in firms is transformed into organizational routines[9] (Nelson and Winter, 1982). Routines are regularities and predictable patterns of behaviour. In small firms, the owner/manager tends to define and exemplify the nature of routines. In apprenticeship institutions, the master personifies the routines and determines the culture and rates of transferring this largely 'hard to pin down skills' to learners.

The nature of tacit and codified knowledge brings us to the issue of formal and non-formal institutions. As Stiglitz (1999), 11) argued, developing countries need to formulate effective ways to promote *local knowledge institutions* because clearly

> the overwhelming variety and complexity of human societies requires the localization of knowledge. ...Practical know-how is largely tacit knowledge that needs to be learned by horizontal methods of twinning, apprenticeship, and seconding.

There is a clear distinction between global public goods and local knowledge and, for this reason, every society should be active in strengthening local knowledge institutions to drive the local learning process. In transforming codified global knowledge to local use, only a proportion can be transferred by formal methods, while the rest would often require a long heuristic process of imitation, reverse engineering, learning-by-doing and apprenticeship. Stiglitz termed these processes of learning 'horizontal methods of knowledge transfer', while the formal codified storable mode is called 'vertical transfer'. On the one hand, these largely practical informal methods take several forms.[10] On the other hand, formal learning is characterized by five distinct characteristics, namely: (1) it has a prescribed framework; (2) an organized learning package or events; (3) the presence of a designated teacher or trainer; (4) the award of a qualification or credit; and (5) the external specification of outcomes (Eraut, 2000).

Formal institutions and learning provided the seedbed for much of the innovation in the past but non-formal learning in factories led to equally momentous technical improvements (Rosenberg, 1976: Landes, 1999). Each served and continues to serve

---

8   Lubit (2001) identifies four categories of tacit knowledge, namely, (a) hard to pin down skills-'know-how', (b) mental models, which show us how the world is constructed, (c) ways of approaching problems, and (d) organizational routines. The word skill implies tacit knowledge which range from the ability to swing golf balls to the dexterity of handling cells in a biology lab, all which are hard to explain in words.

9   According to Nelson and Winter (1982: 167), 'Routines solidify as standard operating procedures and roles are developed and enforced. Routines include ways of producing things, ways of hiring and firing personnel, ways of handling inventory, decision-making procedures, advertising policy, and R&D procedures'.

10   Among these are: study tours to other countries, cross-training which is a form of 'learning-by-observing' in other countries, an implicit knowledge acquisition process that is different from explicit training on how to do things, twinning or seconding which pair together institutions in a horizontal knowledge exchange process (Stiglitz, 1999).

different evolutionary goals. For instance, the French system of polytechnics,[11] with its emphasis on the abstract and theoretical, succeeded in graduating bright individuals that led to building railways, assimilated the best of British metallurgy and formed the cream of French engineering and technocracy. However, there was a lacuna and private based institutions for on-the-job training were established to build on theoretical knowledge. Employers founded them in order to replace the apprenticeship system of old. In other words, the establishment of theory-based scientific institutions was not a sufficient condition for industrial progress, particularly given the example of Britain's industrial revolution that was driven largely by learning-by-doing. The lesson from these is that institutions do serve certain ends, but they are highly conditioned by the social and economic contexts as well as by the national absorptive capacities.

Apprenticeship, a process of skill formation, is a form of local knowledge institution. It often lasts from a period of about six months to three years and tends to be organized by small firms, although not limited to it (Velenchik, 1995). It is a form of learning in which the learner, in addition to learning a skill from the firm, provides labour services to the firm or the owner of a business unit. This institution is widespread in Africa, but has long historical roots in Europe and elsewhere.[12] The practice takes different forms – from highly structured training in large firms, as is the case in Germany, to the more loosely organized 'learning-observing own work mates'. Training is the object and the mode of instruction takes on a variety of forms – from the use of specific instructional manuals (codified) to unspecified and randomly assigned oral tasks (tacit basis) that the supervisor may give - each feeding on the other. The written and unwritten contract is the agreement to teach and to learn for a fixed period of time.

In the African context, apprentices tend to emerge from the young, low ability range with no more than secondary education, but more likely with even less (Velenchik, 1995). Training is of a generalized type that takes place on the job. Findings concerning the types of skill differ. While some findings confirm the generalized nature of the training, others found it to be idiosyncratic with little possibility of skill transfer to other firms. The alternative is for an apprentice to establish his own firm and to replicate the routines he learnt (Frazer, 2002). Frazer found that educated workers in Africa tend to be more productive apprentices, as are apprentices who remained where they trained; although he cautions that this may have no general applicability.

Inter-firm and organizational learning in systems of innovation

Central to the evolutionary and systems of innovation (SI) thinking is the interactions among different actors, namely the organizations and institutions undergirding the

---

11 These were the Ecole Polytechnique (originally named the Ecole Central des Travaux Publics) founded in 1794 (Landes, 1999).

12 Smits (2001) traces the practice to the reign of Tiberius Augustus in AD 36.

exchange processes. Shaped in large part by the technological capabilities of the country and the institutional capacity for innovation, different organizations would provide different types of technical services. For instance, the firm is regarded as the locus of production and research, while universities and PRIs equally carry out research, consultancy as well as scientific and managerial manpower training. However, there are diverse and important sources of technology and innovation in SI, including engineering and maintenance organizations, equipment suppliers and raw material producers (Lundvall, 1988).

The SI is relevant to analysing collaborations precisely because innovation takes place within a network of actors for the production and use of new knowledge (Lundvall, 1992: Freeman, 1987). As these scholars define it, a SI comprises firms and other organizations with their routines and habits interacting in ways to produce, utilize, diffuse and adapt knowledge within a given socio-political and economic context. Mediating this process of innovation are learning and institutions. Learning takes place in interaction among actors within a given context that is socially embedded within institutions. Interaction fosters knowledge flows - both old knowledge used in new ways and new knowledge diffused as innovation. Interactions could be market or non-market mediated but we now know that such interactions are common and widespread. According to Edquist (2004), 62-97 per cent of product innovation cited in the community innovation survey (CIS) was achieved in collaborative arrangements.

A SI is characterized by the heterogeneity of agents that constitute the several sources of external knowledge for augmenting internal technological capability in firms. The non-firm agents include universities and PRIs, both of which rank high although their contribution depends on a number of historical and institutional factors.[13] For instance, universities in developing countries contribute only marginally to industrial research and production and, for this reason, governments have established and relied largely on PRIs, although these organizations suffer perennial funding problems. In the more industrialized countries, public funding of PRIs have been central to the evolution of the research system.

In turn, PRIs and universities are established to produce trained manpower and, in the process, they facilitate the exchange of personnel between academic institutions and industry. This important human capital function, the movement of scientists from universities to industry, and the formation of other formal and informal collaborative arrangements underlie the importance of networking among the SI actors. Academic-industry exchange has grown in recent years for three broad reasons. First, much of

---

13   For instance in highly R&D-intensive countries such as the Netherlands and Sweden, ministries of education provide block grants to universities to carry out R&D in general or specific mission-related funding in specific sectors. In others, specific direct grants are the main instruments and less block grants. The institutions supporting universities also vary widely and, for this reason, the nature of research and innovation might differ. For instance, while regional governments are responsible for the largely autonomous universities in the UK, research councils provide grants on competitive basis (Edquist, 2004).

the knowledge is tacit in nature and transferable only by personal communication between scientists. Tacit knowledge is a bundle of information that is more easily expressed than spoken. It is built from considerable practice and accumulated experience in some narrow tasks, for instance by an apprentice learning from the master. For this reason it is idiosyncratic but not necessarily inapplicable to other situations. There are many dimensions to tacit knowledge,[14] but much of the tacit knowledge in firms is transformed into organizational routines[15] (Nelson and Winter, 1982).

Second, the declining state of funding of university research and training exerts pressure on researchers to find alternative sources of funding. Third, the escalating sunk costs of R&D and the associated risks with innovation outcome makes isolated efforts difficult.

However, there are four broad challenges in achieving fruitful collaborations among SI actors. First, the nature of knowledge generation and transfer between Universities and Public Research Institutes (UPRIs) is complex, highly systemic and context-specific, particularly as a result of the significant, though hardly acknowledged, tacit content of scientific skills required which will therefore require more than codified format. Secondly, there is a wide gap between the motivation, scope and purpose between academic research and industrial research and production. This complicates the transfer process, and restricts the scope for policy incentive (Dasgupta and David, 1994).

Third, external collaboration for purposes of building capabilities and carrying out innovation could be very costly and require prior knowledge and skills on the part of firms, while the outcome of this essentially learning process is uncertain.

Fourth, as a result of differential motivations (put crudely, firms seek profit, academics seek published papers), public research organizations are often ranked low as sources of technical information despite the considerable investments made on them. For instance in a study by Drejer and Jorgensen (2003: 84), only

> one third of the firms found the importance of government laboratories to be either moderate or very significant. No firm indicated that the information from universities or government laboratories was crucial for the innovation process.

On the contrary, over 90 per cent of innovative firms identified suppliers of components and materials as moderately significant sources of information in

---

14 Lubit (2001) identifies four categories of tacit knowledge, namely, (a) hard to pin down skills-'know-how', (b) mental models, which show us how the world is constructed, (c) ways of approaching problems, and (d) organizational routines. The word skill implies tacit knowledge which range from the ability to swing golf balls to the dexterity of handling cells in a biology lab, all which are hard to explain in words.

15 According to Nelson and Winter (1982:167), Routines solidify as standard operating procedures and roles are developed and enforced. Routines include ways of producing things, ways of hiring and firing personnel, ways of handling inventory, decision-making procedures, advertising policy, and R&D procedures'.

Denmark. Previous work confirms this finding. DeBresson et al. (1998) found that universities and PRIs are cited by only an insignificant number of firms (15 per cent) for collaboration. In effect, user-supplier interactions constitute an important and significant source of collaboration within the SI. User and supplier firms build different kinds of relationships with one another in the process of production, innovation and distribution and their roles could be highly sector-specific. For instance, users are very important actors in the instrumentation and agro-food sectors, while suppliers play dominant roles in the downstream component sector (Lundvall, 1988; Von Hippel, 1988; Malerba, 2002). Important as it is, the dynamics of collaboration has hardly been explored in the literature of underdeveloped economies. The modest contribution of this book is to try to fill this gap.

Systems conception of SMEs' support and nature of clusters

Interactive learning underpins the alternative conception of economic agents acting in isolation rather than in a systemic context. The notion of learning is central to the evolutionary economic growth literature and points to the need for continuous change through persistent engagement with other actors in the system. In this book we place the analysis of SMEs support within the systems of innovation framework.

The cognitive basis for the broader NSI framework takes its cue from Lundvall's (1988) argument that market alone is a poor filter for firm-level technical change. Other non-market coordination mechanisms in developing African countries are equally important, but they are notably weak and suffer from poor systemic coordination. Prominent among these are the weak structures of R&D, finance support, metrology, standards and quality centres, and, above all, the inadequate and declining system of education. The SI concept provides a fruitful framework for understanding the ways in which the systemic support mechanisms operate. However, the focus of such analysis will differ from what we know about the SI in advanced industrial economies. In the context of underdevelopment, the weight of empirical analysis would need to take into account three issues. First, the structures of production, which are largely low-cost/low-wage, co-existing with high-cost, technology-intensive industrial systems such as are found in oil-producing countries where the sector employs modern technologies for exploiting crude petroleum. Second, the system of knowledge accumulation would include the role of formal institutions and the processes of learning that build up human capital in addition to the skills employed within firms and S&T knowledge organizations. Third, while the ideal locus of industrial production in a developed market is the private enterprise, the state in underdeveloped areas has controlled the *commanding heights* of the economy and would have to be taken into account.[16] Policy and political

---

16 Edquist (2001: 219–237) rightly pointed to the neglect of education and the role of the state in the SI literature. The pervasive role of the state and the poor market coordination functions makes the issues extremely important.

coordination, rather than the markets, have been the dominant forms of institutional intervention in developing areas.

Evolutionary theories emphasize the interdependence of all actors within the national system, the imperative of learning (Lall, 1980; Mytelka, 2000) and doing so within a network of institutions and other firms, while firms in turn draw upon factor markets for skills, finance, technical assistance and information (Pack, 1993, Lall, 1992).

To this end, the SI concept is particularly suited to analysing the kinds of technological activities carried out in African industry precisely because it emphasizes the systemic and continuous processes that lead from investment to production and design. This contrasts with the view of R&D as the starting point of all innovation. Secondly, it hypothesizes that the nature of innovation in firms cannot be conceptualized as an isolated activity purely within the firm because firms act in complex interactions with other organizations and are governed by institutional rules. In addition to doing business with other firms, firms organize their production and marketing functions in cooperation with other actors such as universities (where this is possible), suppliers, contractors, as well as support agencies providing metrology and quality assurance services.

An industrial cluster is a dense sectoral and geographical concentration of enterprises comprising manufacturers, suppliers, users and traders. However, beyond geography, inter-firm interaction and sectoral specialization are the defining features of a sustainable cluster (Nadvi and Schmitz, 1994). In what follows, we discuss briefly the characteristics of clusters in Africa by looking at the type of clusters, levels of technological development, and the nature of formal and informal institutions supporting cluster development.

Types of clusters

There have been recent attempts to provide a taxonomy of clusters given the diversity of experiences, particularly in developing countries. Pedersen (1997: 23) identified two types, namely, diversified industrial clusters characterized by 'vertical specialisation of individual enterprises and vertical diversity of the cluster as a whole'. In this cluster, there is a broad sectoral specialization, but within the sector, individual enterprises and the cluster as a whole, are not narrowly, but horizontally specialized. Efficiency gains depend on collaboration within and outside the cluster. The second type is the subcontractor cluster, characterized by a narrow vertical and horizontal specialization by both individual enterprises and the cluster as a whole. Its collective efficiency derives from reduced transaction costs due to reliance on larger firms as subcontractors. Amin (1994) identifies three generic kinds, which are craft-based, artisinal or traditional sector industrial clusters (for example, footwear, garment making, metalworking, etc.); high-tech clusters (for example, Silicon Valley); and clusters based on interaction of large and small firms. This is similar to Pedersen's subcontractor cluster. Mytelka and Farinelli (2000) provide a functional categorization of clusters that are either 'public-induced' or 'constructed clusters' such as industrial estates and EPZs or spontaneous clusters that could be informal, organized, or innovative.[17] Low levels of inter-firm linkages characterise informal clusters, but organized clusters have advanced somewhat in this respect. There is relatively greater networking within and outside their national borders, as exemplified by the firms in Nnewi and the surgical instruments cluster in Sialkot, Pakistan.

Levels of cluster development

Clusters vary widely in their levels of development and internal structure and state of embeddedness within the social context. Accounts of the studies of clustering in Africa show that levels of technical competencies correlate closely with the nature and types of clusters delineated above (McCormick, 1999: Adeboye, 1996; Oyelaran-Oyeyinka, 1997b; Van Dijk and Rabelotti, 1997; Brautigam, 1997). In a study of six clusters, McCormick (1999) identified three levels of cluster development: groundwork enterprise clusters, which refer to those at the incipient stages whose basic role is to improve producers' access to markets and for joint action. The second category is industrializing enterprise cluster, which show 'much clearer signs of emerging collective efficiency'. The third category, complex industrial clusters are diversified in size structure and in inter-firm linkages; they exhibit strong external economies, have reached into wider national and global markets and demonstrate joint action in institutionalized professional associations, subcontracting and collaborative arrangements. In terms of internal structural characteristics, the majority of the enterprise clusters, which tend to fall in the first and second categories, operate with low-skilled manpower, exhibit weak inter-firm interactions and lack institutionalized systems of self-help. With notable exceptions of the Nnewi cluster in Eastern Nigeria, the Western Cape clothing cluster in South Africa and the Lake Victoria fish cluster, empirical studies of the relatively more advanced clusters in Africa are limited. Nevertheless, evidence from the literature suggests that clustering 'can and do promote industrialisation' (McCormick, 1999), through improved market access, pooling of labour skills, opportunities for technological upgrading (as proximity promotes exchange of technical information), promotion of joint action in dealing with external shocks.

Clusters in Africa possess unique structural and sectoral attributes and their levels of capabilities vary widely. The most commonly reported are the informal enterprise clusters in the automotive, clothing and garments sectors. Examples include the informal enterprises in the Mathare Valley, Nairobi; auto mechanics

---

17 Most clusters in developing countries fall into the informal and organized type categories. Informal clusters generally contain micro and small firms whose technologies are far from the frontier, and have relatively low technological capabilities. Organized clusters have considerable technological competence, engage in training and invest in apprenticeship system. Firms undertake technical upgrading, undertake design adaptations in response to market and can be highly organized and cooperate among themselves.

in Lagos and Ibadan, Nigeria; blacksmithing and grain milling in Awka, Nigeria and Burkina Faso respectively (McCormick, 1999; Dawson and Oyelaran-Oyeyinka, 1993, Van Dijk and Rabelotti, 1997). The next set of clusters employ relatively higher technical skills and serve a market segment in the higher income bracket.

They are a mix of small and medium firms, but largely small enterprises. Notable examples are the carpentry and metal works in the Suame cluster in Kumasi, Ghana; and footwear makers in Aba and Onitsha, Nigeria (Dawson, 1992; Oyelaran-Oyeyinka, 1997b). At a higher level still are clusters that manufacture more specialized products employing relatively more sophisticated technologies. They are distinguished by their greater subcontracting, more extensive local and global trade and production linkages. The ones reported in the literature include the Nnewi cluster in Eastern Nigeria, the clothing producers in the Witwatersrand in South Africa, and the Lagos clusters (Oyelaran-Oyeyinka, 2001; Rogerson, 2000).

Network cluster capability is as much a function of firm size as it is of its core capabilities. Small firms that possess the most basic technological capability are likely to exhibit limited domestic and probably very weak or no regional and global linkage. Learning in this kind of firm is through apprenticeship, and knowledge bases tend to be tacit, and locked in within a craft-based sector (UNCTAD, 1992; Velenchik, 1995). Small, more dynamic to medium firms tend to engage in greater supplier and trade networking and possess higher levels of production capability. Learning is from both tacit and codified knowledge bases as they tend to be more open to external sources of knowledge. Larger sized firms are engaged in greater subcontracting and have acquired higher linkage capabilities.

Sustainable clusters are characterized by two dynamic elements: the rate and types of technological learning; and the nature and intensity of linkages or networking. SMEs in early industrialization are largely imitative innovators, drawing on a variety of market mechanisms or formal sources such as joint ventures and licencing, and informal sources such as reverse engineering and learning-by-doing (Kim, 1997). As is widely reported in the literature, while these categories of firms may not engage in frontier technologies, the evolutionary technical change processes in which they are engaged constitute important sources of learning and do lead to substantial productivity growth (Bell and Pavitt, 1993; Ernst et al., 1998; Mytelka, 2000). An imitative innovation strategy demands considerable explicit efforts on the part of firms; the process of modifying processes and products leads firms on uncertain, but clearly a learning and competitive trajectory. Even the most competent firms in Africa are technological imitators that import, modify and adapt technologies. From the foregoing review on African clusters, we identify three categories of enterprise clusters, which are dynamic, emergent and static. Table 3.2 and Figure 3.1 are combined to elaborate firm technological capability with network capability in three quadrants which are rather tendencies and fluid since we deal with dynamic agents. We suggest that dynamic clusters are successful learners or imitators; emergent clusters adopt a dependent strategy and tend to react to threats rather than voluntarily imitate and innovate. Static clusters adopt a traditional strategy of non-innovative adoption of production technology. None of the clusters in Africa could be said to belong to the category of dynamic/advanced cluster (quadrant A).

In addition to internal firm-level capabilities, successful firms in clusters develop network capabilities for a number of reasons. First, competitive pressures, which alter the nature of markets and the required technical conditions, induce firms to reach for knowledge bases outside of themselves in order to reinforce extant sources in-house. Secondly, growing firms need to re-invent themselves through the acquisition of new skills and new knowledge and technical information. Third, the need to honour obligational relationships, for instance in a subcontracting or supplier relationship, compels firms to develop linkage capacity for feedback on products and services. In sum, a knowledge network, with which this chapter is concerned, enhances a firm's ability to undertake product and process innovation. Reasons for the formation of networks will vary a great deal depending on the technological capability and strategic focus of firms, the extent and type of market segments and product and the structural characteristics of network agents within the NSI.

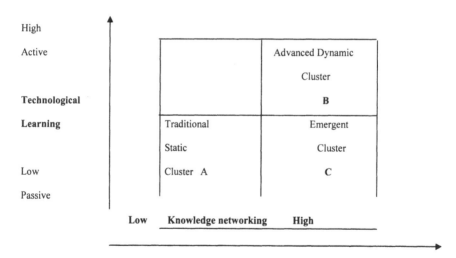

Figure 3.1   A Model of Learning in Clusters

Institutional support for small enterprise clusters

One important lesson from the literature is that clusters are not identical and so too the roles of institutions in their formation and sustenance. However, the differential performance of SMEs clusters in the various countries has opened up the debate on the need to focus policy on the role of institutions in the promotion

Table 3.2 Typology of African Clusters

Quadrant	Cluster description	Network transaction	Product/market
C	Advanced cluster High rate of learning and knowledge creating	Knowledge networking (H) Technological learning (H) R&D intensive	High product specialization and complexity Globally competitive Global linkages (H)
C	Dynamic/ Advanced cluster	Knowledge networking (A) Imitative innovation Propensity Strong linkage Capability	Competitive global/domestic Growing product Specialization Emerging global but strong domestic linkages
B	Emergent cluster	Knowledge network (L) Imitative innovation and learning Average linkage capability largely domestic	Locally competitive Low global but average domestic linkages
A	Static/Traditional	Knowledge networking (None) Poor Learning Supplier networking Mainly agglomerative Benefits Very weak linkage Capability	Not Competitive May be declining

H = High; A = Average; L = Low; N = None

of inter-firm cooperation (Pyek and Sengenberger, 1992; Schmitz and Musyck, 1993). Not unexpectedly, much existing literature focuses on the analysis of successful clusters – notably the Italian variety, which has exhibited considerable versatility and demonstrated that small firms can be successful exporters of traditional products such as shoes, textiles, and so on (Rabelotti, 1995; Cawthorne, 1995). However, there have also been cases of relatively successful clusters in Africa, Asia and Latin America, all existing within considerably diversified institutional and innovation policy settings (Nadvi and Schmitz, 1994; Adeboye, 1996). Evidently, national and industrial features differ, just as other factors driving the success of cluster models differ, as also the roles of the key actors including the state.

The clear variations in structures and the evolutionary history of clusters suggest differentiated approaches and frameworks to understand them and to find the most effective mechanism to promote clustering efficiency. For instance, the Rhine model evolved somehow naturally, while the US model was promoted through active and innovative government initiatives. These dynamic clusters have made in-roads into demanding export markets. Improving the competitiveness of SMEs therefore requires not only better inputs that are supplied by a network of subcontractors, but better use of these inputs and the ability to learn. Close interactions and cooperative arrangements among the firms are likely to raise the competitive prospects of firms. Whatever the trajectory of a cluster's evolution, the process tends to respond to creative support mechanisms through policy initiatives, but equally through the coordinative functions of embedded institutions. From the various literature on support mechanisms and industrial extension, support to clusters could be built around the key constraints that confront SMEs, namely: inadequate credit for investment and operation; low intensity formal and tacit knowledge (human skills), restrictive macroeconomic environment (policy and legal frameworks), inadequate technological, management and entrepreneurial capacity, as well as poor infrastructure. Most of the efforts, through orthodox policy aimed at solving these problems, have been directed at setting up institutions and schemes for providing real services, which may involve direct assistance for designing, building of prototypes, conducting feasibility studies, training, and providing credit and financial services for SMEs. There have been isolated success cases of individual assistance, but clearly there is evident justification for much wider public intervention for systems and clusters (Nadvi and Schmitz, 1994; Pyke, 1992; Oyelaran-Oyeyinka, 1997b) Institutions supporting clusters tend to advance collective efficiency for the following reasons:

- Poor access by small firms to a range of vocational and management training services which large firms are able to provide through internally generated resources;
- Difficulty in accessing specialized technical service centres or agencies to assist SMEs with research and development, technology acquisition, organizational upgrading and information service; and
- Lack of information.

We know very little about how effective cluster institutions support is; however, there is evidence that regions where clusters are located within highly embedded institutions, strong social networks and where high levels of trust exist among economic agents, show superior economic performance in terms of employment growth, low unemployment rates, export market performance and incremental innovation dynamism (Becattini, 1990). Examples of recent success cases which serve to illustrate the efficiency of collective support include UNIDO's support for the leather and footwear industry of Southern and Eastern Africa, the shoe producing clusters of Sinos Valley in Brazil and the surgical instrument clusters of Sialkot in Pakistan (Nadvi and Schmitz, 1994), Box 3.1. The types of support mechanisms for SMEs provided in most LDCs are shown in Table 3.3. The aim of support is, in general, to provide information as well as advise on quality and technical upgrading. Studies of collective support highlight the weaknesses of the existing policy arrangements and argue that supply side measures should be complemented with demand-driven measures such as large firm/government procurement and other market support measures.

There are some similarities in the nature of organizations and institutions supporting particular types of clusters. This is not surprising, given the well known nature of the constraints facing the largely SME clusters in developing countries. For instance, the micro and small enterprise clusters, producing for the low-end product market, lack a broad range of basic literacy skills that tend to keep them producing within the low technology regime. This makes collective support to this kind of cluster clearly important, compare Boxes 3.1 and 3.2.

Box 3.1   Collective Support to Africa's Footwear Industry

The leather and footwear industry of Southern and Eastern Africa receive support through UNIDO. The support has been channelled entirely through the national associations which participate in the programme. The two distinctive features of this programme are that first, it is demand, rather than supply-driven reflected in the support given to manufacturers to participate in international trade fairs. Trade fairs are avenues for producers to learn about competitors and markets as well as customer needs. Shared stands at fairs mitigate the fear of intimidation by larger firms and helps to attract attention to producers. The Bologna and Düsseldorf International shoe fairs provide avenues for African leather and footwear enterprises to measure their products against the best in the world. The second feature is that rather than be public-driven, the industries operate under the Eastern and Southern Africa Leather Industries Association (ESALIA). This organization has proved to be an effective channel for accessing outside assistance and a forum for regular exchange of experience among enterprises with similar problems.

Source: Nadvi and Schmitz (1997).

Box 3.2   Contrasting Structures and Supply Capacity of Meso-institutions in Developing Countries: Nigeria and South Korea

---

Industrial development Centres (IDCs) were first established in Nigeria in 1976 to provide a wide variety of services such as consultancy, extension services, training, Research and Development (R&D) and information services to informal enterprises and SMEs. By 1979 every one of the 21 States of the Federation had an IDC. Each was to be equipped with capabilities for: machine design, technical drawing of parts and components, welding, casting, machining, assembling and finishing; and quality control. While some of the older IDCs have achieved some success in service delivery, overall impact has been poor and limited to small rather than medium enterprises. A host of constraints are advanced for the less than average performance: poor funding, poor transportation, inadequate machinery, little access to technical training, poor remuneration. Entrepreneurs admit that services are highly satisfactory when provided, but lack of awareness and poor response capacity of IDCs remain a problem.

In Korea the Government used a wide array of institutions and incentives. Private sector R&D was *directly* supported through tax-exempt funds; tax credits for R&D expenditures, research-related human capital was heavily subsidized. SMEs were given shop-floor assistance and support was directly provided to upgrade technical capabilities and productivity by the Korean Production Technology Corporation (KPTC).

KPTC assists the Small and Medium Industry Promotion Corporation to give technical training, and other kinds of services to SMEs. Government research institutes operate the 'technology guidance systems' while Korea Academy of Industrial Technology also assists SMEs.

Korea's Meso-institutional support has been an outstanding success and provides useful lessons for LDCs. In over two decades, R&D funding has moved from 20 per cent private/80 per cent public to more than 80 per cent funding by the private sector. Korea aims to achieve R&D to GDP ratio of 5 per cent by the turn of the century.

The lesson here is that policies need to differentiate between LDCs and industrialized first and second-tier NIEs such as Korea in prescribing the kinds and nature of support services to be given.

Sources: Kim (1997); Oyelaran-Oyeyinka (2000).

Clusters of small producers are highly susceptible to sudden policy changes from within and outside the national systems due in part to weak institutional support and their low internal asset base to grow and innovate. According to Nadvi and Schmitz (1994), successful clusters are those that 'have an indigenous growth potential, to be resilient in the face of economic crisis and to be conducive to a process of sustained innovation'. Successful clusters achieve sustained dynamism and compete in the

Table 3.3 Types of Clusters and Institutional Support

Type of support	Institution	Incipient	Emergent	Dynamic/ innovative
Financial	Commercial banks Venture capital Development bank	Basic credit for production	Credit support Export credit Upgrading import of machines Product innovation	Credit support for production Process and product innovation Export support In-plant technical
Technical support and advisory services	Technical and vocational universities R&D institutions	Entrepreneurial guidance and advice	Pre-investment and investment Selection and procurement of machinery Project and production	R&D support for new places and products Systems analysis
Educational training	Universities Technical and vocational institutes	Book keeping and accounting functions Apprenticeship services	Production skills Upgrading management	Management skills Industrial prototypes In-plant systems change Micro-electronics
Educational training	Universities Technical and vocational institutes	Book keeping and accounting functions apprenticeship services	Production skills Upgrading management	Management skills Industrial prototypes In-plant systems change Micro-electronics
Investment & Export	Banks Export promotion councils	Support for adapting local raw materials	Upgrading for export Marketing new products	Competing in the regional and global market, require higher scale of support
Information services	National policy institutes	Information on local techniques and markets	Studies Support on adaptation of new processed products New markets (local and regional)	Changes in trade and export policy New and emerging markets

Learning to Compete in African Industry

regional or global export market not only on price basis but also by becoming an innovative cluster. They do so through continuous learning, through substantial inter-firm linkages and by explicitly investing in skills upgrading.

Traditional technology policy approaches emphasize national level policies but what we here call clustering policy, that is, the incentives and approaches to efficiency in clusters would place far greater emphasis on meso level policies on the assumption that public goods such as infrastructure (roads, water, and telecommunication) are already available. Following from above, we focus on technical, finance, marketing and skills building efforts and institutions supporting clusters and the sources of support, whether public agency, private association, international or non-governmental agencies (Table 3.3).

Support systems and sources of learning

Firms in developing economies pursue a different set of technical objectives from those in developed countries. The most important objective of the firm is to successfully install an operating system at the least possible cost. In doing this, a firm requires skills and knowledge both from within as well as a measure from external sources. The knowledge and skills requirement of the firm increases as the complexity of technology to be acquired increases. The firm needs knowledge and skill to identify, select, purchase, install and commission a system. Sometimes, a set of skills, different from design knowledge, is also required for the firm to successfully commission a plant. This is referred to as investment capability. Subsequently, a firm will aim to raise operating system performance to 100 per cent capacity in the shortest possible time. The complex set of skills and knowledge required to achieve full or partial capacity utilization and subsequent capacity stretching, where required, is referred to as production capability.[18] For instance, capacity-stretching, change in, or dilution of product mix, and plant expansion require significant knowledge of materials and engineering design, supplementary to routine process capabilities that is likely to be the dominant competence in a developing country firm. There is further complexity as electronics inclusion deepens and firms have to acquire process plants and machine tools for more precision-demanding products. The knowledge of electronics and computing skills will be increasingly demanded, more so as firms have to compete in the domestic and global markets with imported higher quality products. The new competition is not based on price differences but on knowledge. Innovation therefore has a far broader meaning for developing countries, different in nature from its codification as R&D or frontier science and technology.

---

18 In reality, uninterrupted production is a long tapestry of technical problem definitions, and resolution, sometime demanding considerable innovation, either minor or major, can only be so defined in the given context. Relatively, minor problems in an advanced economic setting, could be, to a firm in less developed environment, a major, and production-threatening problem. Simple supply problems based on poor inventory practices have led to shortages that closed down an important unit in a steel plant, see Oyelaran-Oyeyinka (1994).

Technology support systems are part of the NSI and, as such, constitute an important node in the network of learning and innovation. Lall (1987), Oyelaran-Oyeyinka (1996) and Mytelka (2000) present cases demonstrating the nature and processes of innovation in developing countries. An increasingly demanding product market has also meant that marketing capability, to search for information on competing products in the export and domestic market, is becoming important. Linkage capability, the knowledge, skills and experience to engage other firms and institutions in the process of production and innovation (Mytelka, 1998), is a most important firm asset that has not been fully explored in relation to the role of support system. It is with this intersection of linkage capability and the role of support systems in the process of learning that this chapter is concerned.

In addition to internal firm capabilities, a firm succeeds on the strength of its ability to access and process a whole range of knowledge outside of itself. It does this by internalizing such knowledge and by continually engaging in networking with sources of knowledge within the national system and outside of it. In doing this, it contends with various actors, diverse knowledge channels and thereby develops process paths to transform knowledge into firm capabilities for production and innovation. Knowledge flows into firms from both within and outside the national system; in this chapter we are primarily concerned with the former. It is useful to look at the learning process as flows and interactions, which take several forms. First, there is inter-firm flow of knowledge and skills in a user-producer type relationship through movement of skilled staff from one firm to another, sub-contracting (manufacturing and trade types), joint ventures, franchises, and supplier-customer relations. These diverse forms of interaction constitute important channels of flows in advanced and developing economies (Pavitt, 1994; Von Hippel, 1988; OECD, 1999). Secondly, we have firm-institution interaction in which public agencies, such as technology development centres (of different varieties across countries) and public R&D laboratories, are among the most prominent in Africa. In broad terms, their mandate is to assist firms in process and product adaptations, and in gaining comparative advantage through the utilization of natural resources. Ideally, through this mode of interaction, support institutions help firms access otherwise expensive information (about processes, products and competitors), and provide or subsidize testing and quality control costs that firms are unable to undertake on their own. These are services which firms traditionally presuppose to be 'public goods', in much the same way as power supply, water and telecommunication, but which are often completely absent, or poorly provided. Oyelaran-Oyeyinka (1997a), Biggs et al. (1995) and Romijn (2001) hypothesize that in addition to and as a result of the lost opportunities for raising firm technical efficiency and competitiveness, considerable learning opportunities are missed by the absence of properly designed and well-delivered support services to African firms.

Technological learning failure may thus be evidence of a breakdown of interaction or possibly lack of knowledge and skills flows between institutions supporting innovation and firms, between firms, and even within the firms themselves. Failure to learn may take the form of little learning, ineffective learning or a complete absence of learning when there is lack of dynamic complementarities (Malerba, 1992). There are two broad modes of interaction that facilitate learning – private and collective. Private interactions and flows involve autonomous firm-level efforts such as technical and managerial training, hiring of local and foreign consultants, and deepening relationships with clients, machinery suppliers and raw materials suppliers.[19] Collective mode is a collection of services provided by public, private and non governmental organizations (NGOs). We propose that these two channels of support and knowledge flows, when properly organized, constitute important learning avenues for firms. There are successful examples of collective support such as group training, information provision, design training, quality assurance provided through industry and trade associations, and public research and developments institutes (RDIs). among others (Schmidtz and Musyck, 1993).   Herein lies the intersection of technological learning and technical support systems.

---

19 As reported in the case study of the Nnewi cluster in Eastern Nigeria, most of the firms pay to have Taiwanese engineers; the technical partners spend time in their factories to teach local engineers skills. They are instructed to 'close mark" the technical partner. This is a metaphor from soccer that typifies close understudying learning-by-doing and observing the technical partners.

Chapter 4

Learning Knowledge and Skills in Industry: Empirical Exploration

Introduction

We have two motivations in this chapter. The first is to understand the sources of learning in industry and in so doing relate it to firm-level performance employing simple statistical techniques. My second motivation derives from the well-debated notion that knowledge growth, validation and transfer is a socially distributed process, mediated by institutions (Lundvall and Johnson, 1994; Metcalfe, 2003; Ducatel, 1998). I therefore hope to highlight the role of institutions underlying firm behaviour using firm-level data in the countries studied. The underlying hypothesis is that African countries' poorly functioning S&T institutions or, in a number of important areas, none at all might well undermine industrial dynamism. In these countries, S&T institutions are embryonic, while indigenous knowledge systems, in medicine and manufacturing crafts such as apprenticeship that once served societies well, have atrophied from neglect or have been swept away by modern techniques. Central to this inquiry is the difficult process of transforming what individual scientists, engineers, and craftsmen know into what one may call *organized knowledge system*. Mokyr (2002: 7) expresses it succinctly: 'In the end what each individual knows is less important than what society knows and can do'. Institutions exist precisely for this role: to store, validate, and distribute knowledge. In this chapter, we concentrate on the forms, role and technological knowledge, its acquisition and the institutions for diffusing it.

The above issues thus beg the following questions: What are the sources of industrial knowledge and skill formation in African manufacturing? What formal and informal systems create industrial human capital? What are the modes of training in firms, and how systemic is human capital creation in manufacturing? How well does the formal educational system prepare the individual for workplace efficiency and is the skill composition of enterprises adequate? This chapter is organized as follows: the next two sections present an analytical framework based on firm-level data and draw a profile of the impact of formal qualification and human skills on the rate of learning and levels of technological capability acquired. The last section concludes and suggests directions for policy.

An analytic framework

Local technological knowledge institutions (LKI) carry out the generation, recreation and diffusion of knowledge available from the local and global domains. It could normatively be defined as a set of agents that act as the repository of creative assets and evolving in a milieu of dynamic interaction with other agents. To be effective, LKIs would have the following three properties: (i) an optimum organizational size (firm size, capacity of a R&D laboratory, and so on), which can be specified only in a given context; (ii) a right mix of formal and experiential knowledge and skills base; (iii) and an environment with a positive systems dynamics. *Optimum size structure* is a well-discussed factor in the literature. Both the dynamic capabilities as well as the resource-based literature emphasize the importance of firms' internal assets (Penrose, 1959; Nelson, 1981; Freeman and Soete, 1997). The weight of empirical evidence suggests that, for the small firm, growth is negatively correlated with firm size and age, while this may not necessarily hold in medium and large firms (Audretsch, 2002). There is a threshold of human and non-human resources required for firm-level effectiveness. African firms are mostly small enterprises, while universities and public research institutions (PRIs) often lack the basic infrastructure and facilities. However, comparative training data for other low-income countries shows the close relationship of size and mode of training. For instance, it would appear from Table 4.1 that all the countries exhibit strong propensity to informal learning with relatively advanced countries like Malaysia showing higher incidence (Biggs et al., 1995). Their report confirms that advanced industrial countries do more formal training while larger firms in developing countries, particularly multinationals, conduct much more formal training for their workers compared with small firms.[1]

Table 4.1 Incidence of Informal Training by Firm Size across Countries

Firm Size	Columbia (1992)	Indonesia (1992)	Malaysia (1994)	Mexico (1992)
<15	67.6	N.A	56.6	7.4
21–100	77.8	15.7	80.5	36.1
101–250	88.6	32.6	88.8	44.7
>250	87.2	16.1	92.4	30.4

Source: Biggs et al. (1995).

1   Large multinational firms in Africa and Asia have well-developed systems of apprenticeship for young engineering and science graduates, who are often referred to as *trainee engineers* or *scientists*. Some have formal vocational schools and highly structured curricula lasting between three to nine months. Even then, this is not the end of training. A trainee is attached to a senior colleague, much like the master craftsman, who is responsible for the progress of the apprentice and makes recommendations on future promotions.

We therefore hypothesize that size correlates with the nature and type of learning (formal or non-formal training) and could be a significant predictor of firms' domestic and export performance.

The role of formal and experiential knowledge From this we observe that the relative proportion of graduates in firms display considerable variation across countries, while the arithmetic means for primary and secondary leavers is relatively low and show no significant difference across countries.

Table 4.2 Test for Equality of Mean Values of Educational Qualifications

Variable							
	All	Nigeria	Kenya	Df	T-value	F statistic	Level of significance
Education No formal education	11.38	10.32	12.96	65	0.449	0.201	0.655
High school	52.09	51.42	54.87	136	0.542	0.294	0.589
University	12.93	17.73	2.60	83	4.222	17.826	0.0001
Employees (size)	38.97	38.85	44.67	202		0.8253	0.439

Though formal education acquired in higher education institutions is important, it is only one source of knowledge, while non-formal sources of skills are equally important and represent important continuation of the human capital build-up. One such form of skills upgrading is adjustment through training in basic and general skills types by firms. However, small firms are normally prone to under-investment in training, and the widespread institutional failure in developing countries to attenuate the skills market failure is well known (Lall, 2000). At the basic level, general skills such as literacy and numeracy are necessary for basic production processes, however, firm-level technological learning and capability acquisition is the primary focus for enterprises. According to Enos (1991: 20):

> To operate modern equipment requires the least training and experience; to improve upon operation requires more; to specify and procure individual pieces of equipment, still more; and to design entire plants and processing schemes the most of all.

In other words, learning technical skills upgrading is an evolutionary, time-consuming process. In addition to the need for progressive addition of skills as society becomes more industrialized, a country needs to maintain an industrial momentum that fosters continuous learning. To this end, time is not the only factor, but the opportunity to foster skills upgrading from the lower to higher levels is important for consistent industrial progress. Appendix 4.1 shows the technological learning and skills formation trajectory of progressing from the simple to complex industrial production. Considerable explicit investment in learning and technological capability building is required on a consistent and sustained basis.

In dynamic economies, a combination of incentives and threats, which both induce and provide the scope for productive technological learning and innovation, arise from a variety of sources. These include possibilities for market expansion, investments in new vintage machinery and equipment, in which the skills of engineers are utilized and competitive pressures bring new entrants into the domestic and external markets. For most developing countries, the opportunity for industrial learning has been limited, but not totally absent. According to Freeman and Lindauer (1999, 5), 'With the majority of the region's labor force still engaged in agriculture, the lack of productive enhancing effects might explain why the accumulation of human capital has done little for economic growth'.

Following from these, we hypothesize that human capital, comprising formal education and human skills acquired in firms, is positively related to firm performance.

Positive systemic dynamics this is the operative environment that promotes, and supports creative capability building and innovation. It depends to a considerable degree on the maturity of institutions of finance, banking, regulation and property rights, in addition to those supporting technical advance. In normative terms, a positive systemic dynamic is said to exist where we have the following: (i) a variety and large numbers of linkages involving suppliers, producers, and service providers; (ii) a high propensity for competitive cooperation and collaboration; (iii) a large number of agents creating and disseminating information and knowledge useful to production of goods and services; (iv) a propensity to foster private initiatives in complementary association with intelligent public service provision; and (v) a strong global-local institution networking at the formal and informal institution levels.

Systems interaction, defined as the organizational competence to generate linkages, is made up of the knowledge, skills and experience to engage other firms and institutions in the process of production and innovation (Ernst et al., 1998). It is an important firm asset that has not been fully explored in the literature of underdeveloped economies. In addition to internal firm capabilities, a firm succeeds on the strength of its ability to gain access to and process a whole range of knowledge outside of itself. Organizations benefit from external agents by internalizing such knowledge, and by continually engaging in networking with sources of knowledge within the national system and outside of it. In this way, organizations develop process paths to transform knowledge into firm capabilities for production and innovation.

Networking could be conceptualized as information flows and knowledge interactions, which may take several forms. They include inter-firm flows of knowledge and skills in a user-producer type relationship, through the movement of skilled staff from one firm to another; sub-contracting (manufacturing and trade types), joint ventures, franchise, and supplier-customer relations (Pavitt, 1984; Von Hippel, 1988; OECD, 1999). Secondly, there are firm-institution interaction in which public agencies such as technology development centres (of different varieties across countries), and public R&D laboratories are among the most prominent in Africa. Their mandate, in broad terms, is to assist firms in process and product adaptations, and in gaining comparative advantage through utilizing natural resources (Oyelaran-Oyeyinka, 1997c; Romijn, 2001; Biggs et al, 1995).

Universities tend to be central to innovation and knowledge creation, but their mandate in developing areas is primarily to train scientists and engineers. As a subset of regional, national and sectoral innovation system studies, considerable attention has been paid to university- industry interaction (Hicks et al., 2001; Salter and Martin, 2001).

Given the theoretical and empirical evidence from the literature, we hypothesize that collaboration in a given systemic context promotes firm-level performance.

Learning and knowledge in African firms: evidence and explanation

Optimum size structure

Our own findings in Table 4.3 show the average firm size in five African countries. In comparison with East Asia and the advanced industrial countries, the enterprise size is only a fraction for comparable economies.[2] Size is imperative for knowledge creation and storage, that is, the building of institutional memory, but this is the precise problem that Africa's small firms face. The death rate of enterprises is high, and exit into non-related activities wipes away tacit knowledge that had been painstakingly acquired over time. The reason crafts knowledge tends to have stagnated at a non-competitive level might relate to its tacit nature. Knowledge that is codified (in texts, pictures, and symbols) is easily transferred and adapted and improved upon by others in the community of practice (Lave and Wenger, 1991). Tacit knowledge, embodied in human skills, is said to undergo 'internalization of knowledge', and vice versa, for the transformation of codified to tacit, transformed through the 'externalization of knowledge' (Nonaka and Takeuchi, 1995). Theirs is a framework in which knowledge creation and re-creation spiral in a ring.[3] According to Nonaka and Takeuchi (1995), there is a perpetual dialogue between tacit and explicit knowledge. In the absence of this sort of dynamic dialogue, or where the

---

2   For instance the Small Business Administration (SBA) in the United States defines a small firm as one employing no more than 500 employees, a figure ten times the mean enterprise size in Africa.

3   The model presents four modes including: *socialization*, a process in which tacit is converted to tacit such as happens in apprenticeship (observation, imitation and practice); *externalization* converts tacit to explicit using metaphors, analogies and models; this is followed by *combination*, the conversion of explicit to explicit through techniques such as reasoning, programming, data mining and information exchange; and, lastly, *internalization*, a process of transforming explicit into tacit routine day-to-day work.

dialogue is a repetitive exchange of old ideas among horizontal actors, very little learning takes place or, in the extreme, none at all.

Table 4.3 Size and Skills Characteristics of Firms in Africa

Variable	Nigeria	Kenya	Ethiopia	Uganda	Zimbabwe
Firm Size (Mean)	38.9	44.7	43.6	25.0	27.81
University degree holder	17.7	10.5	1.88	Low	2.60
High School degree	51.4	52.2	24.64	20.0	54.90
Elementary School	19.6	24.5	18.11		
No formal education	10.3	12.8			6.08

Source: Author's country survey (2002).

Firms are severely constrained by limited knowledge, human skills and experience as well as poor techno-managerial capability of top management or, in the case of the small firms, that of the owner/entrepreneur. This finding applies to almost all African SMEs. We considered two components of human capital – of firm owners or managers – that tend to affect the growth and dynamism of firms. These are: certificated or diploma-awarding qualifications obtained from formal institutions and non-formal learning. The level of human capital shapes the ways in which a firm is managed,[4] and tacit knowledge, a vital but non-quantifiable component of human skills could indeed be a decisive factor of firm performance. Compared with their counterparts in other developing countries and even with the management of larger firms within the same countries, owners/managers of SMEs tend to score relatively low in formal education and experience. We observed a fairly consistent pattern of relatively low qualification and poor managerial competence among the workforce in most cases, with a few exceptions. This is particularly so for the small, rather than medium firms with greater than fifty employees. While firm owners may in fact possess intrinsic entrepreneurial abilities, this attribute does

---

4   In an econometric study of Ghanaian firms, export dynamism was found to be positively associated with the experience of the workforce. Comparative evidence was found for human capital in a number of other African countries: Soderborn (2000), 'What drives manufacturing exports in Africa? Evidence from Ghana, Kenya and Zimbabwe'. Mimeo, Centre for the Study of African Economies, University of Oxford, presented at the Annual Conference on Development Economies Europe, Paris, June 26–28, 2000.

not prove sufficient in the face of the complex demands of modern economies. As firms face both domestic and external competition, the need for new sets of technical and managerial competencies arises.[5]

Conceivably, the considerable gap in management and skills levels between Africa's SMEs and their counterparts in the more industrialized developing countries is understandable given the relatively recent history of industrialization in Africa.

Managing a firm with a limited number of qualified and experienced personnel (the perennial resource allocation constraint) leaves firm owners with little or no time for training. For this reason, non-formal training seems to be the preponderant mode of learning. In the second survey cited in this book, we sought to know from firm managing directors how they train staff and how they themselves learn to use various forms of information and telecommunications technologies (ICTs). Table 4.5 shows that technical apprenticeship is the most common type of training in both small and medium firms.

Table 4.4 Learning ICT Skills by Firm Owners and Firm Size

	Uganda		Nigeria		Kenya		Ghana
Learning Mode	S	M	S	M	S	M	All
Formal Training	21 (28.4)	8 (80.0)	S	47 (66.2)	29 (20.1)	10 (27.8)	13 (14.4)
Apprenticeship	49 (66.2)	7 (70.0)	2 (5.9)	47 (66.2)	82 (56.9)	24 (66.7)	76 (84.4)
Searching the Internet	18 (24.3)	2 (20.0)		5 (7.1)			
Learning from Technical Partners	18 (24.3)	1 (10.0)	1 (2.9)	21 (29.6)			1 (1.1)
Overseas Training	18 (24.3)	1 (10.0)		4 (5.6)			
Total Firms	74	10	34	71	144	36	90

Source: Author's field survey (2002).
Note: Numbers in parentheses are column percentage; Percentage will not add to 100 as this is a multiple response variable.

---

5   This is what Lundvall and Johnson (1994: 33) referred to as learning and forgetting: 'The enormous power of habits of thoughts in the economy constitutes a permanent risk for blocking potentially fertile learning processes. It may be argued that some kind of creative destruction of knowledge is necessary in order to make it possible for radical innovation to diffuse throughout the economy... Forgetting is an essential and integrated part of learning...'

Table 4.5 Correlation of Firm Output and Type of Training

	Nigeria		Zimbabwe		Kenya	
Training Item	Increased output (%)	Improved Technical capability	Increased output (%)	Improved Technical capability	Increased output (%)	Improved Technical capability
In-house Technical Apprenticeship Training	61.7	70.3	64.7	75.0	71.0	66.0
In-house Management Apprenticeship Training	33.3	29.2	–	50.0	45.0	31.0
Overseas Training				50.0		
Local Training	53.8	53.8	40.0		50.0	52.0
Budget on Training (1–5%)	52.3		60.0		57.0	
Budget on Training (6–10%)	64.0		–		60.0	
Budget on Training (> 10%)	71.4		–		70.0	
Better Quality Product	57.7		57.1		55.0	
From training						58.0
More Efficient Workforce	60.9	47.7		57.1		56.0

Tables 4.5 and 4.6 show the correlation of training and different measures of performance, namely, increased firm output, perceived improvement in technical capability and actual increased export performance as a result of training. These are perceptive responses of firm managing directors and the question was framed as follows: 'By how much has your firm increased technical capability as a result of training?' or 'by how much has staff quality improved as a result of training?'. The questionnaire provided for choices in different training types such as 'in-house technical apprenticeship', 'in-house management apprenticeship' and so on. As the response on ICT showed, general technical training also follows the same pattern. Much of the training in small firms is in the form of apprenticeship supplemented by 'local training', often provided by local consultants or some state agency. Small firms could not afford overseas training, but a sizeable proportion attributes improved technical, output and export growth to learning through apprenticeship training. Firms that devote a greater proportion of their budget tend to record higher output, increased technical capability and better export performance.

Table 4.6 Correlation of Capability, Export, Performance and Training

	Nigeria	Kenya	Zimbabwe
Training Items	Increased Export Capability (%)	Increased Export Capability (%)	Increased Export Capability (%)
Management Training	46.2	46.0	50.0
Improved Job Quality	24.1	22.3	21.4
Type of Training			
In-house Technical (apprenticeship)	34.1	38.5	50.0
Local Training	35.3	37.2	40.0
Budget on Training (1–5%)	25.0	30.1	35.3
Budget on Training (6–10%)	53.3	54.2	n.a.
Budget on Training (>10%)	42.9	47.2	50.0
Training Improvement Producing better quality jobs	21.1	23.0	
Higher quality products	50.0	47.2	29.2
Improved Productivity	66.7	65.2	57.3

Source: Author's survey (2001)

The role of formal and experiential knowledge: the limiting value of learning-by-doing

An important point for theory and policy supporting small producers in Africa is why the tacit knowledge base in industry has not been sufficiently externalized and why, despite considerable investment, the process of internalization has yielded so few dividends. Why have institutions of apprenticeship succeeded in the community of medical practice and the legal profession, for instance, but have been far less successful in creating industrial and technological knowledge base in underdeveloped areas? Why has the SI that has been so successful elsewhere not been embedded in Africa? The treatment of apprenticeship and other modes of tacit knowledge learning as a historical anachronism does not fit the facts. Lave and Wenger (1991) cite diverse widely differing historical practices, from Feudal Europe to West Africa and the United States, where much learning, including in highly skill-intensive disciplines such as medicine and the arts, took the form of apprenticeship. From the various examples cited by them, they concluded that apprenticeship learning diverges significantly from popular stereotypes. The cases they cite in their work called into question conventional wisdom of apprenticeship as an informal activity. They note,

It is typically assumed, for example, that apprenticeship has had an exclusive existence in association with feudal craft production; that master-apprenticeship relationships are diagnostic of apprenticeship; and that learning in apprenticeship offers opportunities for nothing more complex than reproducing task performance in routinized ways.

We suggest four main reasons. First, due to the small size nature of firms with little capacity for institutional memory, dispersal of persons with the requisite human skills – a rather common occurrence in firms with high labour turnover – leads to the destruction of such skills. Secondly, the atomistic behaviour of firms, with an aversion to share tacit knowledge, forecloses optimal socialization of such knowledge and, in turn, diminishes the value of knowledge and information. As Fleck (1996) observes, tacit knowledge constrains the social distribution of knowledge and is responsible for the limited circulation of scientific and technological knowledge. The need to maintain asymmetrical power relations within organizations might in fact encourage knowledge hoarding, which in turn might undermine the organization itself. Again, tacit knowledge transfer involves devoting considerable energy and personal time in a mentoring arrangement such as apprenticeship. There are evident disincentives in doing this, especially in competitive environments where individual knowledge is a source of power.

Third, there is a limit to the knowledge accumulated through learning-by-doing. According to Johanessen et al. (2001), tacit knowledge is bounded by negative feedback because, while it promotes continuous improvements, it hardly leads to innovation. 'Thus tacit knowledge promotes continuous improvements only to a certain level, and then declines' (Johanessen et al., 2001: 112). The limiting value of tacit knowledge creation in the absence of innovation is captured in Young's (1993) formulation of 'bounded learning by doing'. He suggests that learning in the course of producing certain goods is finite and, in the end, will approach a limiting value and stop altogether 'in the absence of the introduction of new technical processes'. In other words, *an industry, system of production or firm could not hope to rely indefinitely and exclusively on particular knowledge of production without new knowledge injected through innovation.* This assertion follows the well-known asymptotic behaviour of growth of systems represented in a simple mathematical formulation (Von Bertalanffy, 1968). We could use this to describe the growth of human knowledge[6] assuming, as some scholars have, that knowledge growth takes on an exponential character (David and Foray, 2001).

Consider a simple representation where the growth of knowledge in the system is directly proportional to the number of elements (information, data, etc. in a variety

---

6   This is measured by all kinds of accumulated information and data. Where (a < o) the exponential law would apply as much to radioactive decay as it will the decline of unutilized human knowledge.

of forms) present.[7] When the growth is developed into a Taylor series and solved, it becomes:

$$Q = Q_o \cdot e^{a_1 t}$$

....1)

The growth of the system is positive or negative depending on the value of the constant A_1 and the system increases or decreases accordingly on the sign assumed by A. When we retain only the first term of the series, the simplest solution emerges as equation (1) above. Q_o signifies the number of elements at $t = 0$. This is the well-known exponential law, called the 'law of natural growth'.

When we retain the second term, the solution takes a different form with important implications. The second solution takes on a sigmoid shape with a limiting value, while the first simple solution shows an indefinite growth. Young's formulation, albeit much more complex, echoes the generalized systems solution to which Von Bertallanfy had suggested this simple but powerful equation of growth a quarter of a century earlier. Speculatively applied to our small firm situation, with limiting internal resources in the absence of little or no external innovating inputs, knowledge growth tapers off eventually assuming the logistic curve shown in Figure 4.1. We suggest that the stagnation of African industry may well not be unconnected with the low innovative dynamism of the predominantly small firms that populate manufacturing and services. The solution to the sigmoid or logistic curve is shown in Figure 4.1.

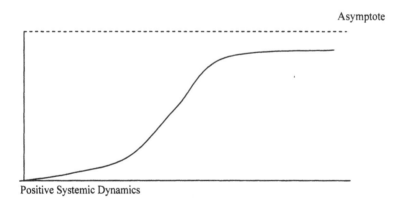

Positive Systemic Dynamics

Figure 4.1   Logistic Curve Representing the Growth of Human Tacit Knowledge

---

7   This is the well-known equation of growth and for knowledge may vary from the volume of books, journals or in the current context, digital materials.

$$\frac{dQ}{dt} = f(Q)$$

Learning to Compete in African Industry

Table 4.7 Equality of Means: Types of Inter-firm Collaboration

Variable	Mean		All	Df	T-value	F-statistic	Significance level
	1. Small	2. Medium					
Horizontal cooperation	1.473	1.212	1.426	182	1.539	2.370	0.1254
Subcontracting	1.285	1.368	1.301	196	0.496	0.246	0.6206
Linkage with Industrial Association	1.641	1.192	1.559	142	2.376	5.646	0.0188
Cooperation with Input Suppliers	0.768	0.795	0.772	196	0.1886	0.0356	0.8506
Collaboration with universities and Technology Institutions	0.781	0.809	0.787	201	0.397	0.157	0.6921

Source: Author's survey (2001).

If we accept the premise that innovative impulse, aside from continuous improvement, would come from external sources outside the small firm, the next question is where from? In order to put the African question in perspective, the question to ask is how well do firms collaborate with knowledge institutions, local or global? Table 4.7 provides a partial answer, revealing that little or no collaboration takes place between small firms in Africa and knowledge institutions such as universities (row five), this with no significant difference between the countries. The normalized scores are rated on a scale of one to five, with five reading strong collaboration and one rated as extremely low or no collaboration. Although the incidence and importance of knowledge spillover is not in dispute, not much of it is associated with university-industry collaboration in the context of African small firms. There seems to be greater collaboration with suppliers and subcontractors at this size level and in this technological regime. There may be three broad reasons for this. First, in positive systemic environments, where knowledge externalities are present, there are three broad sources of knowledge for firms, namely, industry R&D, university R&D (both broadly defined) and skilled labour. The role they each play is self-evident while in particular, new economic knowledge in form of tacit skills and knowledge generally promotes the propensity to innovate. The absence of graduate skilled labour in small firms will therefore deprive them of this impulse to innovate. Secondly, small firms lack the internal capacity to absorb new knowledge. A firm with little or no experience in innovative activity will lack the skills to identify, and adopt the necessary external inputs. Third, acquisition of external knowledge depends on both geographic and knowledge proximity. There is a wide cognitive disparity between small firms and university knowledge bases in African countries, particularly the latter. Where firms are situated near universities, their activity domains are worlds apart as a result of the kinds of markets small firms serve and the publication niche market those university scientists respond to. The mobility of labour is a key source of knowledge transfer, but this kind of exchange hardly takes place except with large, often multinational firms (Oyelaran-Oyeyinka, 2003).

Learning strategies in African SMEs: an illustrative case study

In this final section, we cite a case from a study carried out in four major Nigerian towns: Lagos, Benin City, Ibadan and Nnewi.[8] The sample stratification of firms was based on information collected from trade and manufacturing directories. Three engineering subgroups, covering 47 firms, were examined in this chapter: basic metal and fabricated metal; electrical and electronics; and automotive components and miscellaneous assembly. About 80 per cent of the firms imported between 61–100 per cent of machinery from abroad. All the Nnewi firms had only a handful of imported machinery and equipment from Taiwan. Technical services, both for initial investment and subsequently for production, were foreign. Initial investments were made largely by the desire to exploit perceived market opportunities. The origin of manufacturing investment for Nnewi entrepreneurs was, without exception, found in trading. All started as traders and once enough capital was accumulated, explored technical partnership with a Taiwanese partner. All but one had no previous manufacturing experience.

The Nnewi firms present a particularly interesting phenomenon. Most of the firms were started just before or during the SAP years; they are all fully owned by Nigerians. The owners constitute a distinct category of previous traders with a common ethnic background (all are of Igbo extraction); the firms are spread over a geographic space that has been transformed into a prosperous economic enclave similar to an industrial district. The chapter examined issues of clustering or networking in a systematic manner, and we found a large measure of communalism that is cultural and ethnically determined. Whether this potential of proximity has been usefully explored to enhance local efficiency through the use of available knowledge, skills and information remains to be seen. We do know, however, that Nnewi has explored the external linkages profitably through trading and later investment in manufacturing with Taiwan.

Investment capability which includes searching, sourcing, negotiating, scheduling of investment as well as erection and civil construction seems to have been well mastered by the firms. Since the technology involved in the civil and structural aspects of construction is relatively uncomplicated and has had a long history in Nigeria, it did not pose many problems for Nigerian engineers. Again, it would seem that the entrepreneurs made extra efforts to acquaint themselves with details

---

8   Details of the study can be found in the book, Oyelaran-Oyeyinka (1997b). A journal version was published as 'Technological Learning in African industry: a study of engineering firms in Nigeria', *Science and Public Policy*, Volume 24, No. 5, October 1997.

of the systems either locally or by attachment to suppliers' factories abroad before finalizing transfer agreements.

This chapter examines the learning mechanism in great detail. We conceptualized technological learning as the way in which firms acquire and build up technical knowledge and competencies. Learning represents the dynamic component of the process of capability acquisition. The channels for learning identified are: (a) the apprenticeship system of training; (b) on-site training at supplier's factory; (c) on-the-job training in Nigeria; (d) expert contracting; (e) support mechanism provided by public institutions; (f) learning through transaction with local and external agents; and (g) learning-by-doing production and maintenance.

At the early stages, most firms rely on the technical expertise of machinery suppliers and as such set great store on on-site training at the suppliers' factories abroad. The period of training ranges between three to nine months and essentially emphasizes learning, production and maintenance. Product technology is often quickly mastered, while process technology learning, the skill and knowledge for plant design, to modify plant layout, quality control, maintenance and industrial engineering all take a relatively longer time.

The knowledge and skills acquisition process continue with on-the-job training whereby those who had foreign exposure become trainers to others even while still learning process technology. Expert contracting is a common learning channel with firms at Nnewi. The contract could last for a short or longer time depending on the complexity of the tasks.

Long-term relationships sometime emerge whereby transactional exchange between Nnewi and supplier's factory in Taiwan become a loose network for indefinite time. Services are then paid for as rendered – a sort of 'cash and carry' consulting service. Because most of the start-up staff at Nnewi is semi-literate, without formal technical or engineering training, these initial technical instructions become extremely important. For this reason, entrepreneurs tend to favour their immediate kith and kin for fear of losing a worker who may not be committed to the long-term goals of the firm. 'Close marking' of foreign experts becomes an important technique since the foreigner has a finite time to spend at the factory.

Firms also seem to have gained from visits to suppliers' factories and by exchange with local suppliers, but these tend to be secondary channels. A few benefited from technical advice and information from external support services but again this tends to be on a limited scale. The kinds of horizontal linkages and subcontracting relationships that made the Taiwan model a source of inspiration for entrepreneurs at Nnewi has not fully emerged. Firms rely considerably on internal human and machinery assets and, as such, tend to be vertically integrated. Some acquired special machinery services such as foundries in order to take advantage of economy of scope and to acquire capabilities for minor modifications and maintenance.

Some semblance of R&D is taking place but not in the formal sense. This is particularly so in the area of adaptation of local raw materials where a lot of 'experiments' are being undertaken. For instance, one of the Nnewi firms producing rubber-based products has in time undertaken diversification of its product mix through internal as well as external efforts. The firm has achieved 95 per cent by weight in local content and won the Nigerian Industrial Standard awards in the process. Although the company sends samples to Taiwan for quality assurance tests, much of *compositing* of inputs is done locally.

The decision to train always proves difficult for firm owners as small firms encounter difficulties in retaining competent staff. A strong disincentive is the incidence of high labour turnover among small firms, a situation that results in firms having to opt for one of two distinct choices. The first is to continue as a small firm locked into a low productivity growth path and managed by a low capability technical staff. In taking this route, a firm effectively avoids investments in higher skills, but then forecloses transition to higher technological growth path. For this and other reasons, small firms often foreclose the choice to grow into the medium and large firm categories.[9] In this and other case studies, other skill-related reasons identified by firms as constraints to growth and innovation include: (a) lack of skilled personnel to initiate and sustain growth-inducing activities; (b) fear of losing competent staff once trained; (c) lack of time outside the production routines, this relates particularly to the owner/manager who tends to be over committed while carrying out multidimensional functions; (d) lack of in-house technical skills with enough experience to understand the combined technical and market imperatives of growing competitive economies. The second choice is to follow a path of growth that demands greater explicit investment in human capital. The outcome may not be totally certain, but the promised reward could be substantial in enhanced productivity.

However, firm-specific apprenticeship training is the dominant mode of learning and confers considerable competitive advantage on the enterprise for three main reasons.

First, firms are in a position to identify their specific skills deficiencies as well as the relevant source for bridging the skills gap. Second, firm managers are familiar with the techno-managerial profile of the industry and are best positioned to take advantage of this to improve firm-level capability. While formal education raises general-purpose technical skills and these are important prerequisites for industrial level capacity, they are not sufficient for specific routines of firms such as production, basic and detailed design of products and processes. Third, the process of capability building is cumulative, realized through learning, and consolidated by learning (learning-by-doing), the latter being an important source of experience.

There is a positive association between capital intensity and the level of technical and skill structure of the firm. Small firms tend to be associated with lower quality level of management and skills. This would no doubt affect the firm's ability to adopt, adapt and assimilate technical innovation. Placed in a more dynamic context, the temporary lack of skilled manpower tends to manifest in the long-term accommodation of limiting technological and quality goals. In other words, when

---

9 Some firms retain the choice to remain small in order to benefit from subsidies and other forms of tax protection where these are available.

constrained by skills, small firms tend to 'accept' low-level production/technological regimes and they may be stuck with these for a long time.

Small firms also undertake less training and spend less per worker. When it is undertaken, training is usually of a general-purpose type. There are two implications of this, which our interviews with firms confirmed. First, the predominance of general training in a sector suggests lack of specialization and workers are left with general-purpose-type technology knowledge. Second, firms that undertake specific training and impart skills to workers are less likely to hold on to such staff. The return to general training tends to be less than that from specialized training, but this does not seem to be a sufficient enough disincentive to arrest under-investment in training by small firms.

Summary

In conclusion, we advance some tentative explanations as to the nature, mode and implications of the type of learning and knowledge accumulation in African industry. We suggest three broad but inter-linked trends that draw from our empirical work on firm-level performance. The first is the inability of local knowledge institutions to interact with all but a few productive agents in order to generate sufficient autonomous technical dynamism. Second, the continuing neglect of local knowledge bundled up in the main in firm-level tacit knowledge of small firms that had failed to meet the challenges of high quality product requirements in a new competitive environment. Third, is the lock-in into repetitive learning-by-doing routines among the predominantly small firms with few opportunities for fresh ideas in industries that rely on institutions of apprenticeship. This lack of success by local economic agents and institutions in exploiting global knowledge limits the competitive scope of local firms. Knowledge externalities tend to benefit larger firms, while small enterprises, with little absorptive capacity and limited human skills and knowledge, are disconnected from both local and global knowledge pools. Imported technologies in form of artefacts are of little benefit if not properly mastered and replicated in new processes and products. Institutions that act as the memory of indigenous knowledge have either completely ossified in repetitive techniques or have been abandoned for modern methods, which in turn have not taken root in the local practices. This vicious cycle accounts in part for the lack of dynamism of historically derived learning mechanisms such as the apprenticeship institutions that are so highly prevalent in Africa.

The role of learning institutions is important, but local autonomously generated knowledge is even more critical if transplanted institutions and the knowledge they are expected to transfer are to be successfully embedded in the local milieu. Economic and innovation policies need to support small and medium firms with the right kinds of incentive and the environment to develop their capability through continuous training. An important implication of this chapter is that stocks of knowledge need to creatively change through re-training and that age old habits and routines might benefit from transformation through institutional innovation. The apprenticeship institution is a case a point. Policy will have to provide firms with the incentives to develop workers and to upgrade skills and technologies by linking up with universities and other knowledge centres while continuing to promote inter-firm linkages.

Table 4.8 Typology of Manufacturing Skills and Technological Capabilities

Type of Skill	Elementary Technical	Basic Technical	Basic Production	Advanced Production
Type of technological capability	Simple knowledge of machining, operation and maintenance	Knowledge of production processes	Knowledge and experience of production	Knowledge and experience of production, design and minor innovation
Sources of skills and experience	Technical and vocational schools	University, science and engineering schools	University plus firm-level experience	University firm-level experience, additional theoretical training in production and design
Approximate cumulative number of years of training and experience	3–4 years	4 years	7 years	9–10 years

Note: The approximate years of skills training is derived from the Korean experience in chemicals and steel sector (Enos, 1991).

Chapter 5

Inter-Organizational Collaboration in Systems of Innovation

Introduction

This chapter examines an important dimension of innovation system, which is the nature, structure and dynamics of collaborations among firms, and between firms and other organizations in three African countries. Collaboration between firms and external agents is determined by a number of internal and external characteristics. The internal factors include the knowledge and skills levels of the owner and the workforce; the rate and types of learning; and the history and paths of interactions. Again, the learning trajectory of small firms usually depends to a great extent on the educational level and managerial capability of the entrepreneur (Bougrain and Haudeville, 2002; Oyelaran-Oyeyinka and Lal, 2004). The nature of interaction also influences what firms learn and do not learn. For instance, an enterprise embedded within a strong knowledge milieu and located within the proximity of a hi-tech knowledge saturated environment is likely to learn differently from one within a network of purely trading firms. In other words, external factors, which include geographic proximity, intensity of interaction and the institutional infrastructure, equally determine the rate at which firms accumulate technological capability. In addition, firms benefit from collective learning institutions through general and specific training and also from private professional associations that organize trade fairs and technical visits.

The chapter identifies three types of interactions, namely, competition, transaction and networking. Firms and other actors may be engaged in competitive interaction, the outcome of which may be product or process innovation. Competition promotes learning and the degree of competition tends to determine the intensity of learning. As North (1996: 346) observed, 'competition, reflecting ubiquitous scarcity, induces organizations to engage in learning to survive'. Transaction is a process by which knowledge, goods and services are exchanged between actors. It is often an expensive process which grows more complex as actors in the system multiply and channels of information exchange grow. Networking is a process within which collaboration and competition takes place; different types and roles of networks will be discussed in the section.

In the innovation system framework, interactions involve suppliers of inputs, customers, knowledge institutions such as universities, and regulatory agencies including quality assurance. The chapter proceeds as follows. First, it presents and examines the internal characteristics of firms that foster cooperation among the above set of actors in the national systems of three African countries namely, Nigeria, Kenya and Zimbabwe. Second, we compare collaboration across these countries to map the pattern, if any, of existing networks. Third, the chapter uses discriminant analysis to measure the impact of the various variables on performance indicators, followed by a discussion of the results and a summary section.

Analytical framework

Systems interaction, conceived as linkage capability, is made up of the internal knowledge, skills and experience to engage other firms and institutions in the process of production and innovation (Ernst et al., 1998). In addition to internal firm capabilities, a firm succeeds on the strength of its ability to gain access to and process a whole range of knowledge outside of itself. It does this by internalizing such knowledge and by continually interacting with actors with requisite knowledge both within and outside the national system. In doing this, the firm engages various actors, employs diverse knowledge channels, and develops multiple process paths to transform knowledge into firm capabilities for production and innovation. This chapter is primarily concerned with the interaction between internal and external sources of knowledge, within the national system of innovation.

Collaboration between systems actors is fundamentally a flow of information and knowledge exchange which may take several forms. The first entails inter-firm flows of knowledge and skills in a user-producer relationship, through the movement of skilled staff from one firm to another, sub-contracting (manufacturing and trade types), joint ventures, franchise, and supplier-customer relations. These diverse forms of interaction constitute important channels of knowledge flows in advanced and developing economies (Pavitt, 1994; OECD, 1999; Von Hippel, 1988). Second, there are firm-organizational interactions in which public agencies, such as technology development centres of different varieties across countries and public R&D laboratories, are the central actors. The mandate of these networks, in broad terms, is to assist firms in process and product adaptations and in gaining comparative advantage through the utilization of natural resources. Ideally, through this mode of interaction, support institutions assist firms in gaining access to what would otherwise be expensive information (about processes, products and competitors), and in providing or subsidizing testing and quality control costs. These are services which firms traditionally access as 'public goods', in much the same way as power supply, water and telecommunication, but which are often completely absent or poorly provided (Biggs et al., 1995; Oyelaran-Oyeyinka, 1997c; Romijn, 2001).

There are two broad types of collaborations – external to the national system and within the domestic economy. A developing country relies largely on external linkages for the supply of technology and, in some respects, technical skills. When properly managed, it might lead to the development of capabilities within firms. In the newly industrializing countries (NICs) such arrangements are viewed as cooperative networking. In Africa, the reverse is the case as technology transfer is in the main a vertical transfer relationship and poorer countries remain in a state of complete dependence.

Studies of domestic networks within LDCs (Nadvi and Schmitz, 1994) have, until recently, paid little attention to Africa. However, these networks are central to sustaining production systems and in promoting interactive learning and innovation, as they possess the positive attributes of geographic proximity as well as cultural and economic space that can help to reduce transactional costs. Ernst et al. (1994) identified four broad types of organizational networks, namely, supplier, customer, educational and technology networks. A supplier network includes subcontractors and original equipment manufacturers, while customer networks relate mainly to forward linkages with distributors, marketing channels, value-added resellers and end-users (in both local and foreign markets). Educational networks enable competing producers to pool resources (financial, production capacities, and human) to increase output and boost geographic coverage, while technology networks assist firms to acquire new product designs, production and process technologies, as well as scientific and technological information.

A network of relationships is formed for a number of reasons (Lall, 1992). First, in a bid to introduce new technologies and innovation, firms need to develop an array of technological capabilities. These capabilities include production, investment, minor change, major change, linkage and strategic marketing capabilities (Ernst et al., 1994). All these capabilities are never fully present within a firm. It is through the development of linkage capabilities that a firm is able to reach out and acquire them. Second, external pressures arising from the domestic and external macroeconomic environments also compel firms to seek collaboration with other economic actors. Third, the pressure arising from technological change elsewhere, which changes the nature of competition as well as the technology market, often induces networking among firms.

In sum, the main factors conditioning the growth and character of networks include:

- The resource capacity among large firms for networking (for instance through subcontracting) and the ability of small and medium firms to take advantage of various linkages;
- Transactional exchange, which may be equal among small firms but unequal between large and small firms. This provides opportunities for interactions among firms to facilitate production and innovation;
- The socio-cultural context, which may facilitate or hinder network formation and growth, for example, trust or lack of it between network members;
- Pressure to generate external network formation, which can be viewed as technological efforts to gain greater skills, higher specialization and deeper levels of technology; and
- Linkages facilitated by close geographical proximity, which promote transactions that may be indirect, formal, frequent and even unplanned.

The proximity of firms to one another and to organizations providing technical services is an important determinant of innovation success and firm performance (Freel, 2003; Oerlemans et al., 2001). It therefore follows that there would be considerable lost opportunities for raising firm technical efficiency and competitiveness where channels of collaboration among firms are weak or absent. Interactive collaborations promote learning and contribute in significant measures to building technological capability in firms (Lundvall, 1988 and 1992).

Interactions and knowledge flows involve autonomous firm-level efforts such as technical and managerial training, hiring of local and foreign consultants, deepening relationships with clients, machinery suppliers, and raw materials suppliers.[1] These different channels of knowledge flows, when properly organized, constitute important learning avenues for firms.

Failure to learn in firms may therefore result from poor interaction and lack of knowledge and skills flows between, and among firms and between firms and institutions supporting innovation. Failure to learn may take the form of inadequate learning, ineffective learning, or a complete absence of learning due to a lack of dynamic complementarities (Malerba, 1992).

Methodology and data

The chapter draws from the findings of empirical firm-level studies carried out in the following countries involving about 200 manufacturing firms and distributed as follows: Nigeria (129), Kenya (47) and Zimbabwe (30). The sectors covered include metalworking, food processing, automotive components and repairs. Response rates to our questionnaires in the three countries varied from 60 to 80 per cent. Our primary aim was to understand the nature of collaboration among SMEs and how this determines the performance of firms producing within a network of other economic actors. The chapter is based on primary data[2] collected using structured questionnaires and interview guides. The survey was carried out over a four-month period in the summer of 2001 and based largely on face-to-face interviews with the managing directors, who provided greater qualitative information on the nature and quality of interactions. The survey included specific case studies and visits to production sites, and corroboration of information with partners on the precise nature of collaboration. The research focused specifically on urban SMEs employing relatively modern technologies and producing for medium income consumers. Table 5.1 shows the size and skills structure of the sample firms. Several measures of performance were

---

1   As reported in the case study of the Nnewi cluster in Eastern Nigeria, most of the firms pay to have Taiwanese engineers; the technical partners spend time in their factories to teach local engineers skills. They are instructed to 'close mark' the technical partner, a soccer metaphor typifying close understudying through learning-by-doing and observing the technical partners.

2   Efforts were made to cover as many firms as possible in all the countries, however, the response rate was better in some countries.

Table 5.1 Size and Skills Composition of Firms in Africa

Variable	Nigeria	Kenya	Zimbabwe
Average firm size	39	48	28
Distribution of employees by their qualification (%)			
University degree holder	17.7	10.5	2.60
High School degree	51.4	52.2	54.90
Elementary School	19.6	24.5	36.42
No formal education	10.3	12.8	6.08

Source: Author's survey (2001).

used, namely, speed of delivery of goods and services, sales turnover, profit, quality improvement and percentage of output exported. Innovation is a binary variable and was limited to product innovation. Firm owners were asked if they had 'carried out significant modification to product' in the years under investigation. We asked firms to rate the significance of the identified innovation to the firms' performance on a Likert scale (1 = not significant; 3 = very significant). Internal capability consists of the educational qualification of owners and workers, although the former has primacy of place in small producing firms. Collaboration, a perceptive response, was rated on a Likert scale (1 = weak, 3 = strong) and includes interactions with input suppliers, subcontractors, RDIs and professional associations. The forms of exchange include: information exchange, interaction to improve product quality, joint skills training, and joint marketing (such as trade fairs commonly organized by professional associations).

We are concerned specifically with inter-firm collaboration and its impact on firm performance and innovation. Technical innovation is an important source of productivity change, with innovation broadly defined as change in product and process that is new to the firm but not necessarily new to the country or other parts of the world. The innovations considered in the chapter are largely incremental, and relate to routine product-based technical changes. Going by previous studies, these are the predominant types of modifications carried out by the majority of African industrial firms (Oyelaran-Oyeyinka et al, 1996; Oyelaran-Oyeyinka, 1997c). In analysing the effect of collaboration on performance, a number of mediating factors that influence firm-level behaviour such as perceptive, quantitative and qualitative variables were employed. Among these, firm age, firm size, skills level, and infrastructure indices were used as independent variables. We discuss them briefly.

Employees' and owners' skills

The association of technical skills and general managerial capability with performance is well documented. The proportion of university graduates and technical skills within firms is a proxy of capability. The intensified competitive environment tends to require not only a higher level, but also a wider range of skills (Lall, 2001). The skills market faces persistent market failure, particularly in developing countries. However, market failure is not limited to skills but includes access to information, finance and technology markets. SMEs, in particular, are differentially penalized by information asymmetry, poor access to investment and working capital.

Size of firm

Due to difficulty in obtaining data on sales turnover and assets, size is taken as being the number of employees. The importance of firm size has received considerable attention in the literature. Different schools, including those focusing on dynamic capabilities as well as the resource-based literature, emphasize the importance of firms' internal assets (Penrose, 1959; Nelson and Winter, 1982; Freeman and Soete, 1997). The weight of empirical evidence suggests that for the small firm, growth is negatively correlated with firm size and age, while this may not necessarily hold in medium and large firms (Audretsch, 2002). There is a threshold of human and non-human resources required for firm and organizational level effectiveness.

Age of firm

The age of a firm might be indicative of its learning experience and a pointer to greater internal resources. The literature has treated this variable as a proxy measure of accumulated knowledge and studies have shown it to have a positive impact on innovation and production performance (Love and Ropers, 2001; Freel, 2003).

Infrastructure

Good quality infrastructure is critical for firm performance. Considerable microeconomic evidence in African enterprises suggests that poor infrastructure is associated with low innovation capability and poor export performance, a proxy for competitiveness (Oyelaran-Oyeyinka, 1996; Soderborn, 2000). Firms contend with poor provision of water, bad roads, epileptic power supply, and inadequate telecommunication services that are not only unreliable, but costly. Private associations in a number of African countries are, increasingly, filling this gap, and we will examine the impact of these initiatives on firm performance.

Types of collaboration

SMEs located within a network of firms and other economic actors compensate for, among others, high transport and communication costs and in the process realize higher levels of efficiency. Types of interactions include horizontal links between firms and suppliers (of raw material and machinery/equipment), and between firms and contractors. Small producers do not interact as intensely with universities as large firms do, while the limited number of public RDIs – characterized by poor internal capabilities – are severely resource-constrained in developing countries. In the absence of collaboration between public research organizations and firms, enterprises tend to benefit more directly from user-producer, user-supplier type interactions.

Following from the above, we suggest that all these factors are significantly related to the performance of firms in the national system of innovation. In sum, we would be examining the following types of collaboration:

- Horizontal and vertical such as firm-firm, user-supplier and subcontracting relationships;
- Firm-university and firm-RDI linkages; and
- Firm-industrial association linkages.

Three hypotheses are proposed to organize our findings and discussions.

H1: Effective interaction with external actors is positively related to internal firm capabilities and performance.
H2: SME collaboration with RDIs and universities will promote greater firm-level technical performance and result in better output and product quality.
H3: Firm collaboration with users, suppliers, subcontractors and professional associations will lead to better firm performance and profit.

Univariate analysis

The firm is conceptualized as the locus of production activities, but it carries out innovation in cooperation with other organizations such as universities, standard setting agencies, research institutes, and financing organizations, among others (Edquist, 2001). Small firms, in particular, stand to benefit from collaboration with other firms and organizations. In what follows, we examine the nature of organizational relationships in three African countries for which we have comparable data (Table 5.2). Firms collaborate to a considerable degree with local maintenance organizations and machinery suppliers in all countries. Collaboration is particularly weak between firms and research institutes and universities, and, in most cases, there is no contact.

Learning to Compete in African Industry

Table 5.2 Inter-Organizational Collaboration (%) Responding

Source	Nigeria	Kenya	Zimbabwe
Machinery suppliers	20.0	38.9	8.8
In-House	44.0	50.0	52.9
Foreign technical	8.0	5.6	5.9
Local maintenance	80.0	72.2	32.3
Research institutes/universities	3.8		
Others	5.0	1.9	-

Source: Survey (2001).

Next we sought to examine the nature and intensity of collaboration in greater detail. Based on a Lickert-type rating (1–3) firms were asked to identify and rate the specific forms of activities undertaken in network relationships (Tables 5.3–5.6). A rating of less than 1.5 is weak while one greater than 1.5 signifies some measure of collaboration from average to very strong. We have in addition compared for the countries, the equality of means for different characteristics of the firm namely capability (skill and size) and performance (export intensity), respectively. The data on collaborative tendencies for the three countries were averaged over five years (1996–2000) to minimize point errors that could occur for a single year. Where we are unable to make comparisons for all countries due to unreliability of data, only two countries were compared. In Table 5.3 both horizontal collaboration and subcontracting data averaged over five years show less than average intensity. However there is very strong significant difference in the two countries for which complete data were available.

Table 5.3 Comparison of Interactive Relationships in Countries

Interaction in last 5 years	Nigeria	Kenya	Zimbabwe	F-value	Significance
Cooperation with other firms	0.884	0.796	0.500	10.342	0.0001
Subcontracting	0.814	0.558	0.320	16.955	0.000

Note: Cooperation was measured on a binary scale; 0→ no cooperation, 1 → strong cooperation; Figures show the average value of cooperation.

From our interviews, collaboration intensified by the year 2000 (Table 5.4).[3] When we consider the data for only 2000, there is a significant relative rise in intensity of horizontal and subcontracting relationships, it was however difficult to establish the precise reasons for this. Our conjecture is that as the economic environment became more difficult, enterprises were compelled to search for different ways of improving

---

3   The data for variables shown in Table 5.4 were missing for Kenya.

Table 5.4 Forms of Collaboration in African Industry

	Nigeria	Zimbabwe	T-value (Sig.)	Chi-sq (Sig.)
Collaboration in last 5 years				
1. Cooperation with other firms	1.53	2.32	3.965 (0.000)	36.989 (0.000)
2. Subcontracting	1.83	0.32	9.782 (0.000)	96.818 (0.000)
3. Links with industrial associations	1.59	1.41	0.991 (0.323)	62.109 (0.000)
Cooperation with other firms				
(i) Information exchange	1.52	1.59	0.387 (0.699)	11.344 (0.010)
(ii) Quality improvement	1.33	1.67	2.001 (0.047)	4.503 (0.105)
(iii) Joint skill training	1.95	2.31	1.469 (0.145)	6.612 (0.085)
(iv) Joint marketing	1.98	2.08	0.359 (0.720)	1.357 (0.507)
Cooperation with main suppliers				
(i) Information exchange	1.60	1.58	0.166 (0.868)	1.561 (0.668)
(ii) Quality improvement	1.28	1.52	2.079 (0.039)	12.489 (0.002)
(iii) Speeding up delivery of goods and services	1.50	1.75	1.514 (0.132)	2.361 (0.307)
Cooperation with subcontractors				
(i) Information and experience	1.92	1.87	0.223 (0.824)	4.870 (0.088)
(ii) Product innovation	1.73	1.57	0.729 (0.467)	0.978 (0.613)
(iii) Quality improvement	1.52	1.47	0.288 (0.774)	2.950 (0.229)
(iv) Joint marketing	2.21	1.38	3.163 (0.007)	8.662 (0.34)

Note: Figures in column 2 and 3 show the average value of cooperation that was measured on a Lickert scale (1–3).

performance. Nevertheless, the three types of relationships show considerable variability across countries evidenced by the high significance in the t-values except for the 'links with industrial association' variable. This is not surprising given the growing involvement of private association with firms in all countries.

Much of what goes on between firms involves bilateral contractual arrangements with suppliers, subcontractors, and consulting organizations that organize training and conduct investment feasibility studies for firms. We explored in some details how much and how frequently these contacts are made and for what reasons. Joint skills development and collective marketing as well as information exchange are important activities. In all but a few cases, there is no significant difference in these activities across countries. In other words, the countries undertake fairly similar sorts of activities. The detailed interviews threw light on the preponderance of these types of relationships, and the weak links between firms, RDIs and universities. Network related production and innovative activities focus on product technical change, which requires minimal inputs from organizations outside the firms, particularly in the case of firms with adequate numbers of graduate employees. Export oriented firms, however, tend to seek out new sources of knowledge outside the immediate network. In what follows, we examine the role of skills, markets, and size effects on collaboration.

Collaboration and firm capability: skills level and firm size

In Table 5.5 we compare firms with 'high skills', defined as enterprises with more than 10 per cent of the workforce having a university degree and 60 per cent with high school education, otherwise a firm is classified as having 'low skills'.

Table 5.5 Collaboration and Skills

Variable	Mean			Df	T-value	F-statistic	Significance level
	Low skills	High skills	All				
Collaboration with other firms	1.421	1.430	1.426	182	0.063	0.0039	0.949
Sub-contracting	1.375	1.240	1.301	195	1.0040	1.007	0.3168
Linkage with industrial association	1.508	1.597	1.559	142	0.596	0.355	0.5523
Cooperation with input suppliers	0.713	0.843	0.772	196	1.055	1.113	0.2928
Collaboration with technology institutions	0.789	0.786	0.787	201	0.055	0.0029	0.9566

Note: Figures in column 2, 3 and 4 show the average value of cooperation that was measured on a Lickert scale (1–3).

Table 5.6 Cooperation and Firm Size

Variable	Mean						
	1. Small	2. Medium	All	Df	T-value	F-statistic	Significance level
Cooperating with other firms	1.473	1.212	1.426	182	1.539	2.370	0.1254
Subcontracting	1.285	1.368	1.301	196	0.496	0.246	0.6206
Linkage with industrial association	1.641	1.192	1.559	142	2.376	5.646	0.0188
Cooperation with input suppliers	0.768	0.795	0.772	196	0.1886	0.0356	0.8506
Collaboration with technology institutions	0.781	0.809	0.787	201	0.397	0.157	0.6921

Note: Figures in column 2, 3 and 4 show the average value of cooperation that was measured on a Lickert scale (1–3).

None of the variables, namely, horizontal cooperation, subcontracting, linkage with industrial association, cooperation with input suppliers and technology institutions differ significantly with respect to skill intensity of firms. The results are not surprising because the skill intensity based on the qualification of workers is not as important as the qualification and managerial capability of the owner. The conduct of SMEs is determined largely by the entrepreneurial characteristics of the owner. However, it was not possible to test the differences in the conduct of firms represented by the above variable due to lack of systematic data on the qualification of managing directors.

Table 5.6 presents the results of differences in firm size classified on the basis of total employment; with firms that employ less than 50 workers classified as small enterprises and others treated as medium-sized firms.

From the table only one variable, linkage with industrial associations, differs significantly between small and medium sized firms. This confirms our hypothesis that larger firms are better served by industry associations compared to smaller ones. In other words, larger firms are expected to maintain greater links with industry associations in order to obtain support from local bodies and government.

Collaboration and firm performance

Table 5.7 presents the analysis of variance results of export intensity of firms. Export intensity is a binary variable representing exporting and non-exporting firms.

Table 5.7 Collaboration and Export Performance

Variable	Mean						
	Exporters	Non Exporters	All	Df	T-value	F-statistic	Significance level
Collaboration with other firms	1.508	1.111	1.343	107	2.112	4.462	0.037
Subcontracting	1.318	0.551	0.991	114	5.012	25.124	0.000
Linkage with industrial association	1.500	1.667	1.554	64	0.646	0.417	0.5208
Cooperation with input suppliers	0.894	0.660	0.793	115	1.179	1.392	0.2405
Collaboration with technology institutions	0.896	0.667	0.800	114	3.126	9.773	0.0023

Note: Figures in column 2, 3 and 4 show the average value of cooperation that was measured on a Lickert scale (1–3).

Several indicators of inter-firm linkage, namely, horizontal cooperation, subcontracting and collaboration with technology institutions, differ significantly between export-oriented firms and non-exporters. The results presented confirm what existing literature has to say about inter-firm collaboration. For instance, some export-oriented firms asserted that they avoid subcontracting collaboration for fear of compromising on product quality, while other firms prefer subcontracting in order to avoid high overhead costs. Similarly, export-oriented firms are more predisposed to collaboration with technology institutions in order to keep abreast of new opportunities in the technology and products markets. While firms can survive in the domestic market with relatively low skills and technology, they face considerably stiffer competition in the international market for which higher technical skills are required.

Table 5.8 presents the differences in performance and conduct of firms in the three countries. Performance variables are represented by export intensity, profitability, and sales turnover, while conduct variables are the ability of firm to innovate and speed of delivery.

All the variables, except sales turnover, differ significantly in the three countries. The results suggest that country-specific characteristics and firm performance differ significantly in these countries. In the three countries, firms export largely to regional destinations, but there are relatively more export-oriented and firms reporting innovation in the Nigerian sample. Firms attribute improvements in speed of delivery in the last five years to domestic and international competitive pressures. They respond to internal capability deficiency by conducting more in-house and external staff training, as well as by making improvements to the capacity

Table 5.8 Comparison of Firm Manufacturing Performance in Africa

Variable	Nigeria	Kenya	Zimbabwe	F-value	Significance
Firms that carry out Innovations	1.403	0.667	0.50	63.00	0.000
Percentage of output exported	34.513	7.619	8.963	25.923	0.000
Firm profitability	35.592	23.316	34.038	6.349	0.002
Speed of delivery	1.681	0.653	1.692	32.964	0.000
Quality improvement	1.277	0.940	1.444	10.648	0.000

Note: Innovation, speed of delivery, and quality improvement were measured on a Lickert scale (1–3) and averages are presented; Profitability was measured as percentage of sales turnover.

of product quality testing facilities. In sum, univariate analysis shows that firm-firm cooperation as well as subcontracting relationships exhibit significant correlation with firm performance. Firms in network collaboration tend to show a higher level of performance in terms of export, profitability, sales turnover, and speed of delivery. They also record greater innovative performance.

Multivariate analysis

In this section, we employ multivariate statistical techniques to separate the group of firms classified by specific firm characteristics. Discriminant analysis is used to identify factors that discriminated sample firms. The firms were grouped according to innovative capability of firms, cooperation with subcontractors regarding exchange of information and modification to product, and cooperation with respect to quality improvements. We follow the specification of a knowledge production function by which output is dependent on the availability and volume of internal and external resources (Freel, 2003: 6; Oerlemans et al., 2001: 9).

The model is specified as follows:

$$P = B_0 + B_1 Subcon + B_2 High\_Edu + B_3 Avg\_sto + B_4 Avgexp + B_5 Hor\_cop +$$
$$B_6 Cop\_inp + B7 + B8 Firm\_age + B9 Techsup + B10 Infra$$

where P represents group variable.

The empirical outputs were computed using SPSS package. From the literature, all the variables selected are known to have significant associations with firm performance and innovation outputs. The first set of tests was a multiple discriminant analysis based in part on the insights from the univariate analysis carried out earlier. Discriminant analysis is used in situations where observations (firms in our case) are classified using a combined index based on the known characteristics of population (explanatory variables). The advantage of discriminant analysis over regression analysis is that it does not presuppose causality between a group variable and the known characteristics. The parameters of the model are computed in such a way that the variance of the composite index is minimum with groups and maximum between groups.

Results of multivariate analysis

Tables 5.9–5.13 present the outputs of the discriminant analyses computed for the different functions. All relevant variables were included since the discriminant analysis model computes each variable independently. We discuss them in turn.

Firms that carry out product innovation   (all three countries)

For identifying factors that discriminate firms based on their capability to innovate, we have quantified this variable. We assigned value 1 for those that carried out significant modifications over the period of survey and 2 for others. Discriminant analysis identifies factors that discriminate between firms that carry significant modifications (innovations) and those that do not. In all, nine variables (AVG_EXP, COP_INPUT, HIGH_EDU, TECH_SUP, AVG_STO, SUBCON, INFRA, FIRM_AGE, and HCOP) were included in the analysis. From Table 5.9, eight out of nine variables are significant in discriminating two types of firms. The variable, horizontal cooperation of firms (HCOP) did not emerge a significant discriminant of two types of firms.

Table 5.9 Determinants of Innovation Capability

Variable	Wilks' Lambda	Sig.	Remarks
AVG_EXP	0.63939	0.00	Average exports since 1996
COP_INPUT	0.61125	0.00	Cooperation with input suppliers (binary)
HIGH_EDU	0.56959	0.00	Skill intensity
TECH_SUP	0.55223	0.00	Technological support (binary variable)
AVG_STO	0.53665	0.00	Average sales turnover since 1996
SUBCON	0.52178	0.00	Status of subcontracting (–, =, +)
INFRA	0.49898	0.00	Access to physical infrastructure index
FIRM_AGE	0.48788	0.00	Age of firm

Apart from the significance of variables included in the analysis, another test for goodness of fit of discriminant function is its explanatory power. It can be seen from the classification results (Appendix 5.1) that the total classification power of the function is 93.55 per cent, which is very high. Normally a function whose classification is more than 50 per cent is considered good and more than 75 per cent is considered very good.

Cooperation with subcontractors over the past five years: information and experiences' variable (Nigeria and Zimbabwe)

The group variable in this case has three values namely, '1' for firms that experienced decreased cooperation, '2' where cooperation did not change, and '3' for firms that experienced increased cooperation. The results of the discriminant analysis are presented in Table 5.10. The classification power of discriminant function is 82.61 per cent (Appendix 5.1).

Table 5.10 Determinants of Exchange of Information and Experience

Variable	Wilks' Lambda	Sig.	Remarks
SUBCON	0.77178	0.0750	Status of subcontracting (–, =, +)
AVG_EXP	0.58060	0.0315	Average exports since 1996
AVG_STO	0.46922	0.0261	Average sales turnover since 1996
FIRM_AGE	0.40099	0.0320	Age of firm
INFRA	0.35552	0.0476	Access of physical infrastructure index
TECH_SUP	0.29784	0.0512	Technological support (binary variable)

The results suggest that cooperation with subcontractors with respect to exchange of information is more intense among export-oriented firms that have a comparatively larger size of operation. We conclude from the results presented in Table 5.10 that older firms with better access to physical and information infrastructure assign greater importance to exchange of information and experience. Technological support variable emerged a significant discriminant of firms that assign importance to exchange of information with others. The results confirm our hypothesis as larger firms with higher export-intensity need to exchange information with sub-contractors being more concerned with fulfilling their business commitments (meeting design specification, product quality, and delivery schedule) than smaller firms operating in the domestic market.

Cooperation with subcontractors and innovation over the past five years (Nigeria and Zimbabwe)

In this case also the group variable has three values, that is, '3' for firms that have experienced decreased cooperation, '2' where cooperation has not changed, and '1' among firms that have had increased cooperation. According to our analysis, only average sales turnover emerged significant in discriminating the three types of firms (Table 5.11).

Although sales turnover is the only variable that was significant, the discrimination power of the function (Appendix 5.1) is very high.

Table 5.11 Determinants of Innovations

Variable	Wilks' Lambda	Sig.	Remarks
HCOP	0.81122	0.1112	Cooperation with other firms
AVG_EXP	0.69595	0.1150	Average exports since 1996
SUBCON	0.60652	0.1254	Status of subcontracting (–, =, +)
AVG_STO	0.44401	0.0459	Average sales turnover since 1996

Cooperation with sub-contractors and quality improvement over the last five years (Nigeria and Zimbabwe)

Like other cooperation variables, this group variable also takes three values, that is, '3' representing firms for whom cooperation has decreased, '2' where cooperation has not changed, and '1' for firms that have experienced increased cooperation (Table 5.12).

Table 5.12 Determinants of Quality Improvement

Variable	Wilks' Lambda	Sig.	Remarks
HCOP	0.81122	0.1112	Cooperation with other firms
AVG_EXP	0.69595	0.1150	Average exports since 1996
SUBCON	0.60652	0.1254	Status of subcontracting (–, =, +)
AVG_STO	0.44401	0.0459	Average sales turnover since 1996

Some export oriented firms engage in subcontracting mainly for quality improvement and this is not unexpected. However, the discriminating power of the function (Appendix 5.1) is not very high (40.38). This suggests that in addition to subcontracting, there are other variables that contribute to quality.

Cooperation with subcontractors over the past five yearws using composite index (all three countries)

A composite binary index was generated in order to enable comparisons for all the firms because the Kenya sample index is on a binary scale. Firms were assigned value '1' where any type of cooperation has increased over the last five years and value '0' otherwise. This was the definition used for the Kenya index. The results are presented in Table 5.13.

Although the classification power of the function in only 67.95 per cent (Appendix 5.1), all the variables that were included in the analysis emerged significant discriminants of firms that engage in cooperation with sub-contractors. The results are similar to what have been reported when each factor was considered separately.

Table 5.13 Determinants of Cooperation with Sub-Contractors

Variable	Wilks' Lambda	Sig.	Remarks
AVG_EXP	0.95020	0.0614	Average exports since 1996
AVG_STO	0.92643	0.0744	Average sales turnover since 1996
HIGH_EDU	0.90270	0.0749	Skill intensity

Discussion of results

In the multi-country study that formed the basis for this chapter, we examined a variety of collaboration factors that influence the performance of the firm within the national system. All three hypotheses were confirmed by our analysis, albeit differentially in each country, that is, not all variables emerged as equally significant in every country. In sum, if we take the three countries together, the following represent the findings of the chapter:

- Cooperation between firms is significant, while linkage with knowledge institutions is weak;
- Firm size: medium-size firms tend to collaborate more than small firms;
- Human capital represented by a higher proportion of educated workforce promotes collaboration;
- Cooperation to share information tends to be very significant.

Inter-firm collaboration with clients, contractors, suppliers and input suppliers seems to be the most widespread and the most prominent among small enterprises. Small producers are far more concerned with meeting daily production schedules rather than with medium to long term innovation planning. This consideration, more than anything else, tends to determine the dynamics of collaboration. Again, due to credit and other resource constraints normally associated with small firms, there is a tendency to depend on credit suppliers that in most cases are larger firms. This kind of forced reliance is not inevitable, but a necessity in the absence of alternative state support.

The weakest form of collaboration among the countries surveyed is with the universities. We identified four main reasons for this. First, small firms have relatively small proportions of an educated workforce, although the proportion of owners-entrepreneurs tends to be higher. This lacuna in the skill structure of firms affects collaboration in two ways. In the first place, a well educated management is needed in order to understand and search for information. Firms thus suffer the incidence of inter-organizational knowledge dissonance. In the second instance, the cognitive disability of a firm with a large proportion of uneducated workers sets a limit on its innovation search efforts. The second reason relates to the overall low technological capability base of small firms in underdeveloped areas, which may mean that the types of innovation they carry out will be routine, incremental and with little scientific input. Third, small firms are hardly able to spare the requisite manpower and finance required for innovation search and adaptation, and they are less disposed to take the high risks of innovation failures. Fourth, universities themselves often have little in common with small firms as much of their research work is defined and carried out by individual researchers with an aim to publish rather than disseminate to the local small producers. In developing countries, the most evident contribution of universities to firms is their science and technology training programmes. Such training has a more direct impact on firms than research outputs, which at best would require further tests and resources to be usable at the commercial level.

Small firm collaboration with distant suppliers commonly involves the supply of machinery, equipment and spare parts. In some cases, this is enhanced by technical training provided by suppliers. The case of auto parts producers at Nnewi in South East Nigeria most vividly illustrates this phenomenon. A study of the cluster (Oyelaran-Oyeyinka, 1997b) reported in some detail in Chapter 4, found that more than 90 per cent of firms in the cluster imported machinery from Taiwan and had developed strong trade relations with the Taiwanese firms. This chapter similarly found that there is a strong local network of suppliers and contractors in other parts of Nigeria through which firms place orders for inputs, and this is true, although to a lesser extent, in the other two countries.

In addition to the foregoing reasons, the perceived lack of dynamism in African industry is also tied to poor infrastructure delivery and the poor state of formal institutions of human capital. The low technical and managerial capacity of universities and RDIs, and the subsequent impact on their outputs can be illustrated with the examples of Kenya and Nigeria. In both countries the teaching and research functions have declined considerably in recent years as a result of poor funding, coupled with high growth in enrolment and mass exodus of university lecturers. Paradoxically, the universities face the dilemma of new expectations from the state and society to forge greater links with and provide support for industry.

Table 5.14 shows the absolute increase in R&D expenditure in Kenyan universities over a seven-year period (1988 to 1995) and an almost doubling of R&D as per cent of GDP. However, the 1993 university research expenditure as a per cent of gross academic expenditure (GAE) accounted for only 40 per cent of the level in 1986, a real significant decrease. More importantly, close to 80 per cent of the expenditure

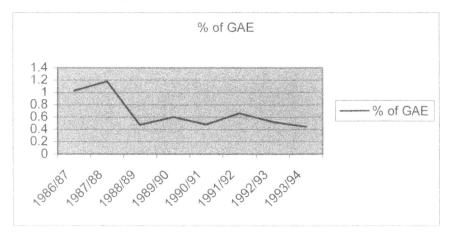

Figure 5.1   Trends in University Funding in Kenya, 1986–1994

for most universities is allocated to staff salaries. At the same time the value of this item fell significantly from 0.15 per cent of total government expenditure in 1988/89 to 0.05 per cent in 1995/96. The trends in university funding (Figure 5.1) shows an uneven but sure decline over time.

This data shows that the percentage of university research expenditure fluctuated in the periods 1986–87 and 1993–94. However, if we consider the entire period, there is sharp decline in the percentage of university research expenditure, from 1.03 in 1986–87 to 0.44 in 1993–94 (Appendix 5.2).

The story is not much different in Nigeria, which has 43 tertiary educational institutions made up of federal, state and recently, private universities. The three private universities (there are a lot more now) are less than 5 years old, while most of the state universities range in age from 10–20 years. In 1996/97 a total of 52 823 students graduated from the universities, twenty thousand more than the 1986/87 period. The growth rate of output from first generation federal universities is lower – Ibadan (9.6 per cent), Ife (2.45 per cent) while in some of the new generation universities, the growth rate exceeds 20 per cent. In the past decade, enrolment doubled to 325 000 students, while the knowledge and physical infrastructure remained largely unchanged until the new democratic government initiated a process of reform. This includes building of new hostels, establishing an IT network to link the universities, significantly raising the salary of lecturers and licensing of private universities to lessen the enrolment pressure on public universities.

The teacher-student ratio (TSR), a proxy measure of quality of education, relates the number of students that a teacher ought to have to the actual situation in a class. A high TSR suggests greater interaction between teachers and students and a tendency to quality instruction. The TSR in Nigerian universities declined from 1:15 in 1995 to 1:22 in 1999, compared to the UNESCO recommended ratio of 1:10. This declining

Table 5.14 Selected Science and Technology Expenditure in Kenya

Year	Total University research (Ksh)	NCST research grant	Other GoK research grant	Total GoK research expenditure	Total private*	Total R&D expenditure	R&D expenditure % GDP
1988/89	7.32	0.15	0.116	48.33	4.83	53.16	0.82
1989/90	7.920	0.09	0.150	56.71	5.67	62.38	0.84
1990/91	9.3	0.066	0.016	7.14	7.81	85.95	1.03
1991/92	11.64	0.050	0.10	87.98	18.78	96.78	1.01
1994/95	13.48	0.050	0.014	185.22	18.52	203.7	1.51
1995/96	14.49	0.050	0.287	159.80	15.98	175.8	1.09

* 10% of total Government of Kenya (GoK)

ratio may well be due as much to higher enrolments as to the mass migration of teachers from the university system to Europe, North America and the Middle East.

For these reasons, the quality of education offered in Nigeria since the mid-1980s has fallen badly, as with the rest of Africa and, overall, considered to be well below world standards and falling further. Education standards are increasingly declining with the gap in achievement between African students and those in industrialized countries 'widening to unbridgeable proportions' (Clarke 2000: 82). Notably, the student/teacher ratios at the primary and secondary schools have steadily increased in the post 1990 period. In addition, there has been a drastic decline in the quality of physical inputs (for example, staff, especially at the senior levels, and learning resources and facilities) that are essential for the successful operations of knowledge institutes(Figure 5.2), for student/teacher ratio.

The declining quality of education is largely a result of constant budget cuts (since 1980) together with rapid increases in enrolment rates. This has made the financing of education recurrent costs more difficult (World Bank, 1988). Proportionally the expenditure per student at the university level declined drastically between 1984/85 and 2000.

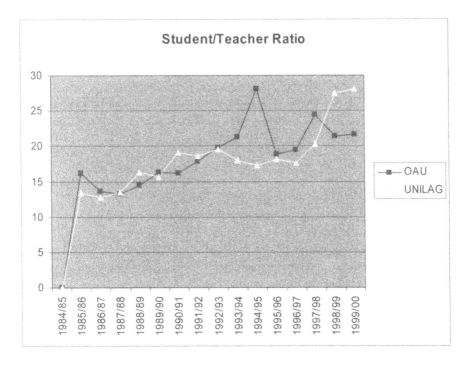

Figure 5.2   Student/Teacher Ratio in Nigerian Universities, 1984–2000

Legend: OAK = Obafemi Awolowo University, Ife-Ife, Nigeria UNILAG= Univeristy of Lags, Lagos, Nigeria.

Summary

This chapter examined inter-firm and inter-organizational networks in African industry. Three sets of interactions were analysed, namely: inter-firm/ firm-industrial association linkages; vertical (subcontracting) relationships; and firm-university linkages. We presented an analytical framework to test three hypotheses that organized our findings and analysed the data within univariate and multivariate frameworks. We expected that SME collaboration with RDIs and universities would promote greater firm-level technical performance and result in better output and product quality, but found little incidence of collaboration between firms and technological institutions. However, there is statistically significant incidence of collaboration among suppliers of inputs, subcontractors and firms and a positive correlation between networking and firm-level performance. There are a variety of channels of interactions, namely, exchange of information, joint marketing, through for instance trade fairs, and subcontracting.

While this chapter identified multiple institutions and channels of exchange that could potentially provide a platform for innovation, it emerged that firms tend to employ only a limited number of these avenues. For instance, the data clearly shows that despite fairly widespread inter-firm cooperation as well as subcontracting relationships, cooperation between SMEs and knowledge institutions is rather weak or, for the most part, non-existent. Another issue has to do with the quality and intensity of the exchanges. Firms and organizations with which they interact introduce modifications largely to products and often in response to certain bottlenecks, but we found no evidence of systematic innovation initiatives. Even though participating firms showed increasing levels of market performance in terms of turnover and profitability in relation to networking, they have not taken a proactive stance on exploiting innovations as a strategic competitiveness tool. This is reflected in the responses of firms to questions on the nature of collaboration with universities. For a firm to progress to greater competitive levels, innovation processes would need to involve not only cooperative relationships between firms, suppliers and subcontractors, but also with technological institutions.

Three sets of issues with implications for policy emerged from our detailed interviews. First, we make tentative conclusions that inter-firm relations, particularly between firms and other economic agents, involve more than the mere exchange of information about prices and volumes, although we are far from fully understanding all the factors that induce networking. However, fostering cooperative interaction between economic agents in industry has not come about naturally, and networking institutions remain weak in all three countries. Second, there is a measure of interaction among economic agents, but this relates largely to maintaining firm daily routines and, to an extent, effecting minor technical modifications that keep plants working. Innovation policy should therefore seek to *move up* the quality of firm level activity as well as promote greater interaction among firms and technological institutions. Policy should also establish or strengthen organizations and institutions to regulate and coordinate innovation functions, which, following the prevailing

Neo-Liberal prescriptions, would be left to the markets. Finally, there is evidence that collaborative exchanges raise economic performance, which provides an economic rationale for intervention to promote inter-firm collaboration. We suggest therefore that developing African countries need to approach the task of developing their national systems of innovation (NSIs) without preconceived ideas of 'ideal' types, as the notion of optimality has no place in systems thinking.

Appendix 5.1　　Classification Power of Discriminant Functions

Function: Innovativeness

Actual Group	Predicted Group Membership		No. of Firms
	Innovating	Non-Innovating	
Innovating	52　(96.3%)	2 (3.7%)	54
Non-Innovating	2　(25.0%)	6 (75.0%)	8

Total discriminating power 93.55%

Function: Exchange of Information and Experience

Actual Group	Predicted Group Membership			No. of Firms
	Decreased cooperation	No change	Increased cooperation	
Decreased cooperation	6　(66.7%)	2　(22.2%)	1 (11.1%)	9
No change		8 (100%)		8
Increased cooperation		1 (16.7%)	5 (83.3%)	6

Total discriminating power 82.61%

Function: Technological Modifications

Actual Group	Predicted Group Membership			No. of Firms
Decreased cooperation	13 (92.9%)		1 (7.1%)	14
No change	1　(12.5%)	5　(62.5%)	2 (25.0%)	8
Increased cooperation			2 (100%)	2

Total discriminating power 83.33%

Function: Quality Improvement

Actual Group	Predicted Group Membership			No. of Firms
Decreased cooperation	10 (33.3%)	9　(30.0)	11 (36.7%)	30
No change	4　(22.2%)	8 (44.4%)	6　(33.4%)	18
Increased cooperation	1　(25.0%)		3　(75.0%)	4

Total discriminating power 40.38%

Function: Cooperation with sub-Contractors

Actual Group	Predicted Group Membership		No. of Firms
Decreased cooperation	38 (79.2%)	10 (20.8%)	48
No change			
Increased cooperation	15　(50.0%)	15 (50.0%)	30

Total discriminating power 67.95%

Note: % is row percentage.

Appendix 5.2   Indicators of S&T Expenditures in Kenya

Year	Personnel* costs as % of recurrent expenditure	University research expenditure as % of GAE**	% of Science Students admitted	Overall enrolment in public universities	Enrolment growth rate
1986/87	68.4	1.03	42.4	8.653	14.9
1987/88	66.5	1.18	39.1	15.116	74.7
1988/89	65.8	0.47	31.2	20.180	33.5
1989/90	71.2	0.60	31.2	24.111	19.5
1990/91	76.1	0.48	29.1	28.353	17.6
1991/92	74.1	0.66	42.1	40.562	78.3
1992/93	76.3	0.52	39.6	38.748	-0.004
1993/94	84.3	0.44	40.0	35.810	-0.001

*University of Nairobi.
**GAE= Gross Academic Expenditure.

Chapter 6

Infrastructure and Industry

Introduction

This chapter examines an important component of the innovation system in continuation of our focus on institutions. It analyses the physical rather than knowledge or non-physical infrastructure such as metrology and R&D services, which are covered in Chapters 7 and 8. Physical infrastructure comprises energy supply, water, telecommunication, transport systems (roads, railways, airfreight and so on). Infrastructure possesses technical and economic characteristics that affect innovation systems in very profound ways. The technical attributes of infrastructure include 'scale, indivisibility, multiple use and generic functions' that separate it from other forms of capital.[1]

Indivisibility confers a systemic attribute on infrastructure that allows it to serve the entire industrial and non-industrial system, with considerable flexibility for multiple extensions. The latitude for multiple use of infrastructure, by urban and non-urban consumers equally, extends its scale economic characteristics. As infrastructure is fundamental to all production activities, it traditionally has been supplied by monopolies or within the public domain. The required scale of investment is often beyond the financial capacity of private investors in developing countries. Infrastructure provision impacts upon three broad groups – firms, industrial systems and consumers.

The absence of necessary utilities such as electrical power, water supply or telecommunication compels firms to make alternative provision. This course of action raises production cost as well as the price of goods and services; thereby depressing demand. Drastic changes in the quality and price at which infrastructure is supplied may equally be productivity enhancing; where such a change is positive or cost-escalating, either the quality deteriorates or prices of utilities rise.

In the second instance, the impact is industry-wide and would relate to the market directly. Low price and high quality infrastructure supply would likely encourage the entry of a greater number of firms into the industry. The resulting competition among firms raises industrial output. Importantly also, the presence of infrastructure is an inducement to the establishment of key industrial facilities and for the diffusion of technologies. Examples include the role of industrial estates, science parks and technology incubators, all of which act to attract firms to specific locations. Clustering

---

1 See Keith Smith, 'Economic Infrastructures and innovation systems', in Edquist and Johnson (1997) for an excellent treatment.

is now well known to provide firms with the benefits of agglomeration that leads to productivity growth. Spatial or geographic concentration leads to 'collective efficiency', whether in organically evolved clusters or in clusters promoted by public policy. The provision of public utilities, such as transportation and communication, has strong externalities and has direct impact on factor prices.

The third and last level where the reduced costs of infrastructure impacts is on consumer behaviour, and this is as a result of their positive impact on product and service prices. Again telecommunication and electrical power tend to be the most prominent. For instance, the introduction of mobile telephony in Africa has greatly improved teledensity in many countries. Improved communication tends to lead to lower information search costs in much the same way that low cost transport and good roads lower transaction costs.

An efficient infrastructure is important to enterprises for two main reasons. First, its absence compels optional provision, a situation that places added financial and material burden on firms. Firms regard the cost of alternative utilities as a major impediment to new investments, as extra financial provision is usually required for major plant vintages as well as for minor plant additions. Second, inadequate national infrastructure makes networking among firms extremely difficult. For example, transaction costs are high where communication is hindered either by poor telecommunications or frequent power outages. In some cases, production linkage is not only made difficult, it is impossible. In most African countries, agricultural and industrial productions are constrained by inadequate backward linkages to exploit agricultural raw materials often located within inaccessible but rich rural communities. This may be due to poor road networks, lack of information, and inadequate storage facilities.[2]

Frequent power outages forces firms to acquire standby electricity generating sets. Firms that are unable to acquire private facilities either cut down on production or in rare cases share power with nearby firms with generating sets. There is the constant risk and realities of damages to sensitive machinery resulting from unplanned power cuts. The perennial poor state of infrastructure leaves manufacturers with little confidence in the ability of public enterprises to meet their supply requirements.

The effect of poor infrastructure on routine production activities could be very significant. To the extent that there is greater propensity for technical change in a regime of continuous production, the availability of infrastructure is critical to achieving competitive advantage. Planning becomes difficult, and coordination among economic agents within the national economy and with international agents, very problematic. Spontaneous inter-organizational linkages made possible by all-purpose infrastructure are a prerequisite for 'networking' – that complex of backward and forward linkages that is taken for granted in dynamic industrial environments. We find that the constraints seem to redirect the focus of firms to unprofitable directions.

---

2   On a 1998 mission to some of Ethiopia's agricultural research stations by road, the journey which on a good road should be no more than one hour took three hours. The station had no functioning telephone.

Rather than take a long-term perspective of 'internal' infrastructure as a component part of a firm's strategic growth process (for example, skill development, re-training to match new technologies and so on), firms are forced to invest in utilities that are largely of public goods.

In effect, firms are penalized for what is essentially failure of public policy, through the provision of alternative utilities. Where such options are beyond firms' capacity, the innovation investments tend to be the first casualty. In sum, issues relating to infrastructural capacity and capability within firms in SSA should be central to discussions on innovation, as infrastructure influences the path and process of inventive activities significantly. It would be misleading to consider them as fixed factors of technical change.

The rest of the chapter is organized as follows: the next section discusses the infrastructure condition of SSA, followed by an analysis of the ICT infrastructure as an infrastructure category and then a firm-level analysis with data from our Nigerian survey. Finally, we present some conclusions.

Infrastructure and economic conditions of Sub-Saharan Africa

LDCs are identified by the United Nations (UN) as low-income countries, with low levels of human capital that are highly vulnerable to natural and man-made shocks. Out of the 49 countries in SSA, there are 33 LDCs, putting the majority of SSA countries in this category. The exceptions, for varying human and material resource reasons, are: South Africa, Mauritius, Botswana, Zimbabwe and Nigeria. There are others which differ only marginally from the African LDCs. In what follows, we present the characteristics of this group of countries.

The 33 African LDCs differ widely in size and resource endowments, however, they share important common characteristics, which distinguish them from other developing countries. Low levels of income, a low degree of industrialization and human capital development, high levels of export concentration, often in one or two primary commodity lines, and a high level of vulnerability to external shocks are common features of these economies.

The average per capita GNP is only a quarter of the developing country average. In fact, in the large LDC countries in SSA, where a majority of the populations live, per capita GNP is barely above 20 per cent of the other developing country average levels. At the prevailing levels of per capita income, the majority of the LDCs' population in SSA lives close to subsistence level. On average, more than 55 per cent of the population has a per capita income below one dollar a day, and about 85 per cent of the population has a per capita income of less than two dollars a day.

The extremely low levels of per capita income reflect the underdeveloped structures of these economies, compared to other developing countries, and their meagre stock of capital. On average, more than two thirds of the population and labour force reside in the countryside and work in the agricultural sector. The share of agriculture in GDP is more than double the average for other developing countries.

The low level of industrialization is also reflected in the extremely low levels of modern sources of hydrocarbon-based energy use, compared to other developing countries. The combined per capita consumption of coal, oil, gas, and electricity is one-tenth the prevailing levels in the developing countries. In contrast, fuel-wood sources of energy still constitute the bulk of energy consumption in much of SSA.

The countries lag far behind other developing countries in educational attainment and other aspects of human capital development required in an increasingly knowledge-based global economy. Available data indicate that adult literacy rate is on average 49 per cent in these countries compared to 81 per cent for other developing countries. Primary and secondary school enrolment rates are on average about 30 and 50 percentage points (respectively) below the other developing country averages. Tertiary enrolment rates are a tenth of what obtains in other countries. The indicators suggest that African countries are fast falling behind other developing countries with respect to human capital formation in spite of the significant progress made since independence. The vast majority of the population is either rural-based or recent migrants to urban areas. The degree of economic retrogression in these countries during the past few decades and the lag between these countries and other developing countries in terms of the stock of human capital is likely to widen in the face of the rapid advances in S&T in the more developed societies.

African countries have comparably weak physical and knowledge infrastructure base, exemplified by poor telecommunications and transport facilities. For example, the number of telephone lines per thousand people is about 5 – one twentieth of the average for other developing countries. The cost of local telephone calls is one hundred per cent higher than the average for the latter. The considerable lag in the development of telecommunications infrastructure within African countries and between SSA and other developing countries is likely to lead to their increasing exclusion from the global economy.

A similar situation exists with regard to the development of transport infrastructure. The poor state of transport infrastructure in SSA is well documented.[3] The situation, however, is not peculiar to African LDCs – though it assumes particularly acute proportions there. As shown in Table 6.1, even after normalizing for population, area, per capita income and regional specificities, other developing countries on average have 60 per cent higher road networks and almost two and a half times higher paved roads compared to these countries. In addition, the much poorer quality of roads and road transport facilities in these countries should be considered.

Rail transport suffers the same fate, but the gap in air transport indicators in the two country groups does not seem to be significant. Another aspect of transportation which further compounds the issue of poor internal transport facilities is that a large number of the countries are landlocked. They depend on long transit routes through adjacent countries with similar poor road infrastructure and borders that are often subject to closures due to political instability. The island LDCs face transportation problems of their own, arising from their small size, isolation and remoteness, and

---

3   See UNDP (1999).

Table 6.1 Transport Indicators for LDCs and Other Developing Countries

t-test for the other developing difference between			
Year/Period	LDCs Average (b)	Country Average	Means
Roads, normalized index (a) 1997 (LDC index = 100)	100	160.3	2.46
Paved Road, normalized index (a) 1997 (100 index = 100)	100	248.5	4.26
Railways, goods transported 1990–97 (1000 ton-km per PPP $ million of GDP)	34.4	321.0	2.91
Railways, 1000 passenger-km 1990–97 (per PPP $ million of GDP)	246	84.7	3.85
Air Transport, passengers carried 1990–97 (per PPP $ million of GDP)	1.5	1.8	0.631
Air transport, freight, 1000 tons 1990–97 per km (per PPP $ million of GDP)	1.5	1.8	0.631

Source: World Bank (1991).
Notes: (a) Normalized taking into account population, area, population density, per capita income and special regional dummies.
(b) Simple averages

the existence of sizable economies of scale in transportation. Apart from reducing international competitiveness and adding to export instability, the weak transportation infrastructure also leads to the fragmentation of the national markets, imposing prohibitive transportation costs on a large segment of the rural population.

Low-income, underdeveloped economic structures and the poor state of infrastructure all lead to high vulnerability to external shocks arising from natural causes or those arising from fluctuations in the world economy. African countries have been subjected to numerous natural disasters such as cyclones, floods, droughts and earthquakes. Some have had more than a fair share of natural disasters, both in terms of frequency and intensity, but what really makes the difference compared to other countries is that economic vulnerability arising from natural events often deepens dire economic and social situations, making such situations persist for much longer. Poor peasants with meagre resources may never recover from the loss of assets resulting from a drought, flood or cyclone.

Economic vulnerability in these fragile environments is further intensified by the fact that much of the activities are engaged with at the subsistence level. Even the mildest natural mishap can easily become a disaster. Similarly, natural disasters can divert a disproportionately large amount of government resources from essential infrastructure investment, thus seriously hampering the long-term resilience of the environment and the economy.

In sum, the foregoing highlights broad aspects of the African economies, which have important implications and policies for attenuating infrastructure constraints. First, the majority of Africa's population lives in countries with very low per capita incomes and underdeveloped production structures. Second, extremely low levels of knowledge and physical infrastructure constrain efficient use of productive resources in these countries. And third, largely as a consequence of the first two characteristics, SSA countries are highly vulnerable to external shocks arising from the vagaries of nature or those arising from factors related to external economies. These factors have important implications for theory as well as policy for mitigating infrastructure deficiencies.

Information and telecommunications infratstructure

ICT infrastructure may be divided broadly into three components: telecommunications, computing and connectivity infrastructure. Historically, the key telecommunications actor had been the Public Switched Telecommunications Networks (PSTNs). However, in the last two decades, privatization and market liberalization led to public divestments as well as the entry of new private telecommunications operators (PTOs) into the sector. Massive restructuring had resulted, but more remains to be done in order to create truly competitive markets in the telecommunication sector in Africa. While some progress has been made in improving connectivity infrastructure, there remains strong reliance on the US Internet backbones for connectivity infrastructure. Skills, innovations and major investments are concentrated in the triad of USA, Japan and Europe. In other words, while users have some form of control on the provision of private computing facilities, access to and the quality of telecommunications and connectivity available to a user depend on geographic space. In effect, the economic environment is a determinant of the access, speed, types of data and, for that matter, information and knowledge to which users have access.[4]

At the very basic level, African countries have highly differentiated access to telephone and electricity services that are taken as given in high income countries. The quality of these basic engineering and physical infrastructure is important for the simple reason that information, coded in files, travels through series of linked nodes within the ICT network. The slowest link in the network node becomes the rate-determining step and thereby defines the overall speed of data transmission (Dholakia, 1997).[5] In other words, local and regional telecommunications infrastructure such as server connectors, local loop telecommunication lines, inter-nodal connections, and switching systems, among others, determine the cost and quality of access. Users in high-bandwidth telecommunications environment are likely to have access to lower

---

4   Castells (1996) cites Porat (1977) and defines Information as simply: 'data that have been organized and communicated'.

5   For example, a 28.8 kbps modem on a home computer may yield a transmission speed of no more than 24.6 kpbs, a speed loss of 14.5 per cent as a result of the quality of telephone lines.

Table 6.2 Correlation of IT Infrastructure and Network Variables in SSA

Variable	Electrical power	Main telephone	Internet use	Internet Hosts	PC use
Electrical Power	1.000 (.000)	0.641*	0.599**	0.838*	0.329***
Main Telephone lines /10,000	0.641*	1.000*	0.965*	0.947*	0.826*
Internet use/capital	0.599*	0.965*	1.000*	0.902*	0.709*
Internet Hosts/capita	0.838*	0.947*	0.902*	1.000*	0.729*
PC use/capita	0.329***	0.826 (.000)	0.709***	0.727*	1.000*

*** .01 level of significance
** .01 level of significance (2-tailed)
* .05 level of significance (2-tailed).

cost connections. Most developing countries face capacity constraints, largely a result of thin-bandwidth and frequent power outages.

The combined effects of poor infrastructure result in high average cost of access to the Internet. Cost components include local calls charges, charges for line rentals, and costs due to ISP services. Historically, there has been a strong correlation between basic domestic and industrial technological artefact adoption such as telephone and computers and levels of development.

The correlation matrix in Table 6.2 shows the indivisibility of the various 'wired' facilities, particularly electrical power and telephone on the one hand, and networks variables comprising personal computers (PCs), modems, and other telecommunication facilities on the other. Internet use and Internet hosts display high correlation among themselves. The correlation derives from a group of 42 African countries, but this propensity equally holds for other highly developed countries and regions (Hargittai, 1999).

Empirical analysis of ICT infrastructure

Using the median of per capita income of US$ 360, we divided African countries into two broad groups of relative low and high income. This exercise is intended only for an analytical comparison in this chapter and does not suggest a permanent category. Not surprisingly, most of Africa's LDCs fall into the low-income group as well as in the low access, poor connectivity category. This confirms what we already know about the correlation of income with Internet access. For instance the 33 LDCs share of Africa's GDP was only 16.5 per cent in 2000, about one-quarter of SSA 46 countries. In Table 6.3, we construct an Internet User index (IUI) for all these countries. The country with the highest per capita IUI, Mauritius, has

Table 6.3 Economic Wealth and Other Determinants of the Internet Use in SSA (2001)

Country	GDP (USD) at 1995	IU density (per 10,000)	IU INDEX	IH density (per 10 000)	PC density (per 1000)	Tele density (per 1000)
Low Income						
Ethiopia	115.88	1.58	0.001	0.01	0.945	3.23
Burundi	140.70	7.47	0.009		..	
Sierra Leone	147.39					
Eritrea	155.05	13.05	0.017	0.05	1.608	8.09
Malawi	168.63	14.51	0.019	0.01	1.161	3.86
Tanzania	190.49	32.75	0.044	0.23	2.847	4.87
Niger	202.80	3.73	0.004	0.16	0.466	1.86
Guinea-Bissau	209.76	24.97	0.033	0.17	..	
Chad	217.84	3.92	0.005	0.01	1.341	1.46
Rwanda	241.77	6.47	0.008	0.47	..	
Madagascar	245.80	18.82	0.025	0.34	2.195	3.43
Burkina Faso	252.05	8.38	0.011	0.32	1.257	4.35
Nigeria	253.60	17.57	0.023	0.07	6.587	3.84
Mali	287.74	16.74	0.022	0.08	1.157	3.36
Sudan	319.08	9.65	0.012	0.21	3.216	11.15
Togo	326.61	86.41	0.118	0.34	21.603	9.22
Kenya	328.20	65.21	0.089	0.53	4.891	10.88
Central African Republic	338.57	4.15	0.005	0.02	1.660	2.80
Uganda	347.95	18.01	0.024	0.08	2.701	2.87
High Income						
Gambia, The	370.48	92.11	0.126	0.12	11.514	24.42
Zambia	392.38	19.19	0.026	0.86	6.717	9.20
Ghana	413.25	14.84	0.020	0.01	2.969	9.93
Benin	414.17	24.6	0.033	0.415	1.640	8.05
Comoros	435.79	21.61	0.029	0.58	4.323	10.27
Mauritania	495.68	18.87	0.025	0.45	9.434	7.17
Angola	506.07	22.84	0.031	0.01	1.142	8.39
Guinea	603.40	10.12	0.013	0.25	3.669	8.16
Senegal	609.24	42	0.057	1.93	16.800	20.71
Zimbabwe	620.70	37.08	0.050	2.16	11.867	27.08
Cote d'Ivoire	742.52	27.05	0.036	0.41	6.087	17.01
Djibouti	783.07	21.94	0.029	0.064	10.188	14.09
Congo, Rep.	841.42	1.75	0.002	0.02	3.492	7.68
Equatorial Guinea	1598.60	15.45	0.020	0.13	2.264	
Namibia	2407.60	170.78	0.234	18.51	34.157	68.35
Botswana	3951.10	154.13	0.211	14.53	36.991	89.93
South Africa	3985.10	549.38	0.754	42.95	61.805	133.63
Gabon	4378.00	122.35	0.167	0.28	9.788	32.28
Mauritius	4429.00	728.91	1.000	27.44	100.539	257.85

IUI = Internet User Index = [X j,i - Min (Xj,i)]/
[Max (Xj,i) - Min (Xj,i)], Xi refers to the Internet user per capita and i, and j refer to the number of countries reporting data.
data source: world development indicators, the World Bank (2002), and ITU (2002).
Data for GDP per capita in US dollars at constant price (at 1995) have been taken from World Bank (2001b).

the maximum value 1.0. Evidently there is higher correlation between IUI and the variables for the relatively higher income countries. South Africa has the next best IUI, while the African LDCs like Burundi and Eritrea with low per capita income have correspondingly low IUI. Our general conclusion is that while low income is generally correlated with low access, countries with the same economic structures may display different patterns of Internet connectivity (Figures 6.1 to 6.3, show the correlation in graphical forms). The main reasons for this may well be historical. It may also be a consequence of policy and approaches to institutional building.

A certain arbitrariness is reflected in Table 6.3, showing that about six of the countries in our category of high income are actually LDCs. However, in this aberrant grouping, we make our first observation that some countries with low income have succeeded in attaining a decent host per capita ratio and a modest IUI.[6] Take for instance the Gambia with an IUI of 0.126 and Ethiopia with 0.001, although both countries are LDCs, the Gambia has more than 120 times the value of IUI as Ethiopia. Mauritius, which leads in the group, has 1000 times the value of Ethiopia. Zambia, another LDC, shares a relatively modest IUI and income per capita with Angola, Senegal and Zimbabwe.

With the exception of Kenya, all the countries that fell into the low IUI and low-income group are the least developed African countries, confirming what we know about the correlation of wealth and Internet diffusion. Figures 6.1 to 6.3 show the graphical correlation of IUI for the two income groups, with Internet host, PC density and telephone density; irrespective of the level of wealth, we found that these variables are correlated with Internet use.

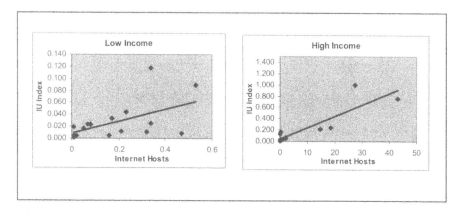

Figure 6.1   Internet Users and Hosts in SSA (2000)

From Figure 6.1, the IUI of some countries for example, Togo and Kenya with income per capita less that half of several countries (Cote d'Ivoire, Djibouti,

---

6   We define IUI as a normalized value using the formula shown under Table 6.3.

Congo, Rep, and Equatorial Guinea) but their level of Internet use is five to ten times higher than these countries. The figure also shows the gradient $\partial(IUI)/\partial(IH)$ of high-income countries to be significantly higher than those of low-income countries. Larger change in per unit of IUI with respect to unit change in Internet Host (IH) suggests that the prerequisites for the Internet, such as telecommunication infrastructure and last mile connectivity, are better in high-income countries where, presumably, the Internet Service Providers (ISPs) are comparatively better able to cover large number of end-users per Internet host.

Figure 6.2 depicts the diagrammatic relationship between IUI and PC density in low- and high-income countries. In this case also the per capita income of Togo, representing a low-income country, is roughly one-fourth while penetration of PCs is about ten times more compared to Equatorial Guinea with a relatively high income level.

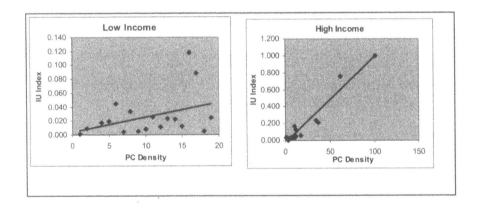

Figure 6.2   Internet Users and PC Density in SSA (2000)

The figure shows that the rate of change of IUI with respect to PC density is much higher in high-income countries than others. We can infer from these trends that PCs are more effectively used for the Internet in high-income countries.

The relationship between telephone density and IUI in two groups of countries is presented in Figure 6.3. It is evident that the range of telephone density in low-income countries varies from 1.46 to 10.88 per thousand persons, while in high-income countries it is 7.17 to 257.85. It is clear that there is a substantial difference in the telephone density in two groups of countries and, not surprisingly, IUI is significantly different in these countries.

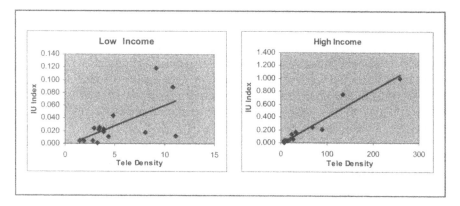

Figure 6.3   Internet Users and Telephone Density in SSA (2000)

Unlike in Figures 6.1 and 6.2, the slopes of the trend lines in Figure 6.3 are similar. This suggests that controlling for the growth in telephone density, all the countries have experienced similar growth rate of Internet users. We conclude that, of the variables considered, telephone density is expected to be the most important factor that influenced the diffusion of the Internet in SSA.

Firm-level performance and physical infrastructure

In this section we report findings of responses from firms in the three countries covered in our survey. Generally all the respondents described the supply of electricity from the national grid as inadequate because of frequent power outages. Information from the survey revealed that power outages forced most of the firms (82 per cent) to acquire their own electricity generating sets while the remaining (18 per cent) rely entirely on the public source. For firms that rely on their own generating sets as well as the public source, a significant percentage still depend on their generating sets for more than half the time on average. 45.5 per cent of the firms use generators for about half the time of their operations while only one in every four firms (27.3 per cent) use their generating sets for less than 50 per cent of the time.

In Nigeria, with the most severe power problems, 45 per cent of the firms combining both the national grid and stand-by generating sets still experience power outages attributed largely to break down of generating sets, fuel shortage, high maintenance cost, and lack of spare parts. The firms' level of satisfaction with physical infrastructure is shown in Table 6.4. A majority of the firms are dissatisfied with physical infrastructure, and electricity is the most problematic of the concerns identified by them (61.6 per cent). This is followed by telephone (53.7 per cent), roads (49.4 per cent) and lastly water (46.9 per cent). Firms provide alternative utilities at great cost and the small firms are less able to afford such costs. The extra costs expended on the provision of these facilities result in increased product prices, according to firms.

In the last five years, a significant percentage of firms (43.6 per cent) claim that the quality of electricity had declined. A similar pattern is observed in a decline in the quality of water, but fewer claim deterioration in the quality of roads. A majority of the firms claim that poor access to infrastructure facilities constrain production activities (Table 6.5). In some cases over 80 per cent of responding firms claim that non-access is a major constraint.

The proportion of the firms' budgets spent on the provision of alternative infrastructural facilities is considerable. The firms spend 22.7 per cent and 20.9 per cent of their capital and operational budgets respectively on less than 10 per cent of the alternative infrastructural facilities while 20.5 per cent and 18.6 per cent of their capital and operational budgets respectively on between 31–40 per cent of the infrastructural facilities. This extra budgetary spending tends to affect the expansion and product diversification of the firms, especially in small firms with no access to loanable funds. 52.9 per cent of firms had in the past abandoned aspects of their operations due to inadequate infrastructural facilities while 47.1 per cent used own savings to carry out their routine operations.

Firms claim that power outages led to cancellation of 52 per cent of production activities, while water shortages accounted for 19.0 per cent and generator breakdown (for those who have one) accounted for 9.5 per cent. These claims confirm the importance of energy for maintaining a steady production regime and subsequently high productivity, which is required for the growth and competitiveness of SMEs in the countries. We also asked how severe the effect of poor infrastructure is on production and firms' responses are shown in Table 6.6. Enterprises fare better in Zimbabwe than in the other two countries. Firms in Nigeria suffer the severest from utilities constraints.

The firm-level finding was complemented with national surveys conducted by the Central Bank of Nigeria (CBN) and the Manufacturers' Association of Nigeria (MAN). CBN survey of manufacturing enterprises in 1995 revealed that total cost of manufacturing operations increased by 26.3 per cent over the comparable level in the previous year owing mainly to high cost of electric energy charges, wages and salaries. More than half the respondents (59 per cent) anticipated improved business performance through the stability of exchange rates and moderation in inflation and interest rates; however, two out of every five respondents (40.4 per cent) attributed high product cost to the poor state of infrastructure, especially incessant power failure.

The Manufacturers' Association of Nigeria (MAN) data on manufacturing performance and available data on electric power supply over the ten years (1987–1997) show that capacity utilization declined from 36 per cent to 28 per cent, largely due to high production cost, low manufacturing performance, low purchasing power and low demand for products. Inadequate power supply and damages to equipment from frequent outages was cited as a major cause.

Table 6.4 Level of Satisfaction with Infrastructure (%)

	Nigeria	Kenya	Zimbabwe	All
Roads	54.5	7.6	63.0	49.4
Water	61.8	38.9	11.1	46.4
Electricity	92.6	38.9	14.8	61.6
Telephone	61.2	24.1	29.6	53.7

Source: Author's survey.

Table 6.5 Provision of Infrastructure in the Last Five Years (%)

	Nigeria		Kenya		Zimbabwe	
Roads	35.2*	(24.1)	83.3	(3.7)	77.8	(11.1)
Water	41.5	(11.3)	25.9	(1.9)	18.5	(11.1)
Electricity	43.6	(30.9)	27.8	(16.7)	22.2	(11.1)
Telephone	28.0	(34.0)	11.1	(40.7)	22.2	(29.6)

Source: Author's survey ( ) Improving, * deteriorating.

Table 6.6 Severity of Lack of Infrastructure

Country	Nigeria	Kenya	Zimbabwe
Severity	3.94	3.77	2.89

Source: Author's survey 1 = not severe, 5 = very severe.

According to the CBN and MAN surveys, frequent power cuts and voltage fluctuations forced almost every industrial establishment in the country to commit extra investments to purchase of electric power generators in order to minimize production losses and prevent damage to machinery and equipment. However, the extra investments raise production costs, making it difficult for local finished products to be competitive. The lower the capacity utilization (CU), the higher the energy intensity – that is, increase in energy per unit of production output.

An earlier survey of manufacturers' responses to infrastructural deficiencies in Nigeria by Anas and Lee (1989) on behalf of the World Bank revealed that nearly all firms installed standby generating sets that have the capacity to run the entire factory. At the time they found that 25 per cent of industrial power consumption was generated from private generating sets while 75 per cent was from the national grid, through the national monopoly, the Nigerian Electrical Power Authority (NEPA). The situation had progressively deteriorated over the years.

There are four ways in which firms might respond to infrastructural deficiencies: (i) relocation; (ii) factor substitution; (iii) private provision; and (iv) output reduction. There is an economic rationale behind each of these responses. Nigerian firms tend not to relocate because infrastructural facilities are almost the same everywhere in Nigerian cities. This tends to limit the gains and improvement in infrastructural quality achieved by moving to new locations. So, instead, firms invest extensively on the acquisition and maintenance of private infrastructural services.

In addition, firms pursue a variety of strategies that include power self-sufficiency, standby private provision, public source as standby, and private electric power provision as main electric power source. A firm is self-sufficient if it provides its own infrastructural services to the point where it does not need any public input. It could switch to its own standby electric generating set when the quality or reliability of public services falls below critical level. On the other hand, a firm may rely primarily on its own power generating facilities, but switch to public supply when public source delivers a high quality service. However, there are a few large firms that have switched off public source completely,[7] while some firms continue to rely on public service exclusively. This is peculiar to those very firms that cannot afford infrastructural capital investment.

Anas and Lee (1989) highlighted some economic incentives for additional regimes of private provision, which are not observed in Nigeria because of government regulations or the supply and trading of infrastructural service by private entities. These regimes are: (i) joint production; (ii) satellite behaviour; and (iii) shared production. Joint production refers to the case where a firm, typically a large one which has already made a substantial investment in infrastructural capital, finds it profitable to sell parts of its infrastructural output to other firms. This has not been possible in electricity production in Nigeria, because private producers of electricity are not allowed to sell surplus power to other firms or even back to NEPA.[8] A satellite firm is one, which purchases infrastructural services from another firm with surplus to sell. For example, in times of power interruption, a satellite firm would switch from NEPA to the generators of a nearby private producer. Shared production refers to the possibility of firms coming together in a club type arrangement to share the cost of infrastructural capital inputs by building their own facilities.

Firms that use standby generating sets as well as those relying on power from the national grid are equally subject to output reduction. This may occur due to the failure of their own equipment or during power outages, as the case may be. It is upon those small firms, with low capacity for alternative response, or

---

7   Cadbury Nigeria Limited is a large foods and beverages firm with truly competitive presence in the Nigerian economy. The firm switched off NEPA completely and adopted full private provision strategy. It recently spent millions of dollars to modernize its generating plant.

8   This is about to change as a result of liberation of the energy sector.

the very large power intensive firms which cannot afford the great costs of the appropriate size of equipment required to meet their service needs (for example, generator) that the major impact of output reduction falls. However, firms that relied solely on public sources were mostly small-scale enterprises that could not afford the purchase and maintenance of private generating sets.

Firms maintain product quality only with a lot of effort, and loss of production output is inevitable in a regime of constantly reduced production time and subsequent reduction in output volume. Power outages increase downtime and production costs, with the subsequent result being a loss of productivity. Chemical firms, for instance, tend to sustain considerable loss of output during extraction processes whenever there is an outage of power. Besides, excess load on generating sets tend to precipitate disequilibrium in the operating systems, leading to reduction in yields.

Other consequences of fluctuating power and outright outages are poor product quality and reduction in output volume. Poor quality of products is particularly common with agro-allied firms, especially food and beverages companies where products are carbonated at very low temperature. Power outages raise storage temperature as the refrigeration process is disrupted during production process thereby leading to de-carbonation. Incidence of product wastage is quite common. Metal manufacturing firms' record damage to the quality of cans produced due to power outages. For instance, in one firm, interrupted power led to air leakages in the cans and produced a defect that caused content contamination when the cans were used by other firms for packaging.

There is a direct correlation between energy intensity and productivity. Energy intensity is defined as energy consumption per unit production output. Firms that rely solely on public utility as their source of electricity power supply experienced increased energy intensity and decline in productivity. This results from decreasing output and/or increased energy within a production regime. Similar trends were observed for some small and medium firms that combine both public and private generating sets as sources of power supply. In general, this may well be indicative of inefficient energy utilization in all the firms. In sum, inefficient energy use has important implications for firm-level operation, the firm's product quality and output volume and, by extension, a country's industrial goods at the domestic and international markets. The high cost of energy translates to high cost of output that makes firms less competitive in the domestic and in the global market.

Again the energy intensity of a firm is a function of the supply source. Table 6.7 shows electricity cost per unit from the national grid and from the generating set of typical private sources, small, medium and large engineering firms over a five year period (1994–1999). The cost of power supply from the generating set was several times greater than the amount spent for electricity from the national grid. Energy cost for small firms is proportionally higher showing that small firms are differentially penalized for poor energy supply.

Table 6.7 Energy Intensity of Public and Private Power Generation

A Firm and Size		B Energy Intensity	C Energy Intensity Generator	D Total Energy Intensity	E % Electricity Cost Per Unit Output	F % Share Generator Cost Per Unit Output
I.	**	0.261	1.58	1.85	15.4	84.6
II.	*	227.7	13.6	196.0	92.0	8.0
III.	**	410	239.6	596.8	64.0	36.0
IV.	*	93.5	293.8	450.0	25.7	74.3
V.	**	19.7	231.3	240.0	8.0	92.0
VI.	***	0.40	1.76	1.83	33.0	67.0
VII.	***	0.63	1.40	2.03	24.3	75.7

* = Small ** = Medium *** = Large.

Summary

Physical infrastructure, which includes modern knowledge-based ICTs, is poorly developed in African countries. Due to the poor quality of public infrastructure and the absence of competitive private alternatives, individual firms in Africa invest relatively high proportions of capital in private facilities. We have, through case studies, established the direct association of high transaction costs and the absence of quality infrastructure, poor communication resulting from widespread low teledensity and low electrical power consumption caused by the twin incidence of inadequate generating capacity and low per capita consumption, which tend to be the most constraining. The indivisibility of network infrastructure was demonstrated by the high correlation of the 'wired' variables among themselves. The systemic imperative of network infrastructure was further demonstrated by the similarity of trend lines of low and medium income countries. Although considerable variation exists in the penetration of telephone and the Internet in African countries, per capita electrical power shows no significant difference. In effect, power supply is uniformly inadequate across countries except in the relatively industrialized ones, such as Mauritius and South Africa.

Firms spend a considerably high percentage of investment and operating capital on private provision. We confirm this by a detailed examination of macro level data, as well as micro level survey results. The severity of infrastructure constraints was evident at the firm level. Over half of enterprise owners abandoned certain projects as a result of power outages. Zimbabwe had the best infrastructure while Nigerian firms suffered the worse fate. Firms in all countries claimed that on average, road, power, telephone and water services declined in the last five years.

It would seem that the SAPs left national infrastructure in an even worse state. From the firms' perception, the poor supply response to reforms had little to do with a lack of willingness, but much more with structural rigidities of institutions. Equally constraining to performance is the slow inflow of domestic and foreign investment to the infrastructure sectors at a time of drastic cuts in government budgets. There is an urgent need to address the declining infrastructure in Africa. Reforms would have to be far more innovative and more sensitive to the needs of SMEs – the main drivers of economic activities.

Chapter 7

Institutions Supporting SMEs in Industry

Introduction

While small and medium firms' development remains central to the economic health of African countries, they lack the scale economy advantage and the capabilities that are often internalized by large firms. The exposure of African industry to international competition from the eighties further revealed the structural fragility of the region's industrial system. The policy response to the internal resource scarcity of SMEs and competitive pressures has been for states and the private sector to attempt to develop institutions and services to promote production within small firms. As we observed in Chapter 1, a systemic approach seeks to upgrade product quality, improve design and packaging, and to improve the overall human skills of firms through *real service* provision.

Employing survey data collected in a number of African countries, we synthesise findings of the types and nature of support systems available to SMEs in African industry. We consider a wide range of institutional support from universities to private associations. This chapter is organized as follows: the next section provides an analytical framework, followed by a section focused on the empirical data from the three African countries, paying specific attention to finance and technology support. We end with a concluding section.

Analytical framework

Support for enterprise involves both real services and the provision of information about technology flows within national boundaries among enterprises, and institutions. For this reason, government policies in developing and advanced industrial countries alike have evolved a battery of measures to assist small and medium manufacturing firms in the technological change process. However, significant market segmentation in underdeveloped countries gives certain categories of enterprises greater access to funds. For instance, large firms are more likely than small firms, to obtain loans (Oyelaran-Oyeyinka, 1996). Even then, this kind of access may be limited to routine operation-type technological activities. In Africa, micro-enterprises are an integral part of the industrial system, yet they do not count in official statistics and, as such, they rank low in priority for state support. Resources for innovative R&D and training are not easy to obtain. Capital market and skills market failures, which are more pronounced in poor countries, have led governments of such countries to formulate policies to selectively channel funds to less favoured groups of firms. They have set up specialized institutions to provide long-term finance. Quite unlike most industrialized economies, private RDIs are practically non-existent and publicly funded laboratories are often isolated from productive enterprises. This phenomenon is not peculiar to African countries. The OECD (1999) found that the most important source of knowledge for firms is the interaction between the firm and its suppliers. Firms learn more by analysing a competitor's products than from government laboratories. In Australia, the most significant sources of knowledge external to the firm are ideas and information from suppliers and customers. Government laboratories and university research are considered relatively unimportant. Working capital and long-term capital are often in short supply, so also is specialized finance for innovative activities. The former poses particularly unique problems, since machinery and equipment are largely imported, and so have to be funded fully or in part, through purchase of foreign exchange. Under recent reform policies, access to the foreign exchange market became more difficult for SMEs due to devaluation of local currencies, which made foreign currencies more expensive. From past studies, we now know that:

- access to technical information and finance is crucial for SMEs survival and growth;
- firm size, scale, type and levels of technological investment activities matter in the growth trajectory of firms; and
- SMEs in Africa rely largely on own savings, not only to grow, but also to innovate; firms often need real services support and formal finance assistance, failing which under-investment in long term capabilities (training and R&D) may result (Oyelaran-Oyeyinka, 2003).

Besides finance, there are critical elements lacking within technology support institutions themselves. These undermine the effectiveness of their support to SMEs and include:

- knowledge,
- skills and experience of staff;
- capacity and quality of internal facilities;
- information and knowledge of market; intellectual and managerial leadership;
- external infrastructure and the incentive system (at the meso and macro levels).

Figure 7.1 shows a diagrammatic model of the support system's contribution to the technological capability building efforts of firms. They include: technology institutions, non-technical institutions and other centres that may be in the public or private domain. Metrology, standards, testing and quality control have become important service categories in light of ISO 9000 and more so by reason of the intensified competitive regime in the domestic market occasioned by liberal import policies.[1] While the benefit of ICTs to innovation support is now clear, a significant proportion of firms still have no access to basic telephone services, let alone the Internet.

External Knowledge Bases

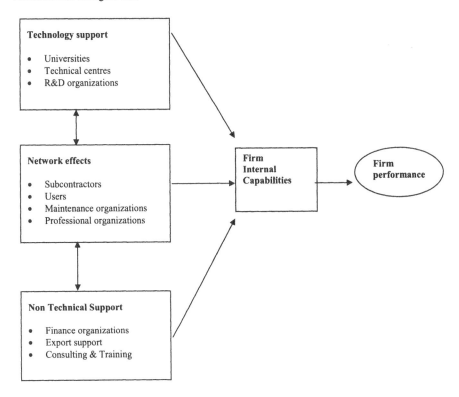

Figure 7.1   A Model of Innovative Support Systems

---

1   In my interviews with footwear manufacturers in Aba, in South Eastern Nigeria, entrepreneurs' main obstacle to meeting the competition largely from Asia was lack of metrological services, and technology upgrading. There were instances where these enterprises had invested in relatively sophisticated machinery but were forced to abandon these equipment resorting to manual operations due to erratic power supply. In this case, the operational deficiency was less a problem of skill and craftsmanship (they possess both) but more of poor quality infrastructure.

Data sources

The data employed in this chapter are taken from two sets of studies carried out at the firm level in a number of African countries in the year 2001, namely, Nigeria, Uganda, Kenya and Zimbabwe.[2] The studies identified a wide variety of mechanisms and institutional arrangements for and confirm some of the hypotheses about, the nature of the support institutions for SMEs. Far from being lone and ineffective economic agents, SMEs are at the centre of production and innovations networks and are capable of contributing significantly to the process of industrialization. The new competitive environment compels small producers in Africa to compete with more organized and technologically more competent firms selling in their domestic markets. The country studies reported in this chapter tend to confirm our assumption that support systems in Africa will have an increasing need to address the question of growth and innovation in firms.

Justification for SMEs support

While technological change is new knowledge about techniques, technical change or change in techniques is the adoption of new techniques. The distinction means that technical change can be said to have taken place even when a new technology that embodies all the principles necessary for the creation of techniques and the knowledge necessary to improve, change, adapt, and alter the basis of techniques has not been adopted. A proper understanding of these concepts is important because it underpins the decision of firms to invest in new physical capital. It is therefore extremely relevant not only to the theory of economic growth, but also to economic policy and technology policy within which the nature of technology support is spelt.

For small producers in relatively poor African countries, the cost of staying competitive is enormous; our findings on the nature of support therefore take on added significance and meaning. There are two main tentative implications. First, it means that support for autonomous technical change should be sought from a much wider variety of sources. It can be from within the firms, on the production lines and from machine shops, among others, rather than focusing exclusively on R&D laboratories. This finding simply reinforces the views that have gained ground in recent years on the nature of firm's behaviour. Secondly, support for technical innovation efforts at improving existing and old vintage plant promises as much economic returns as investment in new vintage plants. This disposes of the need for costly investment in new processes and plants.

---

2   The full reports of each country case study can be obtained on request from the author.

Technology institutions supporting SMEs in Africa

Technology support to industry comes in different forms, while the depth and range of the services vary considerably. In developing countries, RDIs, the universities and technical institutes, local engineering consultants and foreign partners provide support to domestic industry. Support could therefore be divided into three broad categories: domestic private, domestic public, and foreign. In addition to universities and RDIs, there are institutions providing information, metrological services (standards, testing and quality control). Unlike RDIs in industrialized contexts, PRIs in Africa are engaged largely in minor modifications of imported machinery, conversion of local raw materials and improvement of product quality.

Three forms of institutional support, which may be classified as public, private services and network associations, were identified. The last two fall in the private domain, and differ in their motives and governance structure. Government or public support could be provided indirectly within a macroeconomic package, as technical assistance in training, and as finance subsidy. Government support is chiefly delivered through technology centres or public RDIs with broad mandates to assist SMEs in carrying out innovation. Network associations are voluntary trade and manufacturing organizations supported through membership dues. Service providers from the private sector operate as consulting organizations and deliver services at a cost. Three forms of services, namely, technical, financial and market/export support seem the most common. We present comparative experiences of the forms of technical and financial support, drawing from empirical studies carried out in the countries. Under the forms of service we discuss the sources, types, effectiveness and constraints illustrating from country case studies.

Findings: sources, types, nature and limitations of support systems

Sources of technological support

In evaluating technological support, we considered the sources of information and machinery suppliers and whether these were private or public sources. The major sources of technical information for SMEs are shown in Table 7.1. Firms obtain technical information largely from machinery suppliers (31.3 per cent, 53.7 per cent, and 20.4 per cent) in Nigeria, Kenya and Zimbabwe followed by industrial associations (34.4 per cent, 59.3 per cent and 8.2 per cent) in these countries respectively. Technical publications and industrial consultants are also important sources. Other sources are: through attendance of trade fairs, raw materials suppliers, governments' R&D institutions and, lastly, export agents. In spite of the considerable emphasis placed on financing public sector service, the most important source of technical information is the private sector. Over the five year period for which data was collected, firms across the countries indicate that the provision of technical services from the public sector declined, while private provisions to firms improved. Deep budgetary cuts reduced financial allocations to key public support organizations, in particular universities and the PRIs, and resulted in their performance declining, which even at the best of times was not particularly remarkable.

Table 7.1 Sources of Technical Information (%)

Sources	Zimbabwe	Nigeria	Kenya
Machinery Suppliers	20.4	31.3	53.7
Publications	24.5	34.5	50.0
Consultants	18.4	16.5	29.6
Trade fairs	6.1	32.2	24.1
Industrial Associations	8.2	34.4	59.3
Government R&D Export	–	15.8	18.5
Agents	14.3	14.9	7.4
Raw Material Suppliers	6.1	30.6	25.9

Source: Field Survey (2001).

The training function has also been provided to firms largely from private sources. Firms require capability upgrading in the use of new technologies, in product quality improvements, and in the mastery of simple process techniques, such as heat treatment for instance. Not one single organization is able to provide the range of services required in firms. In ideal situations, multiple sources of support should be available, such as productivity centres, RDIs and universities as well as consulting organizations. The limiting factor is as much the low number of training centres as it is the resources and capability of the available training centres. The idiosyncratic nature of firm-level process tends to put a limit on the relevance of external resources in all but the most exceptional of cases. However, there are exceptions such as metrological services, where public presence is one of the very early forms of industrial services that were established by African Governments. However, as product quality requirement become more stringent, national metrology services need to be reformed and modernized.[3]

Table 7.2 How Firms Rate Sources of Technical Services (%)

Sources	Zimbabwe	Nigeria	Kenya
Government	1.57	1.58	1.52
Private	3.0	3.31	2.9
Others	2.56	2.94	2.52

Source: Field survey (2001); 1 = low; 5 = very high.

---

3 Lall (2001) emphasizes the adoption of both quality (ISO 9000) and environmental standards (ISO 14000) in firms. These services are often beyond the resources of individual SMEs.

Finally, firms were asked to assess how important these sources are and the way they rated sources of technical support is shown in Table 7.2. Again, the private sector received the highest rating for the provision of technical support in all the countries, while the government ranks far less in the estimation of firms.

Firms solve their major technical and raw materials sourcing problems largely through in-house innovation efforts and by consulting local maintenance organizations. Machinery suppliers are a major source in Kenya and Nigeria; see Table 7.3. This source seems to be less important in Zimbabwe. In-house effort is uniformly important in the three countries while local maintenance organizations command high patronage in Nigeria and Kenya and again less important in Zimbabwe.

Table 7.3 How Firms Solve Technical Problems (%)

Source	Nigeria	Kenya	Zimbabwe
Machinery Suppliers	20.0	38.9	8.8
In-House	42.3	50.0	52.9
Foreign Technical	8.2	5.6	5.9
Local Maintenance	80.1	72.2	32.3
Others	5.8	3.7	–

Source: Field survey (2001).

A summary of the types of technology support systems to SMEs is provided using the equality of means table, which also gives descriptive statistics on firms. Table 7.4 compares the key firm-level variables in two of the countries, namely, Nigeria and Kenya. Education of the workforce, an important mediating factor, does not differ significantly between the two countries except at the tertiary level. The proportion of graduates in firms in Nigeria is about 30 per cent more than that of Kenya. There is a high level of significance in the way firms solve technical problems (machinery suppliers, in-house efforts, and engagement of foreign partners). The sources of information also exhibit high levels of statistical significance.

Sources of support across countries

In this section, we identify the key support institutions and their effectiveness in Kenya, Nigeria, Zimbabwe and Uganda. There are several institutions established in Kenya to promote innovation in SMEs. The National Council for Science and Technology (NCST) established by the Technology Act of the Laws of Kenya is charged with the governance of S&T activities.[4]

---

4   The NCST functions were spelt out in the 1974–78 Development Plan under the item 'Science and Technology for Development'.

Learning to Compete in African Industry

Table 7.4 Equality of Mean Values of Technology Support System Variables

Variables	All	Nigeria	Kenya	df	T-value	F statistic	Level of significance
Education % No formal education	11.38	10.32	12.96	65	0.449	0.201	0.655
High school	52.09	51.42	54.87	136	0.542	0.294	0.589
University	12.93	17.73	2.60	83	4.222	17.826	0.0001
Employees (size)	38.97	38.85	44.67	202		0.8253	0.439
How Firms Solve **Technical Problems*** Machinery Suppliers	1.92	1.67	2.56	95	5.598	31.33	0.0000
In-House efforts	1.52	1.34	2.86	81	6.411	41.100	0.0000
Foreign Partners	1.89	1.818	4.00	55	7.044	49.62	0.0000
Sources of Technical information:							
Machinery Supplied	1.62	1.37	2.35	89	3.660	13.39	0.0004
Export Agents	2.07	1.54	4.07	75	8.387	70.33	0.0000
Raw Material Suppliers	1.75	1.42	5.00	84	13.149	172.89	0.0000
Publications	1.48	1.38	5.00	72	9.342	87.28	0.0000
Consultants	1.72	1.61	5.00	59	11.363	129.13	0.0000

Source: Survey (2001) * Rated on a scale of 1–5, where 1 = very low, and 5 = strong support.

The NCST is a multi-purpose institution coordinating research, training and pre-investment production functions. In specific terms, the NCST spells out priorities for scientific and technological activities to promote social and economic development. It acts as an advisor to the government in science policy and harnesses scientific results for the development of all sectors including agriculture and industry. Its coordination role is a central function meant to ensure cooperation between all agencies involved in S&T in Kenya. In 1979, an amendment to the NCST act resulted in the establishment of some semi-autonomous research institutes.[5] In

---

5   These were Kenyan Agricultural Research Institute (KARI); Kenya Medical Research Institute (KEMRI); Kenya Trypanosomiasis Research Institute (KEMFRI); and Kenya Industrial Research and Development Institute (KIRDI). A number of additional support

addition to technological infrastructure, the Kenyan government established the Industrial Property Act of 1989.[6] The aims of the Act are: (i) to protect indigenous technology; (ii) to protect foreign patents, to attract foreign investment; (iii) to search for technological information for local technology development; and, finally, (iv) to encourage domestic innovation activities. The Kenya Industrial Property Office (KIPO) administers the Act. Other technical institutions created to assist SMEs include: Kenya Industrial Training Institute (KITI); Kenya Industrial Estates (KIE); Industrial and Commercial Development Corporation (ICDC); Kenya Bureau of Standards (KBS).

Zimbabwe has a fairly well developed infrastructure of technology support systems meant to promote the development of enterprise level competitiveness. However, the number of agencies promoting manufacturing industry technology development and transfer are relatively few compared to those for agriculture and rural development. While manufacturing support services are undertaken mainly through the government, there are a few private sector enterprises and NGOs involved.

While Zimbabwe has been a relatively good performer in the agricultural sector, the country's manufacturing firms are poorly equipped to confront increasing domestic and global competition.

Against this background of intensifying competition, the government established an R&D facility to provide support service for industry, roughly along similar lines as the 'national research service', then called the Department of Research and Specialist Services (DR & SS) that catered for the farming community in the country. This culminated in the launching of the Scientific Industrial and Research and Development Centre (SIRDC) in 1992. SIRDC's mission is to carry out applied research projects in the areas of product design, development, testing, proving and adaptation, developing and upgrading industrial processes.

Potentially, SIRDC could play a greater role in the development of the manufacturing industry in the country and, in particular, facilitate the technology development needs of SMEs. However, the institute's service provision to SME's is limited by its focus on larger enterprises and only to a very limited extent on small firms. In addition, the sustainability of SIRDC seems to depend a great deal on continued government and donor assistance, which had been diminishing, without a clear and sustainable alternative funding mechanism. The mandate and operational strategy of the SIRDC makes it difficult for the institution to support smaller enterprises in need of technological services. The Standards Association of Zimbabwe (SAZ) is another agency supporting development of enterprise technology. SAZ promotes: standardization and quality improvement; information

---

institutions evolved over time. This section draws on: Mwamadzingo, M. and Njuguna Ndung'u (1999) Financing of Science & Technology institutions in Kenya during periods of structural adjustment, ATPS working paper no. 13.

6   In the 1970–78 period, only five of the 1025 patents registered were local, and three out of the five were attributable to subsidiaries of Multinational companies (MNCs).

Learning to Compete in African Industry

services on national and international standards and technical regulations; and also provides technical services for testing of manufactured goods and raw materials.

The SAZ Information Centre provides information services and is a repository of copies of Zimbabwe Standards (SAZs), International Standards (ISO), International Electrotechnical Commission Standard (IEC), British Standards (BS), South African Standards (SAS) and many other standards and technical regulations for public use.

A wide array of technical institutions were established over the years in Nigeria to support SMEs including, the latest, the Small and Medium Industries Development Agency (SMIDA). Other institutions established by the Federal Government by the mid-1980s to advance the development of S&T include: the National Office of Industrial Property (NOIP) now National Office for Technology Acquisition and Promotions (NOTAP), which has responsibility for evaluating and approving all technology transfer agreements between Nigerian users and foreign vendors of technology; the various S&T-related faculties of the universities and polytechnics; and the Patents, Trademarks and Copyrights Department of the Ministry of Trade, which, among other functions, grants and registers patents for Nigerian inventors.

Since the mid-1980s, a number of specialized research institutions were established notable among which is the National Agency for Science and Engineering Infrastructure (NASENI) that advises SMEs in process design.

However, the agencies face the perennial problems of under-funding and lack of skills to operationalize a highly diffused and multi-objective mandate. The agencies lack coordination among themselves and suffer from weak interaction with the productive sector. Although there are isolated success cases where intervention is focused, systematic and sustained, an unsustainable policy process, a poor information environment and high transaction costs, for both firms and support agencies, make such successes the exception rather than the norm.

In Uganda, the state, public and private non-profit organizations provide technical support. Empirical data on Uganda derives from a study of four sectors carried out in 2001 in a collaborative project between the Ugandan National Council for Science and Technology (UNCST) and the UNU-INTECH. Although collective technical support dates back to the early 1970s, these early sources were all not SME-oriented. Several broad-based agencies extending support to SMEs appeared in the early 1990s, once the growing importance of SMEs in Uganda's economy had been recognized. Only since the late 1990s have industry-sector-specific non-profit R&D centres begun to appear, as the technical needs of SMEs became more demanding. There is an extensive network of agencies providing technical support in the form of technical assistance, training programmes, information services and joint research opportunities. Most technical support agencies offer a combination of services, often supported by financial incentives.

The state agencies are led by the Uganda National Bureau of Standards (UNBS), a statutory organization established by an Act of Parliament in June 1983, whose mandate is to promote the use of national standards and to develop quality control and quality assurance systems. Protection of public health and safety, and international trade were high on the mandate of the institute. Several public S&T

policy- and R&D institutions also offer technical services to SMEs as is the case with the Uganda National Council for Science and Technology (UNCST). The mission of UNCST is to develop strategies for the promotion and development of science and technology for the sustainable integration of S&T in the national development process.

Industrial associations have emerged to provide a wide range of services. Among these are Uganda Small Scale Industries Association (USSIA) with 33 regional offices across the country, and a number of industrial associations with their own inspection and testing procedures. They provide technical quality and standards training. Over 200 SMEs received some form of technical assistance in the year 2000, 56.6 per cent of which was provided by NGOs, followed by private agencies providing 36 per cent, the latter including friends, buyers, suppliers and other firms. Firms rank public agencies 'moderately useful', compared to private sources. Again in a study of 16 sources of external technical support for product upgrading, firms indicate that despite government's best efforts, SMEs consistently rate public R&D institutions very low in context of sourcing new ideas.

The ideas for process improvements derive largely from 'local buyers' followed by foreign/domestic equipment suppliers particularly for metal fabrication firms. Order placing firms, imitation of existing products and networking firms engaged in similar business activities were important sources of process improvement for metal fabricating firms. The findings are similar to that of Nigeria, Zimbabwe and Kenya and reinforce our findings on the importance of machinery suppliers as well as local maintenance organizations in these countries.

Types of technology support

The types of technical support services received by the firms are shown in Table 7.5. There is a high level of statistical significance in the type of support between the countries compared. The same pattern is observed for the sources of technical information. A majority of the firms receive technical support from private sources. For example, 43.9 per cent of firms in Nigeria and 61 per cent in Zimbabwe received such private support for quality control, while 44.8 per cent in Nigeria and 60 per cent in Zimbabwe got private support for training. In addition, 40 per cent and 80 per cent received private support for information exchange in Nigeria and Zimbabwe respectively. On the other hand, 20.6 per cent and 22.2 per cent of firms in Nigeria and Zimbabwe respectively received support for information exchange from the government and its agencies. A similar proportion of firms in Nigeria and Zimbabwe got support for quality control from government and its agencies whilst 10 per cent and 11.8 per cent received support for training. In all the countries, state support was far behind that of private sources and largely self-initiated support for firms. The situation is not much different in Kenya, but here, in the provision of quality control and R&D services, public and private services come close in ranking.

Table 7.5 Types of Technical Support (%)

Source	Nigeria	Kenya	Zimbabwe
Information	20.6 (40.1)	3.7 (55.6)	22.2 (80.0)
Training	10.1 (44.8)	9.3 (31.5)	11.8 (60.0)
Quality Control	14.2 (43.9)	33.3 (35.2)	17.6 (61.0)
R&D Services	4.2 (27.7)	14.8 (14.8)	(50.0)

Note: Table shows types of support from public and private sources.
(The latter is shown in bracket)

Financial support system

The literature on the nexus of finance-innovation is almost non-existent, particularly in Africa, and considerable fuzziness exists in defining what stage of firm growth is the most critical. A firm growth cycle consists of start-up, growth and expansion/ innovation stages, each posing its own distinctive challenge to firm owners. In the evolutionary innovation literature, there is a conceptual distinction between the different stages of investment, production and innovation – each demanding its own cognitive requirements. In practice however, the growth of a firm is a tapestry of events in the life of the firm.

Albaladejo and Schmitz (2000) argue that, in order to operate efficiently, SMEs require easy access to short and long term capital. In Africa, the problem seems to be the accessibility of financial institutions rather than the availability of funds. These authors compared degrees of credit availability and accessibility to SMEs (from high to low) in 13 African countries. They also distinguish between formal lending and alternative lending by NGOs. Their findings show that enterprises in most African countries have low access to finance. This is the case of Cameroon, Ethiopia, Gabon, Kenya, Namibia, Nigeria, Senegal and Uganda. In some other countries, namely, Mauritius and South Africa, SMEs appear to have a little more access to finance, but, in general, none of the African countries seem to have an efficient structure of financial institutions providing short and long-term capital to SMEs. In this context alternative means of financing have been developed especially in the countries where formal lending is weak.

The relative importance of different types of financial support has changed over time and across sectors. For example, funds available for co-operative activities have been declining. Where government intervention in financial markets is pervasive, it is difficult to distinguish between sources of private and collective financial support. Such distinctions are useful for both comparative and analytical purposes. Following from Albaladejo and Schmitz (2000), five types of external finance are considered 'private financial support', including: (i) equity funds from public or private offerings of shares; (ii) corporate bonds; (iii) credit from commercial banks; (iv) credit from relatively unregulated non-bank financial institutions (the 'curb' market); and (v) credit from relatives and friends.

Equity funds and 'corporate bonds' are generally less important to SMEs because they are subject to severe information asymmetry hence suffer from adverse selection and moral hazard problems that are easier for large firms to overcome. However, corporate bonds have become an important financial source for larger corporate SMEs in the 1990s. Credit from the 'curb' market has generally been the most important source of private financial support for SMEs. Curb market credit is essentially an aggregation of different components, including: (i) rudimentary credit markets based on the reputation of family relations but with no tradable assets; (ii) rotating credit schemes in which interest rates to depositors and lenders rise with duration; (iii) informal commercial paper markets; (iv) the curb market proper; and semi-regulated financial institutions such as mutual savings and loan funds, 'popular' funds and private finance companies. Private financial support also includes SMEs' loans coming from commercial banks, but, to some extent, subject to compulsory credit allocations and commercial bill discounting and other means of financing that are supported by central bank guarantees and incentives. Two sources of financial support may be considered 'collective' in this chapter. They include: (i) government supported venture captured companies that finance technology based SMEs and (ii) credit guarantee facilities.

In analysing the role of finance, both as a constraint or determinant of growth, we consider a number of issues. First, the role of the different forms of financing such as capital market and private commercial bank loans. Secondly, special state development schemes, made up of development bank loans and special credit programmes for specific sectors such as agriculture and industry. Third, the bias against lending to small firms relative to the size of loans constitutes a disincentive to financial support.

Fourth, small firms' lack of internal human capability to deal with the relatively exacting banking requirements in addition to collateral requirements of banks. Small firms are thus likely to be penalized for this resource limitation by being rationed out of the credit system. Fifth, commercial and state finance organizations may themselves lack adequate credit assessment capability and, as such, tend to favour large firms that need less scrutiny. This applies particularly to those with capital market standing. For these and other reasons, this section will focus on our survey findings about the following:

- Sources of finance for instance, own savings, commercial banking sources, loans from relatives, among others.
- State finance support through special credit and development banks.
- Use to which loans are put, whether for start-up or growth.
- Innovation financing and what kinds of innovation firms undertake (broadly defined);.
- Perception of firms of the above sources of support and their effectiveness.

In Nigeria, there is considerable reliance on own sources – which in fact tends to be underestimated – once account is taken of pre-investment equity and security provided by owners of firms. Added to the eventual capital outlays, these will probably be the most important source for small firms, while medium firms are better favoured by institutional lending. Almost every other firm (48 per cent) in the sample sourced their capital from own savings and slightly fewer (almost 40 per cent) raised their operational finance in the same way. About one in four of the firms (24.6 per cent) raised their capital from friends and relatives and 16.4 per cent sourced operational finance likewise. When asked to rate what they would consider the most important source of loan, 56 per cent rated government, while only 6.8 per cent rated private sources. This demonstrates the perception of enterprises on what they think of the role of the state and private sources in promoting firm' growth.

The reasons why small firms make recourse to personal financing of business are well documented (Liedholm, 1992). High rates of interest on loans are often cited as often as the requirement for security that is far beyond the ability of small firms to provide. Another factor relates to the bureaucratic nature of credit lending from banks, which firm owners consider overwhelmingly tasking and costly. While we did not collect systematic data on the issue, there seems to be some association between the age and size of firms and the propensity to lend by banks. Relatively young and small firms with no track record of consistent performance are considered riskier customers than older firms with track record of investment.[7]

In our sample, 32.9 per cent of firms received a capital loan, while 21.9 per cent received an operational loan. The loans obtained by the firms were meant largely for new machinery (79.5 per cent), expansion of product and process lines (54.8 per cent), while 27.4 per cent needed loans to enter into the export market. Of the firms that succeeded, 70.3 per cent and 46.2 per cent of the firms obtain operational and capital loans respectively.

Credit projects have been the most commonly used method of providing direct assistance to Ugandan SMEs. The proprietors of SMEs typically perceive capital to be the most serious constraint and one of the greatest assistance needs. Much of the perceived need is typically for working rather than fixed capital, but demand for working capital varies significantly by sub-sector and even by type of enterprise within sub-sector groups. The actual need for working capital is often lower than the perceived need for it. Indeed, working capital shortages are often the symptom of some other constraints. For example, a raw material delivery bottleneck may force enterprises to keep their raw material inventories at unduly high levels. Therefore, it is important that financial institutions be able to distinguish between true and perceived needs for working capital.

Ugandan SMEs have access to a significant range of credit sources and the financial system has, to some extent, adopted an increasingly pro-SME orientation over time. The survey results reveal that the most important source of SME financial assistance in the banking sector are commercial banks (at over 20 per cent); whereas among non-bank financial institutions, short-term finance companies (38.9 per cent)

---

7   This claim was made by this category of firms in all our interviews. Banks are reluctant to enter into long-term commitment with firms once they are regarded as unstable.

are ranked highest. Overall the chapter indicates that over 60 per cent of Ugandan SMEs receive some kind of support from numerous financial agencies nation wide.

Taken at the sectoral level, most of the SMEs financial sources (in all sectors) are self generated followed by use of loans from banking and non-bank financial institutions. Government and donor contributions in form of grants are indicated as lacking in all the four sectors examined.

Nevertheless, SMEs suffer from a number of financial constraints. First, shortage and inadequacy of financial institutions for SME support is a major impediment for SME development. Second, access to credit is a major constraint, while most of the SMEs are too small, the financial institutions (banks) tend to focus on the large firms. This resonates with our findings in other countries regarding both technology and finance support. Also, financial institutions perform poorly, due in part to huge non-performing loans and lack of efficient management. High interest rates, high collateral requirements and restriction of collateral to specific assets are requirements that are often too difficult for SMEs to meet. Commercial banks have continued to discriminate against SMEs because they are labelled 'high risk' clients with little or no resources to provide collateral. Real interest rates on loans range between 22 and 27 per cent.

There is a concentration of finance sources in the urban centres. Due to vast distances between major towns and rural settlements, the delivery cost of credit schemes tends to be exorbitant; therefore, making such schemes very expensive to implement. Restrictive clauses on the utilization of funds often come with restrictions on their use – highlighting specific areas to which they ought to be channelled.

Another shortcoming is the lack of effective coordination mechanism to centralize information on possible sources of finance. In most sectors, there is no umbrella institution providing information on possible financial sources. Individual institutions generally advertise the services they provide. In addition, there are quite a number of government agencies, banks and NGOs providing support to SMEs, but the mass of countries lack effective coordination mechanism to centralize SME-related information.

Lastly, we identify misuse of government resources. Financial assistance arising from government sources is often misused to target certain sectors of society that are not supposed to benefit from such schemes. Some of the financial support from government sources has often been directed to political loyalists of the ruling government as rewards for political support.

Credit and finance constraint to small firms is widespread and well recognized by Kenyan enterprises. Firm requirements vary from investment to operational capital. While small enterprise innovation efforts would no doubt benefit from special credit, little is available for Kenyan firms as with other African enterprises. Small firms are as constrained by information asymmetry as by their lot being perceived as being difficult to monitor by institutional lenders. On the supply side, there have been a wide variety of programmes to provide credit to SMEs in Kenya, most of which were considered unsuccessful. The poor programmes record has roots in the political process, faulty design and inadequate managerial capability of senior managers and the workforce. Private lenders remain sceptical of the ability of SMEs to fulfil loan conditions. Banks themselves are subject to regulations, which are at variance with industrial development objectives that seek to promote SMEs.

In the survey, we sought enterprise perception of the sources and types of credit, their effectiveness and the nature of investment for which firms require finance. Private banks and 'own money' are the most prominent sources. Development bank finance has been important but medium rather than small firms are the greatest beneficiaries. However, firms rate own source of finance as the most reliable, with 74 per cent of firms rating government finance as 'poor'. Much of what goes into the rating of firms relates to reliability of source and speed of access, with state finance, a cumbersome bureaucratic process with long and demanding paperwork, being a major disincentive for SMEs.

Private bank demand for collateral and the equally time consuming legal and regulatory compliance requirements also tend to constitute obstacles to firms' access to institutional finance. Investment in new machinery and expansion of existing production capacity, a claim made by 41 per cent and 48 per cent of firms respectively, are the main requirements for enterprise finance. Other reasons for enterprise finance include modifications to plants, and process conversion for local raw material utilization.

Some 44 per cent of SMEs rate lack of financial support as a very severe constraint to their activities and another 28 per cent rate it as simply severe. Given that finance is important at every stage in a firm's life cycle, the significance of this finding to SMEs' development cannot be underestimated. On a scale of 1 to 5, 'own source' of enterprise finance rates high followed by the private sector with state assistance ranked the least.

In general, 68.2 per cent of firms reported having received capital loans and 52.4 per cent having received operational loans. Private banks are the most important sources of financial support for raising capital (as well as operational costs). More than three-quarters of firms cited this to be the case. This could mean that the amount they receive is not adequate, but not necessarily indicate a lack of financing options. There are two other possible reasons. One is the high interest rate charged by banks, which reflect the high cost of capital that small firms can ill-afford. The second are the bank requirements, which may be too stringent for SMEs; lending policies of private banks and other sources of loans may simply not be friendly to manufacturing SMEs. In all the cases, the majority of firms indicated that requirement for financial support for new machinery (63.6 per cent) and expansion into new products (18.2 per cent) are important for their growth. In other words, firms desire funds for innovation, but this is hardly a priority for policy in African countries.

While the government may not be a major source of loans to manufacturing SMEs in Zimbabwe,[8] the establishment of the Small Enterprises Development

---

8   The thrust of government financial support in Zimbabwe is the micro (informal) sector. To spearhead this new thrust, a Minister of State in the Office of the President was appointed in 2001. Her designated portfolio is Informal Sector Enterprises.

Table 7.6 Equality of Mean Values of Finance Support System Variables

Finance (capital loan)(%)	All	Nigeria	Kenya	df	T-value	F statistic	Level of significance
Private Bank	36.90	29.59	54.58				
Development Bank	20.00	12.50	36.00	13	1.123	1.260	0.2818
Special govt credit	0.083	0.111	0.000	10	0.313	0.3125	0.5884
Friends	36.24	38.16	24.00	36	0.932	0.864	0.3575
Own sources	64.71	67.96	48.00	65	1.706	2.909	0.0929
Finance (operational)(%)							
Private Banks	41.94	40.00	27.78	34	0.580	0.337	0.5654
Development Bank	1.50	0.111	4.000	13	1.348	1.818	0.2025
Friends	34.24	37.00	6.67	31	1.5816	2.501	0.1239
Own sources	66.16	70.10	42.50	55	2.1772	4.7401	0.0339

Corporation (SEDCO) in the early-1980s was an important initiative in financial support provision. SEDCO was set up as a development finance institution in the then Ministry of Industry and Commerce following the enactment of the Small Enterprises Development Act Number 16 of 1983. The act came into operation on November 16, 1984 under statutory instrument 368A of 1984. SEDCO was formed to encourage and assist in the establishment of small industrial enterprises.

The government through the Ministry of Industry and Trade wholly funds SEDCO. Donor funds are also channelled through the Ministry. Funds channelled through SEDCO are payable over three years (that is, short-term loans). Medium term loans are payable over five years and long-term loans over 5–20 years. Generally, interest rate is charged at 38 per cent, except for specific government programmes, like the Z$1.3 billion informal sector credit scheme, which attracts 13 per cent interest. The ceiling amount is Z$100 000 per individual.

From its inception SEDCO had drawn support from the Canadian International Development Agency (CIDA), United Nations Industrial Development Organization (UNIDO), The World Bank (WB), and other donors. However, support by bilateral agencies and the International Financial Institutions (IFCs) dwindled in the late 1990s. Allocation to the industrial sector declined sharply since 1996/97. It is therefore not surprising that manufacturing SMEs surveyed reported receiving no financial support from government sources.

Within the banks, the small business services divisions of the main commercial banks and other private sector sources administer financial assistance. The main sources of finance for SMEs are the key commercial banks and the Venture Capital Company of Zimbabwe (VCCZ). Given the relative vibrancy of financial markets in the Zimbabwean economy, the private sector is likely to remain an important source of capital for SMEs.[9] The dynamism that characterizes the financial market is associated with the liberalization, deregulation and promotion of private sector activities in the economy during the 1990s. However, up to 72 per cent of firms rate financial support as a severe-to-very-severe constraint. Two principal constraints affecting SMEs in Zimbabwe are the limited access to finance and the high cost of finance.

Table 7.6 shows the test for equality of mean values for finance support system variables. There are significant differences in the nature of support in provision from private banks, own sources (both capital and operational). Other sources tend to be uniform across the countries.

In sum, the optimal mechanisms for the delivery of financial assistance to SMEs still remain a subject of debate. A wide array of formal financial institutions has been used in the delivery of credit to SMEs. In some instances new institutions have been created, while existing ones have been reformed. Formal financial institutions however have been less useful sources of finance for small and, to some extent, medium enterprises. While this may be partly a result of institutional inertia, administrative costs and risks of lending to them are significantly higher than those associated with regular, larger scale customers. The schemes that have been successful in providing financial assistance to SMEs provided working as opposed to fixed capital. Long term lending to small firms for investment in fixed assets (machinery and buildings) tends to be less successful. Successful lending schemes are largely locally based, have decentralized decision-making structures, and screen for loan requests on the basis of character of entrepreneur and project feasibility, rather than on collateral. The interest rate however has to be high enough to cover operating costs/expenses. As these features resemble those of informal credit institutions, it will appear that the closer formal lending institutions can imitate the practice of informal lenders, the greater the likelihood that they will be successful in creating loans for SMEs (small-scale firms in particular).

Summary

We conclude from the studies that for a firm to grow and maintain a sustained competitive trajectory, the two types of supports described here, namely, technical and finance, are required. This is because small firms lack a broad range of internal capabilities for production, marketing and innovation, and they also do not possess sets of linkage capabilities to tap into the knowledge bases external to them. Small producers are unable to meet some or often all of these prerequisites; therefore, state and private actions are often necessary. On the supply side, technical support actors in Africa are themselves casualties of past reforms. They are depleted in manpower, grossly under funded and staff morale is lacking. Some RDIs have an impressive

---

9   This statement should be qualified in the light of the present crisis in Zimbabwe.

shelf of inventions, which, sadly, are totally irrelevant to SME needs. Universities suffer a similar fate in Africa.

In the finance support systems, banks are risk averse and often hostile to the demand of small firms for support. The capital market is a difficult proposition for small producers and states have set up special credit guarantee schemes and development banks to attenuate the gaps in financial resource flow to firms. In all these institutions, we observe a commonality of attributes. The banks, the capital markets, and the technical support organizations all share the same character of the small firms. In some cases, poorly motivated and sometimes unqualified staff often runs financial institutions, albeit inefficiently. The conditions for SME lending are usually difficult to meet especially the restrictive collateral requirements. Micro-finance schemes launched by NGOs and aid agencies have, to some extent, presented an alternative source of SME finance. These programmes have been growing in recent years, but the small size of loans remain insufficient for SMEs' technological capability acquisition and competitiveness.

This is an internal weakness that makes their collective mandate extremely difficult. At the risk of presumptuous generalization, one policy conclusion seems inevitable. This is that states in Africa will have to raise the qualitative assets of support institutions in the face of the new competitive challenge. The starting point will be the upgrading of extant organizations and the widening of non-public knowledge support bases.

Again, access to finance remains a major problem for SMEs. Most entrepreneurs have had to rely almost entirely on own savings and money borrowed from friends and relatives. Working loans barely sustain production routines, let alone stretch into innovation financing. It is evident from the foregoing that African governments would need to encourage formal financial institutions to enhance their lending to small firms.

Chapter 8

Clusters and Institutions Supporting Clustering

Introduction

The difficulties faced by SMEs are accentuated in poor countries with limited capacity for policy design and implementation (Romijn, 2001). This situation has been made more difficult as a result of the rapid pace of liberalization for which most African countries were ill prepared.

> The recent liberalisation and globalisation of financial markets has made it even more common for developing countries with inadequate banking structures, information imperfection and poor institutions and infrastructure, to suffer from vulnerability through external shocks (Bhalla, 2001: 18).

Developing countries suffer more than financial market failures; pervasive labour and technological market failures are common. Clustering provides an alternative route for SMEs' development, and is potentially a less costly avenue for policy support. As Schmitz and Nadvi (1999) suggest, 'clustering facilitates the mobilisation of financial and human resources', leading to the gains of collective efficiency. Nadvi and Schmitz (1994) provide a number of reasons for this. First, clustering is a significant form of industrial organization for small-scale manufacturing. Secondly, clustering promotes different types of inter-firm linkages. Third, clustering is identified with diverse forms of social networks, which are associated with personal ties, and the notions of trust and reciprocity in competitive behaviour. Fourth, a cluster is not a planned intervention, yet the state has a role in promoting it. While past efforts have concentrated on comparing emergent clusters with advanced clusters, particularly the Italian model, it has become more important to take a more 'dynamic approach, which seeks to understand the processes that lead to success or failure' of cluster growth and development (Schmitz and Nadvi, 1999). This chapter pursues this line of inquiry in seeking to analyse the processes and the dynamics of cluster growth and the informal and formal institutions that promote clustering in Africa.

The role of institutions promoting innovation has been extensively discussed in the theoretical literature (UNCTAD, 1994; Brusco, 1999). To this end, countries have established training institutions and business development centres, while manufacturing associations have emerged, albeit to various degrees of effectiveness. This chapter focuses on the role of institutions in promoting cluster growth with emphasis on the functions and effectiveness of technical, finance, marketing and training organizations in selected African countries. I concentrate on three central issues. The first is that SMEs clusters suffer far more from financial, skills and technology market failures than large firms; therefore, progress up to higher trajectories of production and competition may be slow or impossible without special policy support. Second, clustering policies should be considered separately from the general macroeconomic instruments with emphasis on fiscal and general macroeconomic stability. Clustering policies are specific instruments applied largely at the meso and micro levels and addressing the generic constraints of small producers such poor access to credit and lack of skills for innovation, among others. Third, clusters differ significantly in their levels of development and for this reason the nature of support will differ across countries and clusters. We will attempt to show that differentiated mechanisms for support exhibit close associations with the above variables.

In this chapter, unlike the preceeding ones, we provide qualitative evidence of the different kinds of mechanisms that are used in African countries. The role of private associations is highlighted while the strengths and weaknesses of the different mechanisms are thrown up.

Country-level finding: the types and sources of support to clusters

Support to clusters comes from both state and private sources and could be in the form of technical assistance, credit provision, market support, entrepreneurship and skill training. In what follows we review recent experiences in Africa.

The Small Industries Development Organization (SIDO) in Tanzania, established in 1973, has been active in the promotion of SMEs and clusters, and formalized this process by an official government document issued in 2003 (Musonda, 2004). One of its priority programmes is a proposal to establish/promote industrial clusters in the Mwanza and Marogoro for agricultural and food processing. It has, in the past years, recognized the value of collective support by organizing quarterly zonal fairs and exhibitions in all parts of the country. It ordinarily subsidizes participation of SMEs by paying trade visits to other countries in the region such as Uganda and Kenya. It collaborates closely with local government authorities in allocating industrial lands and premises and in the establishment of common facilities at the district level. Its official mandate include *inter alia*, to provide technology and products support, support technical, business and entrepreneurship training, provide information and advisory services, credit and financial guarantee services, artisinal and youth enterprise support and promote capacity building of business associations.

In Nigeria, two broad types of support services for SMEs can be identified, namely,

- provision of work spaces: industrial estates, industrial infrastructure in areas designated as 'estates',
- real services provision on such sites such as procurement of equipment, buildings, raw materials, centralized utilities and so on,

- export processing zones and business incubator programmes,
- incentives and agency-type support: subsidized credit schemes; vocational and entrepreneurial training; real services provision; and venture capital/risk fund.

The Nigerian experience dates back to the mid-1970s and there have been several initiatives with mixed results. A number of reasons internal to organizations have been advanced for lack of policy effectiveness. These internal constraints include: low technological capacity within support institution (equipment and basic chemicals, and so on); low technological capability of the personnel; and poor management of resources. External constraints, on the other hand, include among others: strong links between domestic enterprises and foreign partners, which prevent patronage of domestic RDIs; and competition with imported machinery and products.

Agency initiatives include the establishment of the National Directorate of Employment (NDE) which was established in 1987 to promote SMEs through: procurement of machinery, managerial advice, and entrepreneurial training. The Raw Materials Research and Development Council (RMRDC) was set up in 1987 to carry out adaptive research and to disseminate information on the country's raw materials resources to manufacturing SMEs. For innovation support, a number of RDIs have evolved over the years to support the growth of and technical change process in SMEs. However, these RDIs face formidable problems, including under-funding and poor infrastructure support, among others.

A recent financing initiative is the Small and Medium Industries Equity Investment Scheme (SMIEIS) conceived by the Bankers Committee of Nigeria, a private association. In this scheme, banks are obliged by law to invest 10 per cent of their yearly pre-tax profit as equity in SMEs, but are not allowed to take more than 40 per cent shares in the enterprises. This arrangement envisages two potential benefits: first, banks are committed to the success of SMEs and therefore bring in their management experience into management of firms. Second, with this diluted shareholding, risk is shared and, moreover, financial discipline and transparency is ensured.

These support institutions were established for a variety of reasons, among which are:

- majority of private small firms tend to start small due to limitations imposed by capital, employee, size and skills required;
- initial and start-up capital is likely to be provided by own savings and from friends; and
- loans from formal institutions to small firms is rare; the propensity to grant loans to firms rise with growth in firm size.

These agencies and institutions were set up to reduce the barriers to entry by SMEs into critical sectors of the economy. On the contrary, large enterprises, with superior financial capacity and/or technical assistance from foreign partners are able to surmount both the start-up, growth and innovation demands in industry.

Industrial training and real services are provided by institutions such as the Federal Institute of Industrial Research (FIIRO), Project Development Agency (PRODA) and other research institutes. Another set of support organizations are the Industrial Development Centres (IDCs) and both sets of institutions are examined in this chapter. The IDCs are expected to provide five broad types of services, which are: consultancy services; extension services; training services; R&D; and information services.

The most recent initiative is the establishment of the Small and Medium Enterprises Development Agency (SMEDAN) as a coordinating institution with a clear mandate for promoting 'sub-contracting, clustering and networking relationships'. SMEDAN will coordinate the IDCs with strong sectoral cluster focus. It is expected to establish systematic links with seven types of service categories, namely: international agencies, training institutions, NGOs, policy advocacy groups, development finance institutions, R&D institutions, and state policy agencies (Bamiro, 2004).

The Uganda Gatsby Trust (UGT) was formed to upgrade the technological capability of small enterprises and now has over 1200 enterprise members from just about 500 in 2000. It recently started a cluster initiative at the request of members through an initiative to construct the Jinja Business Park with 20 'business units', each measuring 20 sq. m. and an anchor tenants' warehouse with an area of 750 sq. m. Another constructed cluster is being started at the Mbarara Club's estate that will house over 50 enterprises. The uniqueness of these constructed clusters is that they were demand-driven rather being a government scheme as seen in different parts of Africa, and that they are being financed in part by enterprise funds with expected full infrastructure services such as water, roads, and constant power supply. The other benefits include security of assets and access to common services, with the resultant gains of collective efficiency through network collaboration.

In addition to their internal capabilities, SMEs depend on an array of external support for the provision of such services as repair of machinery, recruitment of personnel, product development, accounting and staff training. Others include legal and financial services provided mainly by private companies within and outside the local area. Government agencies also provide some of these services to the SMEs, but the effectiveness of state services is constrained by inadequate funding.

In the Nigerian clusters we found that, despite a preponderance of public and private organizations providing support to firms, a huge gap between the demand and supply of services remains. The services lacking in the clusters include: technical assistance, industrial extension, local raw materials identification, R&D, financial and equipment leasing. The chapter probes into the types and the relative importance of such supports in and outside the immediate vicinity of the clusters. The aggregated data for the two clusters is shown in Table 8.1. Firms confirm the relative importance of the support mechanisms as shown in the table and we subsequently provide further disaggregated analysis. We asked firm MDs to indicate the types of institutional support to which they subscribe. There were over 400 and 162 firms within and outside the cluster areas respectively, and overall 73 state agency personnel responded to the questionnaire. The percentage of firms that benefit from institutional support within the clusters far outweigh those outside, suggesting that clustering tended to attract such organizations and vice versa. In almost all cases, the in-cluster beneficiaries double those outside. Heads of state agencies were asked to indicate the proportion of the different services provided by their agencies to firms. Product development and management services are the most common types of services.

Table 8.1 Support Services for SMEs Cluster in Nigeria

Types of Services	State agencies N=73 %	Firms within Cluster N=428 %	Firms outside cluster area N=162 %
Repair of Machinery	10.5	55.8	33.7
Recruitment of Personnel	4.2	78.9	16.8
Product Development	21.1	52.6	24.2
Accounting Function	9.5	73.7	16.8
Legal Services	–	71.6	28.4
Staff Training	12.6	59.0	28.4
Management/ Technical consultancy Service	18.9	59.0	22.1

Source: Author's survey (2001).

Professional ties, informal social interactions and proximity tend to be the most important forms of social networking. Less than 9 per cent of workers employed in firms in the Lagos clusters are related to the owners; whereas at Nnewi, the entire workforce is of Nnewi origin. Most have trading outposts in Lagos that are substantially staffed by families and co-ethnics. In the metropolitan cluster, 32 per cent of firms claim that non-professional other than family ties determine business relations, while spatial proximity and family ties are claimed by 19 per cent and 20 per cent respectively (Table 8.2).

Table 8.2 Informal Institutions Supporting Clusters in Nigeria

Informal Institutions	Total No	%
Family Ties	25	20.2
Spatial proximity	24	19.4
Friends and colleagues	40	32.2
Social Ties	35	28.2

Source: Author's survey.

The role of private associations in clusters

In this final section, we provide detailed empirical cases of support and common services through the activities of private associations[1] within clusters. In doing this, we highlight the content and nature of informal institutional structures that has emerged as an important source of support, particularly among small producers and artisinal groups. While there is competition, there is considerable collaboration particularly through informal social institutions (such as credit from 'trusting brethren').

Local institutions and associations provide critical support and in extreme cases, of failure to provide public goods by the relevant government authorities, private groups have supplanted the state (Brautigam, 1997). Associations expose members to international partners and provide the kind of credibility that individual firms could not possibly have. The promotion of local networking by local institutions has been as important for clusters in highly industrial environments such as Lombardy and Baden-Württemberg (Malerba, 1992) as they have been for Nnewi clusters in Nigeria (Oyelaran-Oyeyinka, 1997b). According to Malerba,

> Local institutions and local associations play a major role in the working of the organization of the district. Regional and local governments, banks, and professional schools provide public support, financial resources and a qualified labour to firms. Export and distribution associations help overcome the problems faced by small firms in selling their final products on international markets(Malerba, 1992: 236).

Private Associations in Nigerian clusters

About 85 per cent of the respondents in the clusters belong to some private industrial association.[2] The working relationships among the various associations are adjudged

---

1   The importance of private associations in filling the gap created by prior public goods and absence of formal institutions has been reviewed in Chapter 6.

2   The major associations in the clusters are the Manufacturers Association of Nigeria (MAN), The major associations in the clusters are the Manufacturers Association of Nigeria (MAN), National Association of Small-Scale Industrialists (NASSI), National Association of

by firm owners to be very good and the services vital for cluster survival in the face of weak infrastructure and poor public goods provision. There are over 20 local manufacturing and services associations in the country. The more prominent and influential associations provide a wide range of services for their members such as capacity building, dissemination of relevant information on government policies/ incentives, tariffs as well as information on the activities of rivals and collaborating enterprises. They also build links between firms and international and national NGOs, organize trade fairs, and lobby state and federal governments for tariff concessions among other things. The associations also provide members a forum for exchange of business ideas, proffer solutions to knotty industrial problems such as environmental, infrastructural and legislative matters.

Table 8.3 Services by Private Association in Nigerian Clusters

Uses	Often		Occasionally		Never	
	No	%	No	%	No	%
1. Advice on legal matters	6	8.2	29	39.7	38	52.1
2. Provide information on other enterprises	17	23.3	12	16.4	44	60.3
3. Capacity building through courses and seminars	44	60.3	22	30.1	7	9.6
4. Dissemination of useful information through bulletins	47	64.4	20	27.4	6	8.2
5. Trade Fair Organization	49	67.1	14	19.2	10	13.7
6. Lobby governments for assistance to members	48	65.8	15	20.5	10	13.7
7. Product Development	–	–	33	45.2	40	54.8
8. Joint Procurement of inputs	–	–	35	47.9	38	52.1
9. Joint Marketing	–	–	35	47.9	38	52.1

Source: Analysis of Field Data.

Some 75 per cent of the surveyed firms are of the view that the associations are abreast of information on market development and are able to assist their members. About 70 per cent of the SMEs suggest that the associations provide useful technical support to their members, while 90 per cent of the SMEs rank the associations as effective leaders of the collective interest of their members, Table 8.3.

The major problems confronting the associations are lack of funds, periodic leadership crises that tend to dissipate organizational resources and lack of informed

---

Small and Medium Enterprises (NASMEN), and Chamber of Commerce. There are over 20 of such associations in the country.

and committed membership. In spite of these problems, the associations are bracing up to the challenges of globalization by encouraging their members to retool, computerize their operations, improve the quality of their products and pressurize government to make the environment investor friendly so that new investments that improve the competitiveness of local products can be attracted into the economy, Table 8.3.

Suame, Ghana private associations

A variety of private associations emerged to support the Suame cluster. In 1983, the Ministry of Industries created the Suame Garages Association to provide a link between government and the artisans as well as to provide welfare support to association members. However, the legitimacy of the association being a state creation was questionable, a situation that was not helped by the heterogeneity of the membership (McCormick, 1998). Other associations operating in Suame include:

- Magazine Mechanical Association (MMA) established in 1957 with current membership of about 98 per cent of the entrepreneurs in Suame numbering approximately 10 000 members, mainly vehicle mechanics.
- The Ghana National Association of Garages (GNAG) was formed with a regional secretariat in Suame cluster in the 1980s with the mandate for land administration and the general welfare of young vehicle mechanics. It controls approximately 1000 building plots in the upland areas of Suame Magazine.
- Association of Micro and Small Metal Industries (AMSMI) was formed in the 1990s by the clients of Suame Intermediate Technology Transfer Unit to address the problems of the metal manufacturing sub-sector. AMSMI is working with the Technology Consultancy Centre and the Ghana Regional Appropriate Technology Industrial Service (GRATIS Foundation) to establish a national network of the association to address issues concerning small engineering manufacturing in Ghana.
- Magazine Spare-Parts Dealers Association: The association was formed by business people involved in importation of spare parts for automobile repair.

Other associations that are in the relatively early phases of formation include the Magazine Auto-mechanics Association, Foundry Association and Scrap Dealers Association (Adeya, 2003). A number of programmes exist devoted largely to skills development and vocational training such as the Business Assistance Fund (BAF) initiated by the National Board for Small-Scale Industries (NBSSI). However, the most well known are the Suame Intermediate Technology Transfer Unit (ITTU) and the National Vocational Training Institute (NVTI). Both were established to transfer new techniques and to institutionalize apprenticeship training by formal certification. Previous short-term training programmes by the World Bank through the Kumasi Technical Institute (KTI) for mechanics and electricians were discontinued for lack of funding.

Efforts to upgrade micro and small enterprises (MSEs) and to develop the skills of artisans has prompted the Government of Ghana to establish institutions and at the same time promoted collaboration between different institutions and cluster MSEs. The areas of focus include technology development and transfer, vocational and apprentice training, business management and entrepreneurship training, working capital and hire-purchase loans, women's enterprise development, business assistance fund, marketing and business promotions programme (Adeya, 2003). The most notable collaborating institutions are:

- the Suame Intermediate Technology Transfer Unit (ITTU),
- the National Vocational Training Institute (NVTI),
- the Ghana Regional Appropriate Technology Industrial Service (GRATIS Foundation),
- National Board for Small-Scale Industries (NBSSI),
- Technology Consultancy Centre (TCC),
- Association of Small-Scale Industries (ASSI),
- Association of Ghana Industries (AGI),
- Council for Scientific and Industrial Research (CSIR),
- Private Enterprise Foundation (PEF),
- Intermediate Technology Ghana (ITG).

While many of these institutions continue to provide consultancy type services to the cluster, very little of their own research output is adopted for two reasons. First, most of the techniques used by Suame artisans change very little, although there is some evidence of learning to gain higher levels of proficiency. There is clearly a limit to repetitive learning-by-doing and without new investment in new vintages the cluster is likely to continue to operate on a very 'low road' of industrialization. Secondly, it is unclear how much the institutions push and market their products and process into the market. The cost of development from laboratory and pilot to commercial scale constitutes an important but particularly expensive step, which organizations such as the CSIR – which is responsible for coordinating other institutes working within the cluster – is ill-equipped to deal with. The CSIR has a number of departments for network coordination of research institutes and other university academic departments to disseminate research findings to the cluster. For instance, the GRATIS Foundation coordinates a network of Intermediate Technology Transfer Unit (ITTU) established within the Suame magazine to develop enterprise capacity to design, manufacture and service agricultural and engineering equipment. One notable success of this initiative of the Suame ITTU is the promotion and establishment of a large number of small foundry businesses in other parts of the country.

The importance of private associations in Africa's informal clusters

An important benefit of clustering is the potential access to common services. This is particularly important within MSE clusters, where individual firms are incapable of providing the full range of facilities taken for granted within large firms. A study of access to a whole range of ICTs including basic fixed line, facsimile, mobile telephone, computer services and the Internet show that clustering facilitates joint action. There is a strong presence of private association within the Nairobi and Suame clusters as the reasons for enterprise participation vary but are broadly similar across countries (Table 8.4).

Table 8.4 The Importance of Private Associations in Clusters

Reason for Joining Association	Nairobi Cluster(%)	Suame (N=69) Clusters(%)
Share Information	13.5	17.0
Small Producers Advocacy	21.6	38.0
Improve Welfare	40.3	4.0
Access to Credit	37.8	1.0
Assist Each Other	27.0	17.0
Secure Business Site	24.3	3.0
Income Generation	18.9	15.6
Benefit from Training		14.0

Source: Adeya, UNU-INTECH (2002) Field Data.

The reasons for and the mandate of the associations reflect the needs and motivation of the enterprises. In the Nairobi clusters, the major reasons for joining national associations were: to meet welfare needs (40.3 per cent); to obtain credit (37.8 per cent); to help each other (27 per cent); to gain access to business site (24.3 per cent); to partake in advocacy for MSE development (21.6 per cent); national umbrella associations for the purpose of starting an income generating activity (18.9 per cent); and sharing information (13.5 per cent). Other reasons for membership relate to savings mobilization and to gain from joint training programmes. Associations are closely involved in providing common services, but particularly striking is the gain in skills transfer among enterprises despite the often fierce rivalrous relationship common to this group of enterprises. For instance, more than half the respondents in the Nairobi clusters transfer skills to other enterprises, notably in apprenticeship skills training. While 65 per cent of trainers charge fees, an expected practice of the apprenticeship institution, some others conduct skills training in exchange for other non-price reasons. Again about half the trained apprentices remain in the enterprise after graduation while the other half seek to establish their own business outside or within the cluster. We established that the process of skill exchange in Suame is equally rampant, with 76 per cent of entrepreneurs acquiring skills through apprenticeship. Apprenticeship ordinarily lasts five years, but there are instances where an apprentice has been learning for a far longer period. ICT skill is largely acquired from formal institutions outside the cluster.

Common facilities sharing in clusters

Another important joint action is the sharing of facilities among enterprise in clusters. In the Nairobi clusters, on average, 46.1 per cent of enterprises here own an ICT facility but 41 per cent confirmed to sharing the facility with neighbours. The most widely owned and shared facility being the fixed telephone for local calls (70 per cent), followed by trunk calls (36.7 per cent) and mobile telephones (30 per cent). In Suame, 36 per cent share these facilities.

In Uganda, two clusters specializing in automotive parts and food and beverages display similar patterns of strong influence of private associations although there is significant sectoral variation. For instance while 40 per cent of the firms in the foods and beverage sub-sector were aware of associations operating within the clusters, only 24 per cent in the auto-parts and metal fabricating sub-sector share a strong affiliation with associations. Most firms in the auto-parts and metal fabrication sub-sector operate independently of each other, and associations are not common in this sector. The association that most enterprises were aware of was the Uganda Small Scale Industries Association.

Table 8.5 Private Association Impact on Small Enterprise Clusters

Item	Food and Beverages (N = 43) (Uganda) (%)	Automotive Components (N = 41) (Uganda) (%)	Suame (N = 69) (%)	Nairobi (N = 107) Clusters (%)
Association within Clusters	40.0	24.0	79.0	77.6
National Association	88.0	80.0	37.0	44.6
Welfare Association	6.0	20.0	5.0	38.6
Association Operating ICTs within Clusters	30.0	14.0		11.2
Type of ICTs: Fixed Line and Computer Services	85.5	50.0		

In the Lagos cluster, the level of inter-firm cooperation and common facility sharing is equally high in some activities: (33.9 per cent) in respect of sharing utilities (electricity), in security arrangements (39.3). There is also joint action in respect of apprenticeship training, sourcing of materials and credit and savings schemes. A summary of the types of private associations in three countries is shown in Table 8.5. National associations are present in all the three country clusters, but, notably, welfare associations predominate and tend to have far greater influence. This is because the clusters comprise enterprises with weak internal resources that are, for most part, neglected by the state and municipal authorities that often lack an understanding of the proper role and the potential force that these clusters could exert. The type of political support that translated to real services instrumented in Emilia Romagna[3] is lacking. This is the context in which private support plays and important role.

Summary

In this chapter, we discussed how different attributes have shaped the evolution and performance of the clusters. We examined, in some detail, the nature of institutions supporting SME clusters in a number of African countries. We found that levels of technology development are closely associated with the types of support and the motivation for joint action, such as roles in private associations. The small producers tend to join associations largely for welfare purposes rather than to pursue technical upgrading. Common facilities sharing is an important alternative remedy to the widespread shortages of physical and communication infrastructure. There is considerable skills transfer among the entrepreneurs within informal clusters in spite of the sometime damaging rivalrous relationship that characterize these clusters. This takes the form of apprenticeship training and represents an important starting point for technical and human capital upgrading. Another striking attribute of the small firm clusters is the differential influence of socio-cultural factors on the evolution of clustering. Economic relation among a group of firms has elements of social embeddedness and can be viewed in three different ways (Granovetter, 1973: McCormick, 1997). The first is the notion that specific and interrelated social and cultural factors give rise to different processes of development. Secondly, the notion that those socio-cultural identities provide a foundation for trust and reciprocity in firms dealing with one another; and, third, that the social milieu exerts strong influence on and is influenced by the processes of innovation and technical change. There is evidence that investment decision by firms and the subsequent cluster formation in clusters was strongly predicated on ethnic, family and geographic factors. In the more metropolitan clusters, family and kinship factors were less influential, but social and professional networks were very important.

The role of education of entrepreneurs seems to be neutral in the choice of location for the rural cluster, as other factors tend to be more powerful. We did not systematically investigate the consequences of low educational attainments for firm performance, but this will become crucial in an increasingly competitive, skill-based economic milieu. The compelling need for investment security and the unavailability

---

3   See Best (1990) and Brusco (1992) or full discussion of the Italian Clusters in Emilia Romagna.

of land, for instance, in Eastern Nigeria meant that entrepreneurs locate factories within their own 'father's compound', even in the face of high transaction costs (poor road networks and poor power supply). In the Suame and Nairobi clusters entrepreneurs join welfare type associations for purposes of gaining access to land. However, in the metropolitan medium sized clusters, social and professional networks are based on educational attainment of owners and, for that reason, tend to be a strong determinant of business formation and growth.

Spatial proximity plays different roles. Nnewi firms are part of business associations as are the Lagos firms, but the two clusters tend to leverage professional networks in different ways and to different degrees of intensity. The Suame and Nairobi clusters claim definite benefits from geographic proximity, particularly common facility sharing, easy access to information and product markets, as well as training opportunities. Collaboration with foreign firms is more crucial to the Nnewi entrepreneur, while firms in Lagos have developed greater inter-firm links among themselves. The informal Suame and Nairobi clusters have virtually no foreign affiliation. While in the medium-sized cluster collaboration has grown with input suppliers and traders within and outside the country, the Lagos clusters engage local firms in maintenance, purchase of spares and in sharing of information on technical and market matters. Nnewi firms trade and conduct much of their financial transactions in Lagos where they maintain trading outposts.

There is little formal support from the central and local authorities beyond the provision of basic amenities. It is evident that the emergent clusters have accumulated considerable competences and may well be ready to compete outside the sub-regional market if assistance is provided for technology upgrading, and quality assurance for inputs and products. There is a need to upgrade the quality of infrastructure such as electric power, communication and water supply. Much of SSA suffers from these constraints and it would be useful to deepen and widen our study on how institutional support could transform these clusters into strong centres of quality manufacturing. This chapter shows how little we yet know of the African variety, and suggests the direction for future research efforts on clusters in Africa.

Chapter 9

Conclusions and Policy Suggestions

Introduction

This book has explored the institutional root of industrialization with a focus on SMEs. It started with two explicit assumptions. The first is that institutions in their broadest sense are important to the process of industrialization and that technical change is the motivating force for industrial progress, although policy makers in Africa underestimate the role and importance of institutions. Second, while much of the enterprises in Africa are small and medium sized firms, this structural characteristic should not be an impediment to industrial progress. Contrary to the notion of small firms being simply a survivalist category with no scope or capability for innovation (Galbraith, 1975), studies of small firms in clusters show that they can be dynamic and innovative (Brusco, 1992).

We made the point that policy makers in many African countries have erroneously assumed that the process of technology acquisition is costless and effortless once a country could mobilize the resources to import machinery and equipment; from that point on, engineers and technicians would automatically learn-by-doing. As for endogenous technical efforts, the assumption was that the imitation of western type R&D institutes would result in the development of prototypes. These would further develop a dynamic transformation of local raw materials into goods and services and that would result as indigenous enterprises build plants and develop processes. In this linear conception of the innovation process, the critical role of institutions was assumed away. The neo-institutionalist proposes three roles for institutions (Lundvall and Johnson, 2003):

- they define property rights and contracts, and spells out who gains and loses;
- institutions channel information about markets, actors and products; and
- influence the nature of competition (promote or hinder).

However, these conditions are inadequate for creating firm-level dynamism where continuous learning and un-learning are important factors for accumulating critical technological capabilities. Beyond innovation, the necessary process of doing daily routine by firms and thereby growing is in itself an asset creating process. According to Penrose (1959: 56), 'The very process of operation and of expansion are intimately associated with a process by which knowledge is created' (cited in Best, 1990:128).

What this means is that in the new economic context, where firms must compete in the domestic market with imports and in the international market, knowledge becomes a critical resource and learning an inevitable activity. Large firms enjoy scale economy and possess the secure resources to internalize much of what small firms lack, namely, skills, experience and knowledge.

However, new forms of industrial organization such as networking and clustering have emerged to attenuate this shortcoming of small firms. As Pyke et al. (1990: 4) perceptively formulated the issues: 'the key problem for small firms appears not to be that of being small but of being isolated'. This has led to the policies on technology incubation, science parks and the promotion of clusters in order for firms to gain the benefits of collective efficiency. This is where the study of the 'third Italy' has caught the imagination of scholars and policy makers. In this book we call attention to the less emphasized aspects of the success of the Italian cluster, the institutional roots of autonomous technical change in the transformation of small firms.

Institutions act to promote collaboration between firms. Such a collection of collocating firms act as a fully entrepreneurial industrial district through a combination of 'productive decentralization and social integration' (Best, 1990): 207). This is an ideal form of economic collaboration, which has arisen from a combination of historical accidents, political and social action at the local and municipal levels, and through active innovation policy.

As this book demonstrates, African governments are only beginning to pay attention to the underlying principles of innovation policy support that other countries in Europe and Asia have practised for years.[1]

In what follows, we raise the following issues and discuss their implications for policy making:

- What implications do the institutional forms currently existing in Africa have for long term industrialization?
- How does the innovation systems framework apply to African conditions?
- What did we find of the size, structure of firms and where do they go from here?
- What types of learning and capability building is taking place and how should policy promote the dynamism of small firms?
- What kinds of knowledge and skills should be promoted?
- What forms of SME clustering policies are appropriate for the African context?

---

1   Japan's prefecture governments established scores of public testing and research centres as well as technology centres to promote the productions of particular products. The first technology centre in Japan was established in 1894 at the Hyogo prefecture to support textile spinning. Subsequently 46 centres were opened in the 1927-45 period and 57 in the 1946–64 period (Yamawaki, 2002).

Sector specific innovation support has been a guiding principle of the Emilian Romagna cluster. Government at the municipal level as well as quasi-public agencies such as ERVET recognized and established centres for design information services to promote competition.

Implications for institutions, technology and African industrialization

Different types of organizational ineffectiveness manifest as system inefficiency (Niosi, 2002b). The relevance of existing research and training institutes, for example, has been questioned; the former for their lack of linkages with the productive sectors and the latter for their limited ties to dominant actors in the economy such as small and SMEs. This gives rise to the poor coordination of knowledge and economic production functions leading to imbalances in the demand and supply for skills of the right kinds, quantity and quality mix at sectoral levels and overtime. Poor resource commitment for meeting organizational objectives, including poor funding and inadequate staffing, are also common and may lead to x-ineffectiveness. While there is a general agreement that developing countries need to create organizations and institutions where they do not exist and reform those that are functioning poorly, institutions for policy making themselves lack both broad and specific competencies in their coordination functions. This is a serious drawback for developing countries and leads to a situation in which policy coordination is largely politically driven in the absence of strong market coordination. Maintaining these organizations to achieve effective service delivery depends to a considerable extent on available public resources. However, government involvement tends to create its own idiosyncratic lock-in conditions for two main reasons. First, governments have the authority to override market forces thereby creating alternative institutions to which actors have to respond. Second, state institutions tend to persist for much longer periods due to in-built processes that make essential alterations to constitutional rules slow and difficult. However, institutional gaps may, in part, be traced to the inability of African governments to establish necessary agencies due to financial constraints or poor or a lack of information on what institutions are required. Private involvement in institutional creation is very limited.

Innovation and systems of innovation: application to the African condition

In a number of important respects, our ideas and assumptions of how development and industrialization should proceed are being increasingly challenged. Central to the new thinking about development is the role of innovation in transforming particularly traditional sectors into dynamic innovative systems. We adopted a broader definition of innovation in this book as, '... the process by which firms master and implement the design and production of goods and services that are new to them, irrespective of whether or not they are new to their competitors – domestic or foreign' (Ernst et al., 1998: 12–13). This view of industrial transformation rests on three main assumptions. First, firms do not innovate in isolation but do so within a network of other economic agents, making interaction an important element. More importantly, innovation takes place in all sectors (not only in high-tech sectors like biotechnology and information technology, but equally in traditional sectors such as foods and beverages); and across all firm sizes (small and medium). However, depending on the context, innovation has elements of size-bias being more skewed in favour of larger sized firms. Second, all agents are involved in a continuous process of learning and, as such, the notion of knowledge 'producer' and 'user' has limited conceptual and policy relevance. Learning in turn is heuristic, taking place over a long period of time and possessing a systemic and incremental character. This makes proximity an important factor, although mere co-location of firms does not predispose agents to innovation. Third, the role of knowledge has become increasingly central to an analysis of economic progress, and institution, a carrier of knowledge. Innovation will be the main driver of competitive industries and enterprises.

Chapters 3 and 4 in particular underlie the importance of these concepts to the situation of developing areas. The findings in this book confirm our three theses relating to networking and clusters. First, that enterprises and cluster transformation succeeds on the strength of increasing links with other innovating agents. Second, formal and tacit knowledge of critical actors strongly influence enterprise performance and should ultimately impact on the nature of the shift from clusters to innovation systems. Third, cluster competitiveness is closely correlated with continuous learning and support from local institutions. Firms are severely constrained by limited knowledge, human skills and experience, as well as poor techno-managerial capability of top management – and in the case of the small firms – that of the owner/ entrepreneur. This finding applies to almost all African SMEs although pockets of sound technological capabilities and excellent managerial skills abound particularly in medium enterprises.

We considered two components of human capital – of firm owners or managers – that tend to affect the growth and dynamism of firms. These are: certificated or diploma-awarding qualifications obtained from formal institutions; and non-formal learning. The level of human capital shapes the ways in which a firm is managed, and tacit knowledge, a vital but non-quantifiable component of human skills, could indeed be a decisive factor of firm performance. Compared with their counterparts in other developing countries, and indeed the management of larger firms within the same countries, owners/managers of SMEs tend to score relatively low in formal education and experience. We observed a fairly consistent pattern of relatively low qualification and poor managerial competence among the workforce in most cases, with a few exceptions. This is particularly so for the small rather than medium firms with more than fifty employees. While firm owners may in fact possess intrinsic entrepreneurial abilities, this attribute does not prove sufficient in the face of the complex demands of modern economies. As firms face both domestic and external competition, the need for new sets of technical and managerial competencies arises.

Managing a firm with a limited number of qualified and experienced personnel (the perennial resource allocation constraint) leaves firm owners with little or no time for training. For this reason, non-formal training seems to be the preponderant mode of learning. We found that technical apprenticeship is the most common type of training in both small and medium firms.

We demonstrated the statistical correlation of training and different measures of performance, namely, increased firm output, perceived improvement in technical capability and actual increased export performance as a result of training. Training in small firms is largely in form of apprenticeship supplemented by 'local training' (within the cluster or local area) often provided by local consultants or public agency. Small firms hardly engage in overseas training, while enterprises attribute much of the technical improvements as well as output and export growth to learning through apprenticeship training. We found strong association between levels of investment in training and higher output, increased technical capability and better export performance.

However, learning-by-doing attains a limiting value and tacit knowledge is bounded by negative feedback, because, while it promotes continuous improvements, it hardly leads to innovation. In other words, an industry, system of production or firm could not hope to rely indefinitely and exclusively on particular knowledge of production without new knowledge injected through innovation.

In Chapter 4 we showed that little or no collaboration takes place between small firms in Africa and knowledge institutions such as universities. There seems to be greater collaboration with suppliers and subcontractors at this size level and in this technological regime. We advance three broad reasons for the poor linkages between universities and SMEs. First, in positive systemic environments, where knowledge externalities are present, there are three broad sources of knowledge for firms, namely, industry R&D, university R&D (both broadly defined) and skilled labour. The role each of these play is self-evident, while, in particular, new economic knowledge in form of tacit skills and knowledge generally promote the propensity to innovate. The absence of graduate skilled labour in small firms will therefore deprive them of this impulse to innovate. Second, small firms lack the internal capacity to absorb new knowledge. A firm with little or no experience in innovative activity will lack the skills to identify and adopt the necessary external inputs. Third, acquisition of external knowledge depends on both geographic and knowledge proximity. There is a wide cognitive disparity between small firms and university knowledge bases in African countries, particularly the latter. Where firms are situated near universities, their activity domains are worlds apart as a result of the kinds of markets small firms serve and the publication niche market those university scientists respond to. The mobility of labour is a key source of knowledge transfer, but this kind of exchange hardly takes place except with large, often multinational, firms.

Much of what goes on between firms involve bilateral contractual arrangements with suppliers, subcontractors and consulting organizations that organize training, and conduct investment feasibility studies for firms. We explored in some detail how much and how frequently these contacts are made and for what reasons. Joint skills and collective marketing as well as information exchange are important activities. In all but a few cases, there is no significant difference in these activities across countries. In other words, the countries undertake fairly similar sorts of activities. The detailed interviews threw light on the preponderance of these types of relationships, and on the weak links between firms, RDIs and universities. Networks focus on production and innovative activities are centred on product technical change, which require minimal inputs from organizations outside the firms particularly with firms with some level of graduate employees. However, firms with export orientation tend to seek out new sources of knowledge outside the immediate network. In what follows, we examine the role of skills, markets and size effects on collaboration.

None of the collaboration variables, that is, horizontal cooperation, subcontracting, linkage with industrial associations, cooperation with input suppliers and technology institutions, differ significantly with respect to skill intensity of firms. The results are not surprising because skill intensity, based on the qualification of workers, is not expected to be a dominant influence on the conduct of firms. The conduct of SMEs is determined largely by the entrepreneurial characteristics of the owner.

Export-oriented enterprises differ in many respects from inward-looking firms. Several indicators of inter-firm linkage, such as horizontal cooperation, subcontracting and collaboration with technology institutions, differ significantly between export-oriented firms and non-exporters. The findings confirm what existing literature has to say about horizontal collaboration as well as our hypothesis. For instance, some export-oriented firms asserted that they avoid subcontracting collaboration for fear of compromising on products quality while other firms prefer subcontracting in order to avoid high overhead costs. Similarly export-oriented firms are more predisposed to collaboration with technology institutions in order to keep abreast of new opportunities in the technology and products markets. While firms can survive in the domestic market with relatively low skills and technology, they face considerably stiffer competition in the international market for which higher technical skills are required.

We examined enterprise performance, represented by export intensity, profitability and sales turnover, while conduct variables are the ability of firms to innovate and speed of delivery. All the variables except sales turnover differ significantly in the three countries. The results suggest that country-specific characteristics and firm performance differ significantly in the countries. In the three countries, firms export largely to regional destinations, but there are relatively more export-oriented and firms reporting innovation in the Nigerian sample firms. Firms attribute improvements in speed of delivery in the last five years to domestic and international competitive pressures. They respond to internal capability deficiency by conducting more in-house and external staff training as well as making improvements to the capacity of product quality testing facilities. Small firm collaboration with distant suppliers commonly involves supply of machinery, equipment and spare parts supply, and this is in some cases, attended by technical training.

Three sets of issues with implications for policy emerged from our analysis. First, the chapter came to the tentative conclusion that inter-firm relations, particularly between firms and other economic agents, involve more than exchange of information about prices and volumes; although we are far from fully understanding all the factors inducing networking. However, fostering cooperative interaction between economic agents in African industry has not come about naturally; therefore, networking institutions remain weak in all three countries. Second, there is some measure of interaction among economic agents, but these relate largely to maintaining firm-level daily routines and, to an extent, effecting minor technical modifications that keep plants working. Innovation policy should therefore seek to move up the quality of firm level activity as well as promote greater interaction among firms and technological institutions. Policy should also establish or strengthen where they already exist, organizations and institutions should regulate and coordinate innovation functions, which, following the Neo-Liberal prescriptions, would be left to the markets. Finally, there is evidence that collaborative exchanges raise economic performance; therefore, there is an economic rationale for intervention to promote inter-firm collaboration. We suggest therefore that developing African countries need to approach the task of developing their NSIs, but with no preconceived ideas of 'ideal' types since the notion of optimality has no place in systems thinking.

Creating and promoting networking and clusters

The notion of clusters fits into the innovation systems framework given its systemic, networking features as well as reliance on institutions as sources of dynamism. However, clusters are not necessarily innovation systems (Mytelka and Farinelli, 2000) and transforming clusters into innovation systems require sustained policy support. The process of policy learning is itself heuristic, while strengthening local actors takes time and requires explicit investment in learning. An important lesson for developing countries is the fact that traditional sectors in advanced industrial countries have made the transition from low technology sectors into successful innovative clusters.

Policies to build dynamic clusters therefore need to take account of a number of issues one of which is the uniqueness of clusters, the fact that a 'best practice' does not exist in practice much in the same way that an innovation system does not have an 'ideal form' (OECD, 2001). The others are the cluster origin, type of cluster, level and stage of development, extant and potential forms of interaction, types and roles of institutions and knowledge to support clustering. Thus, when considering an effective and appropriate means of cluster support, the structure of the entire system of innovation and the harmony of the structure or mode of support within the given industrial context is of vital importance.

Policies to transform small firm clusters into innovative clusters should take account of the following: Origin and evolution of the cluster: history matters (path dependence) and where a cluster originated from would, in large parts, condition where it is going. A sudden imposition of ideas at variance with its basic practices and routines might derail rather than promote the trajectory of development. An important first step in designing support is the mapping of critical actors and understanding the *institutional systems features* of a cluster.

Uniqueness of a cluster There is no 'best practice' and all systems have their own unique attributes. Successful clusters thrive as much on the skill and technological capabilities of actors, as on the social context and the effectiveness of the institutions in which they are embedded.

The critical role of institutions Institutions are not just organizations. Organizations become institutionalized and secure their legitimacy in the long process of serving and being effective in their mandate. Local formal and informal institutions are particularly critical to long term growth of systems and, for this reason, policy should be to foster the co-evolution of both the technological and institutional regimes. Private associations, the apprenticeship systems and the indigenous credit finance systems could be important roles in upgrading clusters into innovative systems. Ultimately, the institutional structure and organization of SME support system should be conditioned by: (a) the roles and services that are already provided in the country by other institutions; and (b) the need to fill institutional gaps rather than the desire to create new structures.

Learning and pattern of interaction What kinds of linkages exist and between what knowledge bases; and to what other wider sets of critical knowledge and skill bases clusters could be linked, should be sought throughout the economy. Incentives to encourage and promote learning in clusters should consider not only formal but experiential learning within firms in clusters. Promoting inter-firm cooperation between small firms may require some level of external inducement, whether from private associations or from the state or both. The lesson from successful clusters is that approaches vary as much as diversity of institutions that are present in different contexts.

The role of the state Governments have a critical role to play inasmuch as it already provides public goods and could better upgrade it and in most countries, the state and its agencies already have in place a number of technical services. What may be required are new ways of adjusting to knowledge-based systems of support that take into account not only the needs of production, but continuous innovation.

One thing that organized professional bodies and the state could jointly facilitate is trust. Trust is an important feature of collaborative relationships and we found for all successful clusters that cooperation thrives where social groups know and trust each other. This is a long term undertaking and the African credit system of esusu (as the Yorubas in Southwestern Nigeria call it) thrived for centuries on the basis of trusted brethrens and trusting brothers. For this reason geographical proximity and common culture form the basis of trust to promote local collaboration.

In sum, the combination of local institutions, local learning and local capabilities is indispensable to transforming clusters into innovation systems.

Infrastructure and performance

Firms maintain product quality only with a lot of effort, and loss of production output is inevitable in a regime of constantly reduced production time and subsequent reduction in output volume. Power outages increase downtime and production costs with the subsequent result being a loss of productivity. Chemical firms, for instance, tend to sustain considerable loss of output during extraction processes whenever there is an outage of power. Besides, excess load on generating sets tend to precipitate disequilibrium in the operating systems, leading to reduction in yields.

Other consequences of fluctuating power and outright outages are poor product quality and reduction in output volume. Poor quality of products is particularly common with agro-allied firms, especially food and beverages companies, where products are carbonated at very low temperature. Power outages raise storage temperature as the refrigeration process is disrupted during production process thereby leading to de-carbonation. Incidence of product wastage is quite common. Metal manufacturing firms record damage to the quality of cans produced due to power outages. For instance in one firm, interrupted power led to air leakages in the cans and produced a defect that caused content contamination when the cans were used by other firms for packaging.

There is a direct correlation between energy intensity and productivity. Energy intensity is defined as energy consumption per unit production output. Firms that rely solely on public utility as their source of electricity power supply experienced increased energy intensity and decline in productivity. This results from decreasing output and/or increased energy within a production regime. Similar trends were observed for some small and medium firms that combine both public and private generating sets as sources of power supply. In general, this may well be indicative of inefficient energy utilization in all the firms. In sum, inefficient energy use has important implications for firm-level operation, the firm's product quality and output volume and, by extension, for a country's industrial goods at the domestic and international markets. The high cost of energy translates to high cost of output that makes firms less competitive in the domestic and in the global market.

Physical infrastructure, which includes modern knowledge-based ICTs, is poorly developed in African countries. Due to the poor quality of public infrastructure and the absence of competitive private alternative, individual firms in Africa invest relatively high proportions of capital in private facilities. We have, through case studies, established the direct association of high transaction costs and the absence of quality infrastructure, for instance:

- poor communication results from low teledensity;
- low electrical power consumption.

The indivisibility of network infrastructure was demonstrated by the high correlation of the 'wired' variables among themselves. The systemic imperative of network infrastructure was further demonstrated by the similarity of trend lines of low and medium income countries. Although considerable variation exists in the penetration of telephone and the Internet in African countries, per capita electrical power shows no significant difference. In effect power supply is uniformly inadequate across countries except in the relatively industrialized ones, such as Mauritius and South Africa.

Firms spend a considerably high percentage of investment and operating capital on private provision. We confirm this by a detailed examination of macro level data, as well as micro level survey results. The severity of infrastructure constraints was evident at the firm level. Over half of enterprise owners abandoned certain projects as a result of power outages. Zimbabwe had the best infrastructure, while Nigerian firms suffered the worse fate. Firms in all countries claimed that, on average, road, power, telephone and water services had declined in the last five years.

It would seem that the SAPs left national infrastructure in a worse state. From a firm's own perception, the poor supply response to reforms had little to do with a lack of willingness, but much more with structural rigidities of institutions. Equally constraining to performance is the slow inflow of domestic and foreign investment to the infrastructure sectors at a time of drastic cuts in government budgets. There is an urgent need to address the declining infrastructure in Africa. Reforms would have to be far more innovative and more sensitive to the needs of SMEs – the main drivers of economic activities.

We conclude from the studies that for a firm to grow and maintain a sustained competitive trajectory, technical and finance supports are required. This is because small firms lack a broad range of internal capabilities for production, marketing and innovation, and they also do not possess sets of linkage capabilities to tap into the knowledge bases external to them. Small producers are unable to meet some or, often, all of these prerequisites; therefore state and private actions are often necessary. On the supply side, technical support actors in Africa are themselves casualties of past reforms. They are depleted in manpower, grossly under funded and staff morale is lacking. Some RDIs have an impressive shelf of inventions, which sadly, are totally irrelevant to SME needs. Universities suffer a similar fate in Africa.

In the finance support systems, banks are risk averse and often hostile to the demand of small firms for support. The capital market is a difficult proposition for small producers and states have set up special credit guarantee schemes and development banks to attenuate the gaps in financial resource flow to firms. In all these institutions, we observe a commonality of attributes. The banks, the capital markets and the technical support organizations all share the same character of the small firms. In some cases, poorly motivated and sometimes unqualified staff run financial institutions, often inefficiently. The conditions for SME lending are usually difficult to meet especially the restrictive collateral requirements. Micro-finance schemes launched by NGOs and aid agencies have to some extent presented an alternative source of SME finance. These programmes have been growing in recent years, but the small size of loans remains insufficient for SMEs' technological capability acquisition and competitiveness.

This is an internal weakness that makes their collective mandate extremely difficult. At the risk of presumptuous generalization, one policy conclusion seems inevitable. This is that states in Africa will have to raise the qualitative assets of support institutions in the face of the new competitive challenge. The starting point will be the upgrading of extant organizations and the widening of non-public knowledge support bases.

Again, access to finance remains a major problem for SMEs. Most entrepreneurs have had to rely almost entirely on own savings and money borrowed from friends and relatives. Working loans can barely sustain production routines, let alone be stretched into innovation financing. It is evident from the foregoing that African governments would need to encourage formal financial institutions to enhance their lending to small firms.

The role of the state and innovative systems

The process of technological accumulation takes place within a national system of innovation (NSI), which regulates the process of adoption, and diffusion of innovations, (Freeman, 1987; Lundvall, 1992). The NSI places innovation at the centre of economic activity and consists of a network of institutions, which include organizations. The kernel of innovation systems approach is a focus on the nature of actors and their interaction as well as interdependence. The firm is often the locus of innovation but it carries out innovation in cooperation with other organizations such as the universities, standard setting agencies, research institutes, financing organizations, among others (Edquist, 2001). Three characteristics of the NSI relate to the theme of this book. The first is inter-firm relations particularly between firms and other economic agents. These 'involve more than exchange of quantitative information about prices and volumes. They often constitute ongoing cooperative relationships that also involve exchange of other kinds of knowledge and information that shape learning and technology creation'(Edquist, 2001). Fostering cooperative interaction between economic agents in African industry has not come naturally. Atomistic behaviour of small actors, lack of information on rivals and support agents makes interaction very difficult.

The second characteristic is the focus of innovation policy. Rather than attending only to the innovation, system of innovation policy also focuses on the interactions between economic actors. There is a reason for this – 'interactions should be facilitated by means of policy – if they are not spontaneously functioning smoothly' (Edquist, 2001: 219). In the case of developing countries a ready example will be the interaction of research and development institutions with firms – which for most countries – remain weak and ineffectual. Another is the absence of such organizations and institutions to regulate and coordinate innovation functions, which, following the Neo Liberal prescriptions would be left to the markets. The third characteristic of the NSI is that it recognizes the role of the state in creating organizations where they do not exist. The state can also redesign and re-engineer both the organization and the institutions particularly in answer to deep-seated structural changes.[2] 'To change organizational actors and institutional rules is what innovation policy makers already do in their

---

2 Edquist (2001) cites such functions of the state in Eastern Europe at the time of transition, as well as the general development strategies in Japan, South Korea and other Asian countries. Lall (1994) makes a strong case for selective intervention, which is the kernel of innovation policy within the NSI framework.

efforts to develop the ability of the public sector to pursue innovation policy...such creation or redesign of organizations and institutions might be more important policy instruments than subsidies and other financial instruments.'

State action is required in correcting markets, in creating new ones where they do not exist, and also complementing them, where they are not functioning perfectly. Developing countries in several respects have underdeveloped markets, and this become more pronounced in periods of fast structural changes such as the liberalization of markets undertaken by African countries. The input and factor markets for skilled and unskilled labour, capital, foreign exchange, and the product market for consumer, intermediate and capital goods are the most problematic for developing countries (Bhalla, 2001). Unemployment, credit rationing, weak and unstable currencies (evident in parallel foreign exchange markets) reflect the imperfections in these markets.

A concluding statement

This book concludes that African enterprises have a lot to learn in an attempt to compete in regional and global markets. However, this much has been evident in other studies. What we have attempted to do in this book is call attention to the roots of the problem located in the ways an enterprise innovate and within a particular context and historical period. Policies matter, but institutions that are more enduring and with longer reach into the past, tend to matter even more. I have focused very narrowly on institutions supporting innovation systems and in the process identified some that are missing and those that are present but weak. The major elements relate to institutions for interactive production, knowledge bases, finance, as well as technological and information support mediating inter-firm and organizational learning. While we have taken some tentative steps we are far from a full understanding of the ways institutions shape the rate and nature of technical change in Africa. Chang (2003) made a passionate plea for a more open discussion of institutions in the present developed countries as well as greater and concerted intellectual effort to understanding the policies and institutions in the present developing countries. While Chang addressed a broader set of institutions, the effort in this book has been narrowly focused on those of them undergirding innovation. Our plea is for a systematic study of institutions in developing countries, particularly in Africa.

References

Abramovitz, M. (1986) *Journal of Economic History*, **46**, 385–406.

Abramovitz, M. and David, P. A. (1994) Stanford University, Stanford.

Acemoglu, D., Simon, J. and Robinson, J. A. (2000).

Adeboye, T. (1996) *Science, Technology and Development*, **14**.

Adeya, C. N. (2003) UNU/INTECH, Maastricht, The Netherlands.

Akyüz, Y. and Gore, C. (2001) *Cambridge Journal of Economics*, **25**, 265-288.

Albaladejo, M. and Schmitz, H. (2000).

Allen, C. (1995) *Review of African Political Economy*, **22**, 301–320.

Amin, A. (1994) UNCTAD, Geneva.

Amsden, A. H. (1989) *Asia's next giant: South Korea and late industrialization*, Oxford University Press, New York and Oxford.

Amsden, A. H. (2001) *The Rise of 'The Rest': challenges to the West from Late-industrializing Economies*, Oxford University Press, Oxford.

Anas, A. and Lee, K. S. (1989) In *World Bank*, Working Papers 325, Washington DC.

Ariyo, A. and Jerome, A. (1999) *World Development*, **27**, 201–213.

Arocena, R. and Sutz, J. (1999) *Industry and Innovation*, **7**, 55–75.

Aron, J. (1996) In *Africa Now: People, Policies & Institutions* (ed., Ellis, S.), James Currey Ltd and New Hampshire: Heinemann: 93–118, London.

Aryee, B. (2001) *Resources Policy*, **27**, 61–75.

Audretsch, D. B. (2002) In *Small Firm Dynamism in East Asia* (eds, Iqbal, F. and Urata, S.), Kluwer Academic Publishers, Dordrecht, NL.

Aunty, R. M. (1993) *Sustaining Development in Mineral Economies: The Resource Curse Thesis*, Routledge, London.

Bairoch, P. (1988) *Cities and Economic Development: From the Dawn of History to the Present*, University of Chicago Press, Chicago.

Bamiro, O. A. (2004) In *The African Cluster Book* (eds, Oyelaran-Oyeyinka, B. and McCormick, D.), forthcoming.

Becattini, G. (1990) In *Industrial Districts and Inter-Firm Co-operation in Italy* (ed., Pyke, F. e. a.), Geneva International Insitute for Labour Studies, Geneva.

Beije, P. (1998) *Technological Change in Modern Economy: Basic Topics and New Developments*, Edward Elgar Publishing, Cheltenham.

Bell, R. M. and Pavitt, K. (1993) *Industrial and Corporate Change*, **2**.

Best, M. H. (1990) *The New Competition: Institutions of Industrial Restructuring*, Harvard University Press, Cambridge, Massachusetts.

Bhalla, A. S. (2001) Palgrave.

Biggs, T. (2001).

Biggs, T., Shah, M. and Srivastava, P. (1995) *World Bank Technical Papers*, **288**.

Blakemore, R. and Cooksey, R. (1982) *A Sociology of Education For Africa*, George Allen and Unwin, London.

Bougrain, F. and Haudeville, B. (2002) *Research Policy*, **31**, 735–747.

Brautigam, D. (1997) *World Development*, **25**, 1063–1080.

Brusco, S. (1992) (eds, Pyke, F. and Sengenberger, W.), pp. 177–196.

Brusco, S. (1999) *Journal of Economic Theory*, **87**, 356–378.

Burke, F. G. (1969) *Journal of Comparative Administration*, **1**, 3345–3378.

Callaghy, T. M. (1987) In *The African State in Transition* (ed., Ergas, Z.) Macmillan Press Ltd, London, pp. 87–116.

Cantwell, J. (1997) In *The New Globalisation and Developing Countries* (eds, Dunning, J. H. and Hamdani, K. A.), United Nations University, Tokyo, New York, pp. 155–179.

Carlsson, B. (1997) *International Journal of Industrial Organization*, **1**, 775–799.

Castells, M. (1996) Blackwell Publishers.

Cawthorne, P. M. (1995) *World Development*, **23**.

Chang, H.-J. and Cheema, A. (2001) In *United Nations University, Institute for New Technologies* (ed., Learning Rents, S. S. a. I.), 2001–2008, Maastricht, The Netherlands.

Cimoli, M. (2000) *Developing Innovation Systems: Mexico in a Global Context*, Continnuum 2000, London; New York.

Clark, N. G. (2000) *Journal of Economic Studies*, **27**, 75–93.

Coriat, B. and Dosi, G. (1998) In *Institutions and Economic Change New Perspectives on Markets, Firms and Technology* (eds, Nielsen, K. and Johnson, B.), Edward Elgar Publishing: 3–31, Cheltenham, UK.

Dasgupta, P. and David, P. A. (1994) *Research Policy*, **23**, 487–521.

David, P. A. (1994) *Structural Change and Economic Dynamics*, **5**, 205–220.

David, P. A. and Foray, D. (2001).

Dawson, J. (1992) *IDS Bulletin*, **23**, 34–38.

Dawson, J. and Oyelaran-Oyeyinka, B. (1993) International Labour Office, Geneva.

DeBresson, C., Hu, C., Drejer, I. and Lundvall, B.-Å. (1998), OECD Draft Report.

Dholakia, N. (1997) *Telematics and Informatics*, **4**, 197–207.

Dia, M. (1996) The World Bank, Washington DC.

DiMaggio, P. J. and Powel, W. W. (1983) *American Sociological Review*, **48**, 147–160.

Dosi, G., Freeman, C., Nelson, R., Silverberg, G. and Soete, L. (1988) *Technical change and economic theory*, Columbia University Press, New York and London.

Drejer, I. and Jorgensen, B. H. (2003) *Technovation*, **25**, 83–94.

Ducatel, K. (1998) Danish Research Unit for Industrial Dynamics (DRUID), Aalborg University, Aalborg.

Easterly, W. (1997) *Quarterly Journal of Economies*, **CXII**, 1203–1205.

Easterly, W. and Levine, R. (1995) In *World Bank Policy Research* Working Paper no. 1503.

Edquist, C. (1997) *Systems of Innovation Technologies, Institutions and Organizations*, W.W. Norton, London and Washington.

Edquist, C. (2001) In *The Globalizing learning Economy* (eds, Archibugi, D. and Lundvall, B.-Å.), Oxford University Press, Oxford, pp. 219–237.

Edquist, C. (2004) In *The Oxford Handbook of Innovation* (eds, Fagerberg, J., Mowery, D. and Nelson, R. R.), Oxford University Press, Oxford, pp. 1–28.

Edquist, C. and Johnson, B. (1997) In *Systems of Innovation Technologies, Institutions and Organizations* (ed., Edquist, C.), Pinter, London, pp. 41–63.

Engerman, S. L. (2000) *Journal of Economic Perspective*, **3**, 217–232.

Engerman, S. L. and Sokoloff, K. L. (1997) In *How Latin America Fell Behind* (ed., Haber, S. H.), Stanford University Press, Stanford, California, pp. 260–304.

Enos, J. (1992) *The Creation of Technological Capabilities in Developing Countries*, Pinter, London.

Enos, J. J. (1991) *The Creation of Technological Capability in Developing Countries*, Frances Pinter, London.

Eraut, M. (2000) In *The Necessity of Informal Learning* (ed., Coffield, F.) Policy Press, Bristol.

Ernst, D., Ganiatsos, T. and Mytelka, L. (1994).

Ernst, D., Ganiatsos, T. and Mytelka, L. (1998) *Technological Capabilities and Export Success in Asia*, Routledge, London.

Fabayo, J. A. (1996) *Technovation*, **16**, 357–370.

Fleck, J. (1996) *International Journal of Technology Management*, **11**, 104–128.

Frazer, G. (2002) University of Toronto, Toronto.

Freel, M. S. (2003) *Research Policy*, **32**, 751–770.

Freeman, C. (1987) *Technology Policy and Economic Performance: Lessons from Japan*, Frances Printer, London.

Freeman, C. (2002) *Research Policy*, **31**, 191–211.

Freeman, C. and Lindauer, D. L. (1999).

Freeman, C. and Soete, L. (1997) *The Economics of Industrial Innovation*, Pinter, London and Washington.

Galbraith, J. K. (1975) Houghton Miffin, Boston.

Granovetter, M. S. (1973) *American Journal of Sociology*, **78**, 1360–1380.

Gu, S. (1999) UNU-INTECH, Maastricht.

Hallberg, K. (2000) In *The World Bank*, Discussion Paper no. 40, Washington DC.

Hannah, M. and Freeman, J. (1984) *American Sociological Review*, **49**, 149–164.

Hargittai, E. (1999) *Telecommunication Policy*, **23**, 701–718.

Hawkins, T. (1991) In *Africa 30 years on* (ed., Rimmer, D.), The Royal African Society/James Curry Ltd/Heinemann Education Books Inc, London and New Hampshire, pp. 130–154.

Henderson, R., Orsenigo, L. and Pisano, G. (1999) In *The Sources of Industrial Leadership* (eds, Mowery, D. and Nelson, R.), Cambridge University Press.

Hicks, D., Breitzman, T., Olivastro, D. and Hamilton, K. (2001) *Research Policy*, **30**, 681–703.

ITU (2002).

Johannessen, J.-A., Olaisen, B. O. and Olsen, B. (2001) *International Journal of Information Management*, **21**, 3–20.

Johnson, B., Lorenz, E. and Lundvall, B.-Å. (2002) *Industrial and Corporate Change*, **11**, 245–262.

Johnson, B. and Lundvall, B.-Å. (2003) In *Putting Africa First* (eds, Muchie, M., Gammeltoft, P. and Lundvall, B.-Å.), Aalborg University Press, Aalborg.

Kayizzi-Mugerwa (ed.) (2003) *Reforming Africa's Institutions Ownership, Incentives and Capabilities*, UNU-WIDER.

Kenwood, A. G. and Longhead, A. (1992) *The Growth of the International Economy 1820-1980*, Rudolp, Richard and Good, London and Sydney.

Kim, L. (1997) *Initiation to Innovation: the Dynamics of Korea's Technological Learning*, Harvard Business School Press, Boston.

King, K. (1991) In *Africa 30 Years on* (ed., Rimmer, D.) The Royal African Society, James Currey Ltd and Portsmouth: Heinemann, London and New Hampshire, pp. 73–90.

King, K. and McGrath, S. (eds) (1999) *Enterprise in Africa, Between Poverty and Growth*, Intermediate Technology Publications, London.

Kuznets, S. (1965) *Economic Growth and Structure*, W.W. Norton, New York.

Lall, A. (1980) *Oxford Bulleting of Economics and Statistics*, August, 203–226.

Lall, S. (1987) *Learning to Industrialize: The Acquisition of Technological Capability by India*, Macmillan, London.

Lall, S. (1992a) In *Alternative Development Strategies in Subsaharan Africa* (eds, Stewart, F., Lall, S. and Wangwe, S.), MacMillan, London, pp. 103–144.

Lall, S. (1992b) *World Development*, **20**, 165–186.

Lall, S. (1993) *Development Policy Review*, **11**, 7–65.

Lall, S. (1994) *World Development*, **22**, 645–654.

Lall, S. (1995a) In collaboration with UNCTAD, Geneva.

Lall, S. (1995b) *World Development*, **23**, 2019–2031.

Lall, S. (2000) In *Technology, Learning and Innovation: The Experience of Newly Industrializing Economies* (eds, Kim, L. and Nelson, R.), Cambridge University Press, Cambridge, pp. 13–68.

Lall, S. (2001) *Competitiveness, Technology and Skills*, Edward Elgar Publishing, Cheltenham, UK/Northampton M.A. USA.

Lall, S. and Pietrobello, C. (2003) *Failing to Compete: Technology Development and Technology Systems in Africa*, Edward Elgar Publishing, Cheltenham.

Lall, S. and Wignaraja, G. (1998) Commonwealth Secretariat, London.

Landes, D. S. (1999) *The Wealth and the Poverty of Nations – Why some are so rich and some so poor*, W.W. Norton, New York and London.

Lave, J. and Wenger, E. (1991) *Situated Learning Legitimate Peripheral Participation*, Cambridge University Press, Cambridge.

Levy, B., Berry, A. and Nugent, J. B. (1999) *Fulfilling the Export Potential of Small and Medium Firms*, Kluwer Academic, Boston.

Liedholm, C. (1992).

List, F. (1885) In *The National System of Political* (ed., Translated from original

German by S.S. Lloyd, C. X.), Longmans, Green and Co., London, pp. 149–162.

Love, J. and Ropers, S. (2001) *Research Policy*, **30**, 643–662.

Lubit, R. (2001) *Organizational Dynamics*, **29**, 164–178.

Lundvall, B.-Å. (1988) In *Technical Change and Economic Theory* (ed., Dosi, G. e. a.), Printer, London.

Lundvall, B.-Å. (1992) *National Innovation Systems: towards a theory of innovation and interactive learning*, Frances Printers, London.

Lundvall, B.-Å. and Johnson, B. (1994) *Journal of Industry Studies*, **1**, 23–42.

Lundvall, B.-Å. and Johnson, B. (2003) In *Systems of Innovation and Development Evidence from Brazil* (eds, Cassiolato, J. E., Lastres, H. M. M. and Maciel, M. L.), Edward Elgar Publishing, Cheltenham, UK/Northampton, USA.

Lundvall, B.-Å., Johnson, B., Andersen, E. S. and Dalum, B. (2002) *Research Policy*, **31**, 213–231.

Mahoney, J. (2000) *Metal Finishing*, **98**, 402.

Malerba, F. (1982) *Economic Journal*, **102**, 845–859.

Malerba, F. (1992) *Economic Journal*, **102**, 845–859.

Malerba, F. (2002) *Research Policy*, **31**, 247–264.

Marx, K. (1973) *Grundrusse*, Vintage Books, New York.

Mass, W. and Lazonick, W. (1990) Department of Economics, Columbia University, New York.

McCarthy, D. M. P. (1982) *Colonial Bureaucracy and Creating Underdevelopment 1919-1940*, Iowa State University Press, Ames.

McCormick, D. (1997) (Ed, al, v. D. e.).

McCormick, D. (1998) In *University of Nairobi*, IDS Discussion Paper 366, Nairobi, Kenya.

McCormick, D. (1999) *World Development*, **27**, 1531–1551.

Mensch, G. (1978) *Research Policy*, **7**, 108–112.

Metcalfe, J. S. (1994) *The Economic Journal*, **104**, 931–944.

Metcalfe, J. S. (1997) In *Economics of structural and technological change* (eds, Antonelli, G. and De Liso, N.), Routledge, London.

Metcalfe, J. S. (1998) *Evolutionary Economics and Creative Destruction*, Routledge, London.

Metcalfe, J. S. (2003) In *Growth and Development in the Global Economy* (ed., Bloch, H.), Edward Elgar Publishing, Perth, Australia, pp. 15–38.

Mikesell, R. F. (1997) *Research Policy*, **23**, 191–199.

Mkandawire, T. (2001) *Cambridge Journal of Economics*, **25**, 289–313.

Mokyr, J. (2002) *The Gift of Athena: Historical Origins of the Knowledge Economy*, Princeton University Press, Princeton, New Jersey, USA.

Muche, M., Gammeltoft, P. and Lundvall, B.-Å. (2003) *Putting Africa First: The Making of African Innovation Systems*, Aalborg University Press, Aalborg.

Musonda, F. M. (2004).

Mytelka, L. (1998) Centro Cultural de Belem, Lisbon.

Mytelka, L. (2000) *Industry and Innovation*, **7**, 15–32.

Mytelka, L. and Farinelli, F. (2000) In *Meeting on Local Clusters and Innovation*

Systems in Brazil: New industrial and technological policies for their development, Rio de Janeiro.

Nadvi, K. and Schmitz, H. (1994) In *Brighton Institute of Development Studies* (ed., agenda, R. o. e. a. r.), 339, Brighton.

Nadvi, K. and Schmitz, H. (1997) In *New Trends and Challenges in Industrial Policy, Proceedings and Seminar Paper*, UNIDO, Vienna.

Nadvi, K. M. (1999) *World Development*, **27**, 1605–1626.

Nelson, R. (1981) *Journal of Economic Literature*, **XIX**, 1029–1064.

Nelson, R. (1993) *National Innovation Systems. A Comparative Analysis*, Oxford University Press, New York and Oxford.

Nelson, R. and Nelson, K. (2002) *Research Policy*, **31**, 265–27.

Nelson, R. and Winter, S. (1982) *An Evolutionary Theory of Economic Change*, Belknap Press, Cambridge.

Nelson, R. R. (1987) *Understanding Technical Change as an Evolutionary Process*, North Holland, Amsterdam.

Nelson, R. R. and Sampat, B. (2001) *Journal of Economic Behavior and Organization*, **44**, 31–54.

Ng, F. and Yeats, A. (2002) World Bank.

Niosi, J. (2002a) *Research Policy*, **31**, 291–302.

Niosi, J. (2002b) *Research Policy*, **31**, 291–302.

Nissanke, M. K. (2001) *Cambridge Journal of Economics*, **25**, 343–367.

Nonaka, I. and Takeuchi, H. (1995) *The Knowledge-creating company: How Japanese companies create the dynamics of innovation*, Oxford University Press, New York.

North, D. C. (1989) *Journal of International and Theoretical Economies*, **145**, 238–45.

North, D. C. (ed.) (1996) *Economic Performance through Time*, Cambridge University Press, Cambridge.

North, D. C., Summerhill, W. and Weingast, B. (1998) In *Unpublished Manuscript*, Hoover Institution, Stanford University.

North, D. P. (1990) *Institutions, Institutional Change, and Economic Performance*, Cambridge University Press, Cambridge.

OECD (1998) Paris.

OECD (1999) Paris.

Oerlemans, L., Meeus, M. and Boekema, F. (2001) *Papers in Regional Science*, **80**, 337–356.

Ogbu, O., Oyelaran-Oyeyinka, B. and Mlawa, H. M. (1996) *Technology Policy and Practise in Africa*, IRDC Publishers, Ottawa.

Oyelaran-Oyeyinka, B. (1994) *The Steel Industry in Nigeria*, Caltop Publications, Ibadan.

Oyelaran-Oyeyinka, B. (1996) *ATPS Monograph*, **1**.

Oyelaran-Oyeyinka, B. (1997a) NISER, Ibadan.

Oyelaran-Oyeyinka, B. (1997b) *Nnewi: An Emergent Industrial Cluster in Nigeria*, Technopol Publishers, Ibadan.

Oyelaran-Oyeyinka, B. (1997c) *Science and Public Policy*, **24**, 309–318.

Oyelaran-Oyeyinka, B. (2000) UNCTAD.

Oyelaran-Oyeyinka, B. (2001) UNU-INTECH, Maastricht.

Oyelaran-Oyeyinka, B. (2003) *Science, Technology and Development*, **8**.

Oyelaran-Oyeyinka, B. (2004) *International Journal of Technology and Sustainable Development*, **3**, 91–113.

Oyelaran-Oyeyinka, B. and Barclay, L. A. (2003) In *Putting Africa First: The Making of African Innovation systems* (eds, Muche, M., Gammeltoft, P. and Lundvall, B.-Å.), Aalborg University Press, Aalborg, pp. 93–108.

Oyelaran-Oyeyinka, B., Laditan, G. O. A. and Esubiyi, O. A. (1996) *Research Policy*, **25**, 1081–1096.

Oyelaran-Oyeyinka, B. and Lal, K. (2004) In *UNU-INTECH*, DP 2004–2007, Maastricht.

Pack, H. (1993) *World Development*, **21**, 1–16.

Parson, S. (1956) In *Structure in Modern Societies* (ed., Parsons, T.), Free Press, Glencoe, pp. 16–58.

Pavitt, K. (1984) *Research Policy*, **13**, 343–373.

Pavitt, K. (1994) *Research Policy*, **13**, 343–373.

Pedersen, P. O. (1997) (Ed, al, V. D. e.).

Penrose, E. T. (1959) *The Growth of the Firm*, Basil Blackwell, Oxford.

Pierson, P. (2000) *Amercian Political Science Review*, **94**, 251–267.

Pietrobello, C. and Rabelotti, R. (2004) Inter-American Development Bank, Washington.

Porat, M. (1977) US Department of Commerce, Washington DC.

Porter, M. E. (1998) *Harvard Business Review*, November-December 1998.

Pyke, F. (1992) Geneva.

Pyke, F. (1994) In *Geneva* (ed., Studies, I. I. f. L.).

Pyke, F., Becattini, G. and Sengenberger, W. (eds.) (1990) *Industrial Districts and Inter-firm cooperation in Italy*, International Labour Organisation, Geneva.

Pyke, F. and Sengenberger, W. (1992) (ed., ILO, I. f. L. S.), Geneva.

Rabelotti, R. (1995) *World Development*, **23**, 29–41.

Rogerson, C. M. (2000) *Development Southern Africa*, **17**.

Romijn, H. (2001) *Oxford Economic Papers*, **29**.

Rosenberg, N. (1976) *Perspectives on Technology*, Cambridge University Press, Cambridge.

Rosenberg, N. (1986) *Perspectives on Technology, Cambridge*, Cambridge University Press.

Sachs, J. and Warner, A. (1997) *Journal of African Economies*, **6**, 333–376.

Salter, A. and Martin, B. (2001) *Research Policy*, **30**, 509–532.

Sampat, B. and Nelson, R. R. (2002) *The New Institutionalism in Strategic Management*, **19**.

Sandberg, L. G. (1982) *Journal of European Economic History*, **11**, 675–697.

Saxenian, A. (1991) *Research Policy*, **20**.

Schmitz, H. (1992) *IDS Bulletin*, **23**.

Schmitz, H. (1995) *Journal of Development Studies*, **31**, 529–566.

Schmitz, H. and Musyck, B. (1993) Brighton.

Schmitz, H. and Nadvi, K. M. (1999) *World Development*, **27**, 1503–1514.

Schulpen, L. and Gibbon, P. (2002) *World Development*, **30**, 1–15.

Scott, W. R. (1992) *Institutions and Organizations*, California: Thousand Oaks, Thousand Oaks, London and New Delhi.

Scott, W. R. (1995) *Institutions and Organizations, 2nd edition*, Thousand Oaks, London and New Delhi.

Scott, W. R. (2001) *Institutions and Organizations*, Thousand Oaks, London and New Delhi.

Selznick, P. (1948) *American Sociological Review*, **13**, 25–35.

Selznick, P. (1949) *TVA and the Grassroots*, University of California Press, Berkeley.

Soderborn, J. (2000) University of Oxford, Oxford.

Stein, H. (1994) *World Development*, **22**, 1833–1849.

Stiglitz, J. E. (1999) Department for Trade and Industry and Centre for Economic Policy Research, London.

Tortella, G. (1990) *Education and Economic Development since the Industrial Revolution*, Generalitat Valenciana, Valencia.

Tortella, G. (1994) *Economic History Review*, **47**, 1–21.

UNCTAD (1992) United Nations, New York and Geneva.

UNCTAD (1994) *Technological Dynamism in Industrial Districts: an alternative approach to industrialization in developing countries*, United Nations, New York and Geneva.

UNCTAD (1999) United Nations, Geneva.

UNCTAD (2000) UNCTAD, Geneva.

UNCTAD (2001) *World Investment Report 2001*, UNCTAD, New York.

UNDP (1999) Oxford University Press, New York.

Unruh, G. C. (2000) *Energy Policy*, **28**, 817–830.

Van Arkadie, B. (1995) In *The Role of the State in Economic Change* (eds, Chang, H.-J. and Bowthorn, R.), Oxford University Press, Oxford, pp. 187–211.

Van Dijk, M. P. and Rabelotti, R. (1997) *Enterprise Clusters and Networks in Developing Countries*, Frank Cass, London.

Vartainen, J. (1995) In *The Role of the State in Economic Change* (eds, Chang, H.-J. and Bowthorn, R.), Oxford Unversity Press, Oxford.

Velenchik, A. D. (1995) *The World Bank Economic Review*, **9**, 451–477.

Viotti, E. B. (2001) In *Center for International Development, Harvard University*, Science, Technology and Innovation Discussion Paper No. 12, Cambridge, MA, USA.

Vitta, P. B. (1990) *World Development*, **18**, 1471–1480.

Von Bertalanffy, L. (1968) *General System Theory: foundations, development, application*, George Braziller, New York.

Von Hippel, E. (1988) *The Sources of Innovation*, Oxford University Press, Oxford.

Walker, W. (2000) *Research Policy*, **29**, 833–846.

Wangwe, S. M. (1995) *Exporting Africa: Technology, Trade and Industrialization in*

Sub-Saharan Africa, Routledge, London and New York.

Williamson, O. (1997) University of California, Berkeley.

Witt, U. (Ed.) (1993) *Evolutionary Economics*, Edward Elgar Publishing, Aldershot.

Witt, U. (2002) *Industry and Innovation,* **9**, 7–22.

Wittfogel, K. A. (1957) *Oriental despotism: a comparative study of total power,* Yale University Press, New Haven, CT, USA.

Woerdman, E. (2003) Ghent, Belgium.

World Bank (1981) *Accelerated development in Sub-Saharan Africa: an agenda for action*, World Bank, Washington DC.

World Bank (1988) *Education in Sub-Saharan Africa: Policies for adjustment, revitalisation and expansion*, International Bank for Reconstruction and Development, Washington DC.

World Bank (1991) *World Development Indicators 1991*, Oxford University Press, New York.

World Bank (2001a) *African Development Indicators 2001*, The World Bank, Washington DC.

World Bank (2001b) *A Chance to Learn: knowledge and finance for education in Sub-Saharan Africa*, The International Bank for Reconstruction, Washington DC.

World Bank (2001c).

World Bank (2002).

Yamawaki, H. (2002) *Small Business Economics*, **18**, 121–140.

Young, A. (1993) *Journal of Political Economy*, **101**, 443–472.

Young, C. (1994) *The African Colonial State in Comparative Perspective*, Yale University Press, New Haven.

Zysman, J. (1994) In *Systems of innovation: growth, competitiveness and employment, volume II* (eds, Edquist, C. and Mchelvey, M.), Edward Elgar Publishing, Aldershot, UK, pp. 243–263.

Index

Learning to Compete in African Industry

Ducatel, K. 50–51

Edquist, C. 13–14, 54, 175
education systems and educational levels
    39–43, 71, 107, 116, 162, 168; *see
    also* universities
Egypt 2
electricity supplies 114, 123–8, 172–4
enclave societies 30–31
energy intensity 127–8, 173
Enos, J. 71
enterprise clusters 58–66
entrepreneurship 9–10, 168
Equatorial Guinea 121–2
equity finance 143
Eritrea 121
Ernst, D. 89, 167
Ethiopia 45, 121, 142
evolutionary economics 12–14, 36,
    56–7
exchange of information and experience
    101, 169–70, 175
experiential knowledge 48, 172
export-oriented firms 98, 170
export trade 1–5, 76–7

factor endowments 30
Farinelli, F. 57
financial support for firms 142–9, 174–5
firm age 92
firm size 73–7, 92, 97, 103
First Tier System of Learning Innovation in
    Development (SLID1) 34–5
Fleck, J. 78
footwear industry 63
France 10
Frazer, G. 53
Freeman, C. 20
Freeman, J. 37

Gabon 142
Galbraith, J.K. 38
Gambia 40, 121
Germany 53
Ghana 9–10, 30, 43–5, 59, 158–9
globalization 1, 11, 21, 151
government intervention in industry 172
growth, constraints to 83
growth theories 56

'growth tragedy' of Africa 31
Guinea 43

Hannah, M. 37
heuristic learning 168, 171
'hollowing out' of the state 7
'horizontal' knowledge transfer 52
human capital 20–22, 39, 44, 51, 71–4, 83,
    103–4, 116, 168
hysteresis 33

import substitution industrialization (ISI)
    strategy 8
income per capita 115
incubation 166
industrial districts 166
industrial policy 8, 11
industry associations 97, 141
information and communication technology
    (ICT) 76, 118–23, 128
infrastructure, physical 92, 113–17, 123–9,
    173–4
    and economic conditions 115
    and firm-level performance 123–9
    levels of satisfaction with 124–5
    responses to deficiencies in 126
    see also institutional infrastructure;
        technological infrastructure; trans-
        port infrastructure
initial conditions 5, 12, 29, 39
    persistence of 33–6
innovation
    characteristics of 21–2
    definition of 167
innovation capability, determinants of
    100–102
innovation investments 115
innovation policy 108, 166, 171, 175–6
innovation systems 5–15, 20–21, 32, 37–8,
    53–7, 87, 168, 171
    in developing countries generally 45
    institutional and evolutionary basis of
        12–14
    national 109, 175
innovative impulse 80
institutional gaps 45–6
institutional infrastructure 6
institutional inertia 36
institutional innovation 12–14, 28